Django for Beginners

A few words about Django

So, what is **Django**?

In the world of programming, it's one of the popular, if not the most popular, frameworks for building websites and web applications.

You might be wondering, what do **YouTube, Google, Dropbox**, and **Instagram** have in common?

Correct! They are all built using the **Django** framework!

You might be asking, what exactly is this framework?

A framework is a software structure, a framework consisting of multiple components, where common problems are already solved, and based on which a programmer can write their own code and ensure the server-side operation of the website.

For example, many websites require forms for filling in data, an admin panel, logging procedures, authentication, as well as the need to work with databases, and so on.

All these tasks are essentially repetitive.

By solving one task in one place, you can solve the same task in another place in the same way.

So, a framework solves all these and other tasks.

If you go to the documentation on the main **Django** framework homepage,

docs.djangoproject.com/en/4.1/

you will see a complete list of tasks that **Django** has already solved, and accordingly, you can use all these functions.

Common web application tools

Django offers multiple tools commonly needed in the development of web applications:

- **Authentication:** Overview | Using the authentication system | Password management | Customizing authentication | API Reference

- Caching

- Logging

- Sending emails

- Syndication feeds (RSS/Atom)

- Pagination

- Messages framework

- Serialization

- Sessions

- Sitemaps

- Static files management

- Data validation

So, what is **Django**?

For instance, there are tools here that allow you to solve problems such as caching, logging, sending emails, and so on.

It's also worth noting that the framework provides us with coding rules that we must adhere to:

To fully work with this framework, the following knowledge is necessary:

1. Python language and its Object-Oriented Programming (OOP).
2. Template handling.
3. Basic knowledge of working with SQL queries.
4. Regular expressions.
5. Fundamentals of ORM (Object-Relational Mapping), i.e., interacting with a database through class models.

Table of Contents

The purposes of the Django framework

In short, **Django** framework is used to facilitate server-side website operations.

In more detail, the interaction process between a user and a website can be described as follows:

The client initiates a request, for example, **google.com**.

The informational packet from the client starts moving towards the server where the **google.com** site is hosted.

On the server (computer), there are specialized programs, including a web server (usually **Apache, Nginx**, etc.).

So, this web server constantly "listens" to incoming channels. And at the moment a user's request arrives, the web server needs to redirect the request for processing to the appropriate website.

Different websites on the server can handle incoming requests differently, using **PHP** or **CGI scripts**, or they can use frameworks. In this case, **Django** serves as a wrapper for the **Python** language.

In this context, the web server interfaces with **WSGI** (Web Server Gateway Interface), a standard for interaction between a **Python** program running on the server-side and the web server itself. The web server hands over the request processing to this framework.

Next, a specific view within this framework is activated, which is associated with a particular client request, resulting in the creation of an **HTML** page.

This **HTML** page is first passed back to the web server, which in turn sends it to the client. The client (user) in their browser sees a ready-made page that was generated by the corresponding view within the framework.

Running a web server at home for educational purposes.

(Setting up a web server at home for project development purposes)

How to run the **Django** framework for home or project development purposes?

There's good news. All modern computers have an internal network called "localhost" at **127.0.0.1.**

Additionally, the **Django** framework comes with a built-in debugging server that can be launched on your home computer, eliminating the need for an external server.

Of course, after full development and debugging, websites are typically hosted on external servers, often referred to as hosting, where they operate in a "live" mode.

Now, let's begin the process of setting up your project on your home computer.

There are several approaches, but we'll start with creating a new virtual environment.

Django often interacts with various **Python** packages, and the version of **Python** itself matters too. To ensure consistent and expected results, it's recommended to use the same versions across your working server environment, starting from **Django** and ending with a specific version of the **Python** language.

However, your computer might already have certain packages installed, or you might need to install specific packages for your project in the future. But this could negatively impact existing projects and installed modules on your computer.

To prevent this, you need to isolate the current project reliably from other projects/environments, including the global environment.

So, let's create a virtual environment and install the current versions of **Django** and the **Python** language within it.

Creating a virtual environment.

You will need a **Python** interpreter for this. If you don't have it, you should first download it from the official website **www.python.org/downloads/**

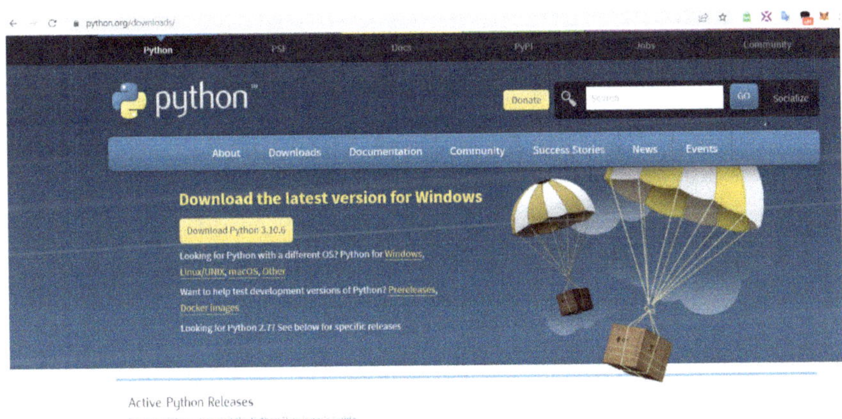

Navigate to the "**Downloads**" tab and select the appropriate operating system.

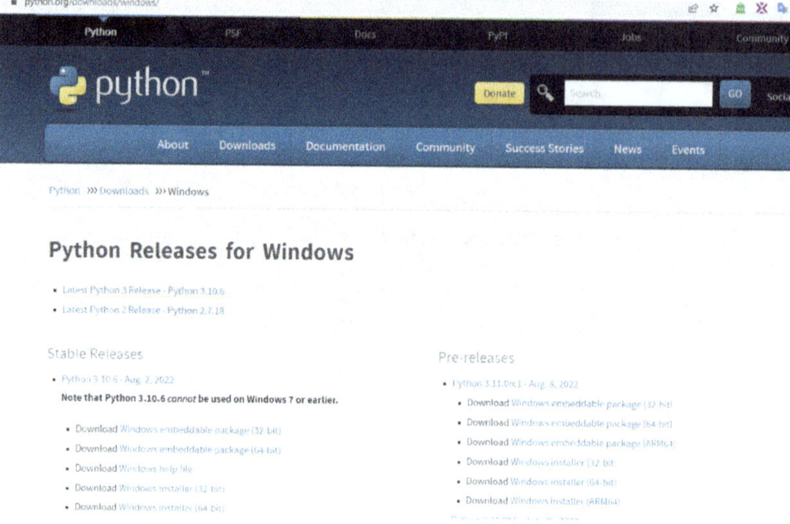

Proceed to download the latest official release and install it. I recommend installing it in the "**Python**" folder on the "**C**" drive. Additionally, you'll need to work with the command line.

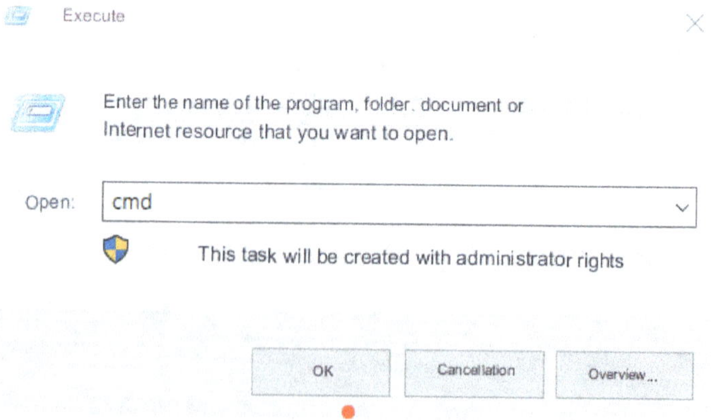

Next, I'll provide instructions for working with the **Windows** operating system. The process is similar on **Linux or macOS**.

To open the command prompt, press the **Win+R** keys together, then type **"cmd"** and press **Enter**. This will open the command prompt window:

In this **window**, you can enter the relevant commands. To check the functionality of the **Python** interpreter, type the following command: **python -V**

As you can see, the required version of **Python** has been installed.

Note that if you are using **Linux or macOS**, you would use the command **python3 -V** (if you have **Python 3** installed).

To see the installed packages, you can use the command **pip** list.

You might encounter a similar notification in your console:

```
C.Administratortop: C:\Windows\system32\cmd.exe

Microsoft Windows [Version 10.0.14393]
          (c) Microsoft Corporation. 2016. All rights reserved.

C:\Users\User>python -V
Python 3.10.6

C:\Users\User>pip list
Package     Version
---------- --------
pip         22.2.1
setuptools 63.2.0

[notice] A new release of pip available: 22.2.1 -> 22.2.2
[notice] To update, run: python.exe -m pip install --upgrade pip

C:\Users\User>
```

This indicates that a new version of **pip** is available, and we can update it. To do so, you can use the command:

python.exe -m pip install --upgrade pip

Ready!

Please note the fact that you are in a global environment, and all packages currently installed are also visible in the global space.

Let's move on to the next point, namely to creating our virtual environment.

First, we need to create a folder where the virtual environment will be located.

My project will be located at the following path:

C: - > Python -> Django -> travels

You might have a different path. Accordingly, the path can vary widely.

In the console, if you are on a different drive, switch to the appropriate drive immediately. For example, if you've created the project on drive **D**, switch to that drive using the command **D:**

I will navigate directly to the required folder and provide the following command:

cd C:/Python/Django/travels

Sure, while being in this folder, let's create our virtual environment using the following command:

Python –m venv venv

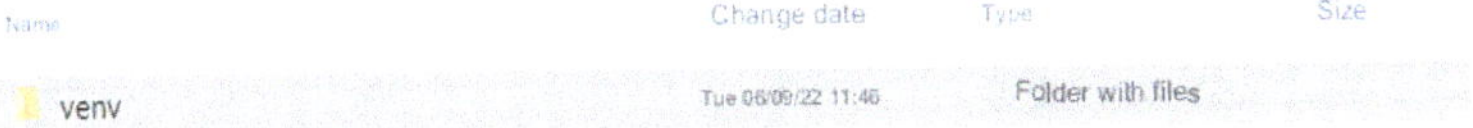

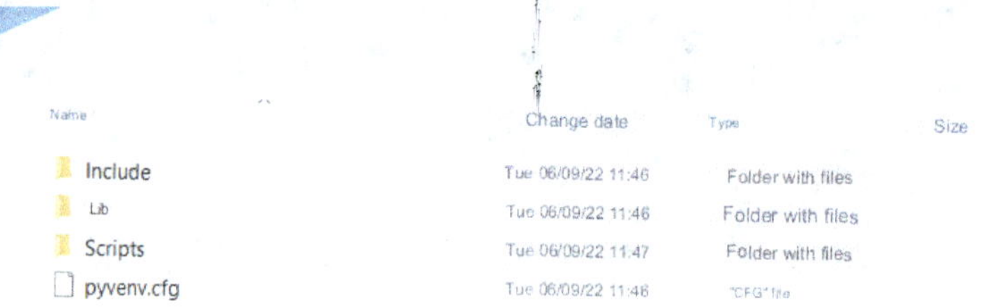

Name	Change date	Type	Size
Include	Tue 06/09/22 11:46	Folder with files	
Lib	Tue 06/09/22 11:46	Folder with files	
Scripts	Tue 06/09/22 11:47	Folder with files	
pyvenv.cfg	Tue 06/09/22 11:46	"CFG" file	1 KB

As you can see, a folder named **"venv"** has been created (the name is arbitrary and is specified at the end of the command **Python –m venv venv**).

All that's left is to activate the virtual environment we created. While being in the folder with this address:

C:/Python/Django/travels

we should execute the following command:

.\venv\Scripts\activate

At the very beginning, don't forget to add a "."

```
Administratortop: C:\Windows\system32\cmd.exe

C:\Users\User>pip list
Package     Version
---------- -------
pip         22.2.2
setuptools  63.2.0

C:\Users\User>cd..

C:\Users>cd..

C:\>Python
Python 3.10.6 (tags/v3.10.6:9c7b4bd, Aug  1 2022, 21:53:49) [MSC v.1932 64 bit (AMD64)] on win32
Type "help", "copyright", "credits" or "license" for more information.
>>> cd Python
  File "<stdin>", line 1
    cd Python
       ^^^^^^
SyntaxError: invalid syntax
>>> exit()

C:\>cd D:/Python/Django/travels
  The device is not ready.

C:\>cd C:/Python/Django/travels

C:\Python\Django\travels>Python -m venv venv

C:\Python\Django\travels>.\venv\Scripts\activate

(venv) C:\Python\Django\travels>
```

With the prefix at the very beginning "(**venv**)", we understand that we are in the created virtual environment, and everything we do will happen within the isolated scope of our virtual environment, separated from the global environment.

If you're working under **Linux**, you should execute the following command:

Source venv/bin/activate

If we now execute the command "**pip list**", we will see the following:

```
C:\>cd D:/Python/Django/travels
The device is not ready.

C:\>cd C:/Python/Django/travels

C:\Python\Django\travels>Python -m venv venv

C:\Python\Django\travels>.\venv\Scripts\activate

(venv) C:\Python\Django\travels>pip list
Package    Version
---------- -------
pip        22.2.1
setuptools 63.2.0

[notice] A new release of pip available: 22.2.1 -> 22.2.2
[notice] To update, run: python.exe -m pip install --upgrade pip

(venv) C:\Python\Django\travels>python.exe -m pip install --upgrade pip
Requirement already satisfied: pip in c:\python\django\travels\venv\lib\site-packages (22.2.1)
Collecting pip
  Using cached pip-22.2.2-py3-none-any.whl (2.0 MB)
Installing collected packages: pip
  Attempting uninstall: pip
    Found existing installation: pip 22.2.1
    Uninstalling pip-22.2.1:
      Successfully uninstalled pip-22.2.1
Successfully installed pip-22.2.2

(venv) C:\Python\Django\travels>
```

If you had modules installed in the global environment, you won't see them here. Additionally, you should perform the update again, as we did earlier.

To exit the virtual environment, you need to enter the command "**deactivate**".

Integrated Development Environment (IDE) PyCharm

(For working with Python code)

Understood. Since you use the PyCharm integrated development environment for your work, you will perform all further actions with the virtual environment within this environment.

```
Admintop: C:\Windows\system32\cmd.exe
The device is not ready.

C:\>cd C:/Python/Django/travels

C:\Python\Django\travels>Python -m venv venv

C:\Python\Django\travels>.\venv\Scripts\activate

(venv) C:\Python\Django\travels>pip list
Package    Version
---------- -------
pip        22.2.1
setuptools 63.2.0

[notice] A new release of pip available: 22.2.1 -> 22.2.2
[notice] To update, run: python.exe -m pip install --upgrade pip

(venv) C:\Python\Django\travels>python.exe -m pip install --upgrade pip
Requirement already satisfied: pip in c:\python\django\travels\venv\lib\site-packages (22.2.1)
Collecting pip
  Using cached pip-22.2.2-py3-none-any.whl (2.0 MB)
Installing collected packages: pip
  Attempting uninstall: pip
    Found existing installation: pip 22.2.1
    Uninstalling pip-22.2.1:
      Successfully uninstalled pip-22.2.1
Successfully installed pip-22.2.2

(venv) C:\Python\Django\travels>deactivate
C:\Python\Django\travels>
```

As we can see, the (**venv**) prefix is no longer present.

Since you use the **PyCharm** integrated development environment for your work, you will perform all further actions with the virtual environment within it.

To download this **IDE**, you can follow the link:

https://www.jetbrains.com/ru-ru/pycharm/

In the beginning, using the free version of **PyCharm** Community should suffice. Now, let's open the created project. Follow these steps:

Go to the "**File**" menu.

In the dropdown menu, select "**Open.**"

Please note that the exact steps and user interface may vary based on the version of **PyCharm** you are using.

In the next window, select the "**travels**" folder

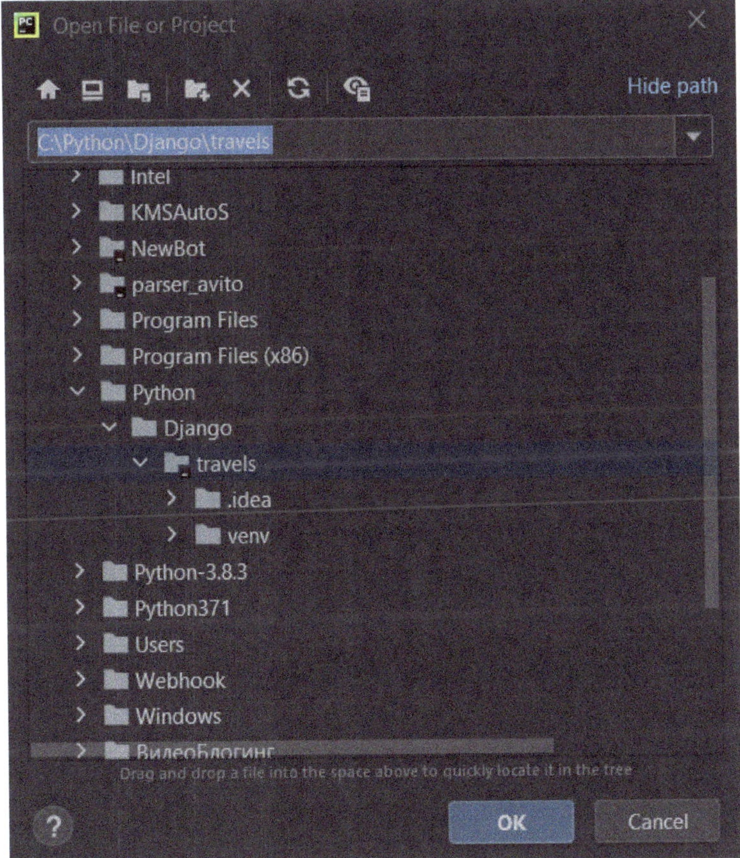

And click "**OK**".

After this action, the project will be loaded.

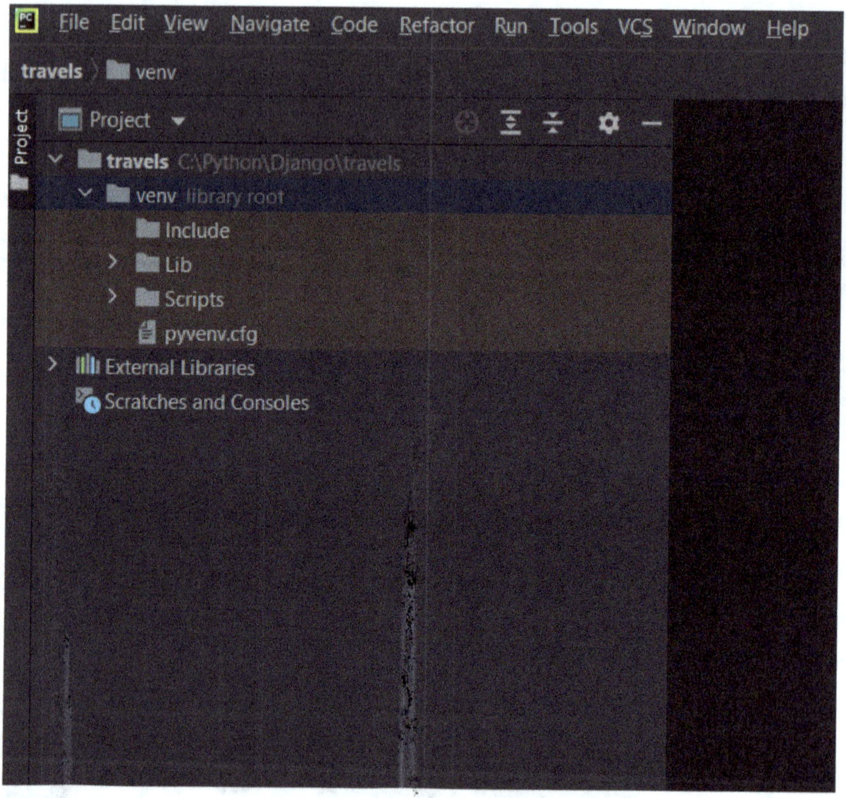

If you go to the terminal at the bottom part:

We will see the activated virtual environment.

If, for some reason, this didn't happen... for example:

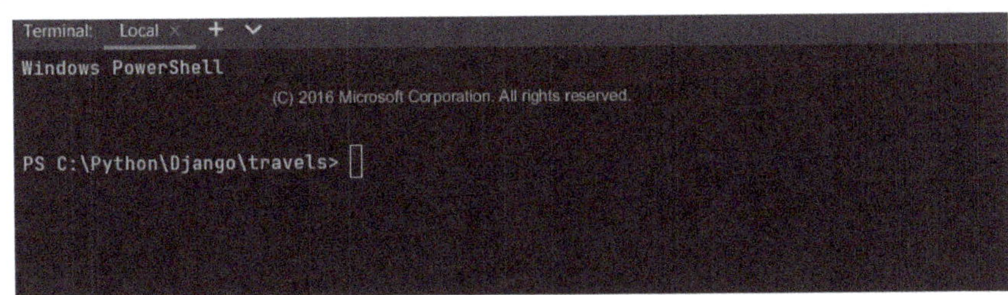

it's necessary to manually activate the environment by following these steps:

Open the "**File**" menu.

Select "**Settings...**"

In the opened window, go to "**Project:travels**" and choose "**Python interpreter**."

Then, click on the arrow on the right and choose the desired interpreter from the list.

Please note that the exact steps and user interface might vary based on the version of **PyCharm** you are using.

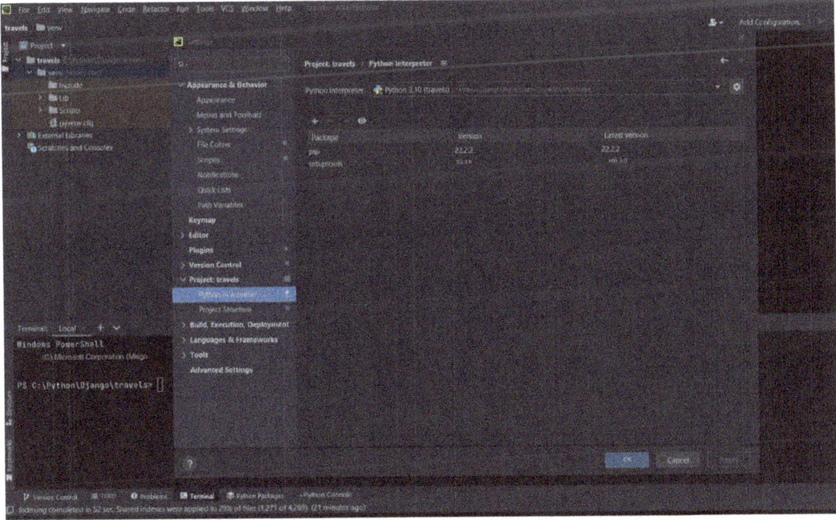

 Quite often, when opening the terminal, an error appears:

```
.\venv\Scripts\activate : Невозможно загрузить файл
C:\path\venv\Scripts\activate.ps1, так как выполнение
сценариев отключено в этой системе.
Для получения дополнительных сведений см.
about_Execution_Policies по адресу
http://go.microsoft.com/fwlink/?LinkID=135170.
строка:1 знак:1
.\venv\Scripts\activate
~~~~~~~~~~~~~~~~~~~~~~~~~
    CategoryInfo          : Ошибка безопасности: (:) [],
PSSecurityException
    FullyQualifiedErrorId : UnauthorizedAccess
```

The solution involves the following steps:

1. Open the **PowerShell** terminal as an administrator. Click the Start button, type "**PowerShell**," right-click on "**Windows PowerShell**," and select "**Run as administrator**."

2. Paste and execute the command: **Set-ExecutionPolicy RemoteSigned**
3. When prompted, respond with **-A**

You can read about the impact of disabling execution policies in **PowerShell** on security through the following link:

https://docs.microsoft.com/ru-ru/powershell/module/microsoft.powershell.core/about/about_execution_policies?view=powershell-7.2

If you've followed all the steps correctly, after the manipulations, your terminal should look like the screenshot below:

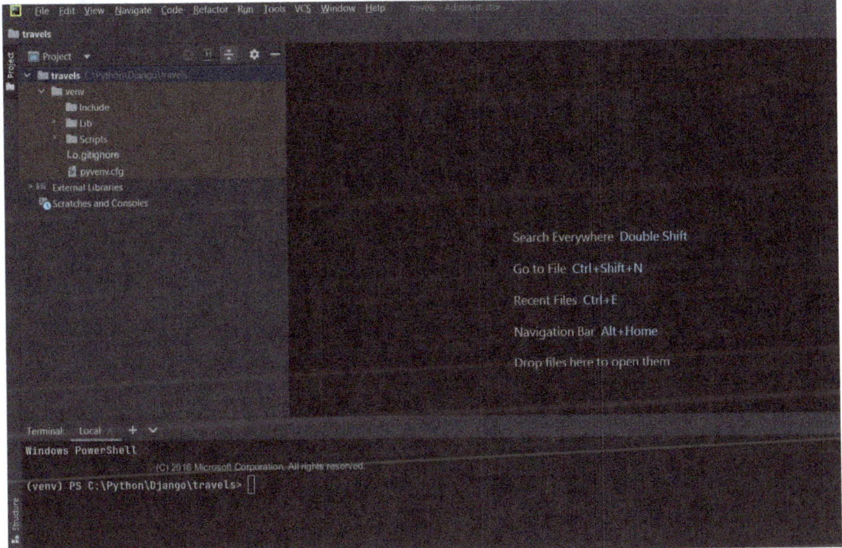

Installing the Django framework.

At this stage, let's proceed with installing **Django** while being in the project's root folder. To do this, in the **PyCharm** terminal, you should enter the command:

pip install django

If you enter the command **pip list**, you will see that the **Django** package has been added to our list.

To view the list of core commands of the **Django** package, simply type the command **django-admin**

```
[django]
    check
    compilemessages
    createcachetable
    dbshell
    diffsettings
    dumpdata
    flush
    inspectdb
    loaddata
    makemessages
    makemigrations
    migrate
    optimizemigration
    runserver
    sendtestemail
    shell
    showmigrations
    sqlflush
    sqlmigrate
    sqlsequencereset
    squashmigrations
    startapp
    startproject
    test
    testserver
Note that only Django core commands are lis
 the environment variable DJANGO_SETTINGS_M
(venv) PS C:\Python\Django\travels>
```

Creating our project.

To create our project, type the following command in the terminal command line:

Django-admin startproject travels

After running this command, we discover a new folder within it...

	Date of change	Type
.idea	Cp 07.09.22 13:52	File folder
travels	Thu 08.09.22 11:54	File folder
venv	Cp 07.09.22 13:42	File folder

Name	Date of change	Type	Size
travels	Thu 08.09.22 11:54	File folder	
manage.py	Thu 08.09.22 11:54	JetBrains PyCharm ...	1 KB

Name	Date modified	Type	Size
__init__.py	Thu 08.09.22 11:54	JetBrains PyCharm ...	0 K5
asgi.py	Thu 08.09.22 11:54	JetBrains PyCharm ...	1 KB
settings.py	Thu 08.09.22 11:54	JetBrains PyCharm ...	4 KB
urls.py	Thu 08.09.22 11:54	JetBrains PyCharm ...	1 KB
wsgi.py	Thu 08.09.22 11:54	JetBrains PyCharm ...	1 KB

The name of the website usually coincides with the domain name where the site will be hosted. We intend to name the site **"travels."**

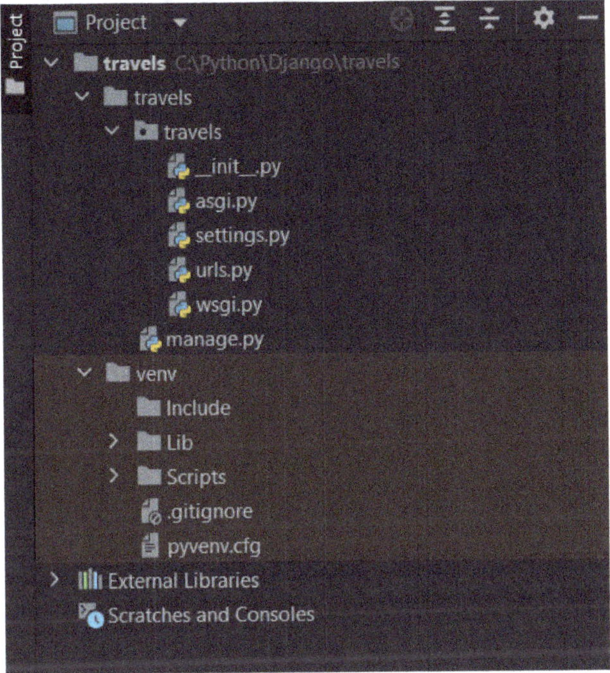

In the screenshot, it's evident that two "**travels**" folders were created. Inside the nested "**travels**" folder, there's another folder containing files that define the current project configuration. This folder is also referred to as the configuration package. The purpose of the files in this package will be explained later.

We also see the "**manage.py**" file. This file is used to manage the current website. For instance, we'll create applications, perform database migrations, run a test web server, and so on through this file.

Everything is ready to set up a test web server!

To do this, we will navigate to the "**travels**" folder using the command:

cd travels

Start our server using the command:

python manage.py runserver

```
(venv) PS C:\Python\Django\travels> cd travels
(venv) PS C:\Python\Django\travels\travels> python manage.py runserver
Watching for file changes with StatReloader
Performing system checks...

System check identified no issues (0 silenced).

You have 18 unapplied migration(s). Your project may not work properly until you apply the migrations for app(s): admin, auth, contenttypes, sessions.
Run 'python manage.py migrate' to apply them.
September 08, 2022 - 12:13:30
Django version 4.1.1, using settings 'travels.settings'
Starting development server at http://127.0.0.1:8000/
Quit the server with CTRL-BREAK.
```

The main page of our website will be accessible at the following address: **http://127.0.0.1:8000/**

Clicking on this link will open a browser, and the following page will appear:

The advantage of the debugging web server is that it automatically reloads when we make changes to our project's code. Unfortunately, this doesn't always work. So, if you find that nothing happens after making code changes, simply restart the web server. You can do this by pressing the **CTRL-BREAK** combination.

Please note that when we initially launched this emulator of a real web server, a file named "**db.sqlite3**" appeared. This is **an SQLite3** database file. By default, **Django** uses this type of database. In the future, we can switch to any other database management system supported by this framework, such as **PostgreSQL, MariaDB, MySQL, Oracle**, and **SQLite**.

If for any reason you decide to run the test server on a different port, you can do so by adding the desired port number to the command string.

Python manage.py runserver 4000

```
(venv) PS C:\Python\Django\travels\travels> python manage.py runserver 4000
Watching for file changes with StatReloader
Performing system checks...

System check identified no issues (0 silenced).

You have 18 unapplied migration(s). Your project may not work properly until you apply the migrations for app(s): admin, auth, contenttypes, sessions.
Run 'python manage.py migrate' to apply them.
September 08, 2022    12:32:07
Django version 4.1.1, using settings 'travels.settings'
Starting development server at http://127.0.0.1:4000/
```

As you can see, our server has reloaded on the new port.

With that, we've completed all the preparatory steps and launched the test web server.

Model-View-Template (MVT)

According to **Django**'s philosophy, we should create a new application within the scope of our website. **Django** developers have decided that each part of the site should be represented as a separate application.

For instance, when creating a blog, we would define an application for creating the blog's pages. Later, if we need a user comment feature, we create a new application for this functionally independent part. The same applies to features like creating a survey, which would also be separated into its own application, and so on.

Every logically and functionally independent part of the site implies the creation of a separate application. **Django** applications should be designed to be as independent as possible, so that when creating a new website, you can simply copy the code and move it to the new project. At the very least, this is what we should strive for.

So, let's create the first application within our site to handle the basic functionality. To begin, let's navigate to the directory named "**travels**" located inside the "**travels**" directory. To do this, use the following command in the terminal:

cd travels

And once inside this directory, execute the command:

python manage.py startapp traveler

    traveler – the name of our application.

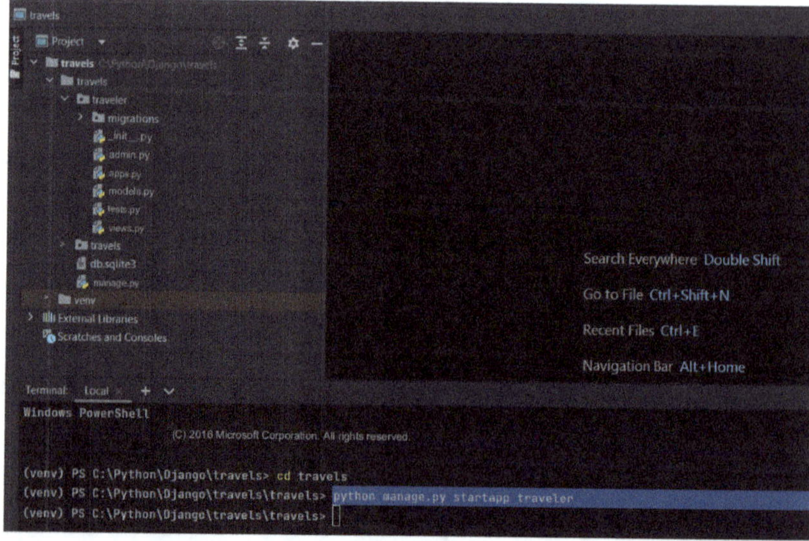

As you can see, a new directory named **"traveler"** has appeared, containing certain files.

Firstly, we see the file named **"init.py"**. It indicates that this **"traveler"** directory is nothing but a package. Additionally, there's a **"migrations"** folder. It's meant for storing database migrations.

"admin.py" is used to connect our application with the site's admin panel.

"apps.py" involves configuration and setup for the current application.

"models.py" is where **ORM** models are stored.

"tests.py" is a module for testing procedures.

"views.py" stores the views or controllers of the current application.

Next, we need to register our application in the project of our site so that **Django** is aware of its existence and can work with it correctly. To do this, open the **"travels"** folder, find and open the **"settings.py"** file. In this file, locate the **"INSTALLED_APPS"** list and add the name of our application to the end of the list, as shown in the screenshot below.

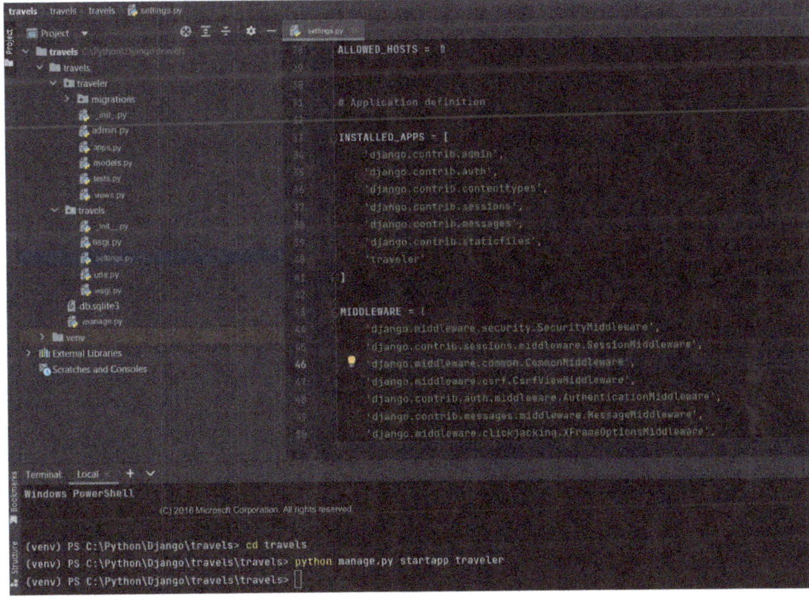

 # Application definition

INSTALLED_APPS = [

'django.contrib.admin',

'django.contrib.auth',

'django.contrib.contenttypes',

'django.contrib.sessions',

'django.contrib.messages',

'django.contrib.staticfiles',

'traveler'

]

Here's an improved version:

If you open the "**apps.py**" file:

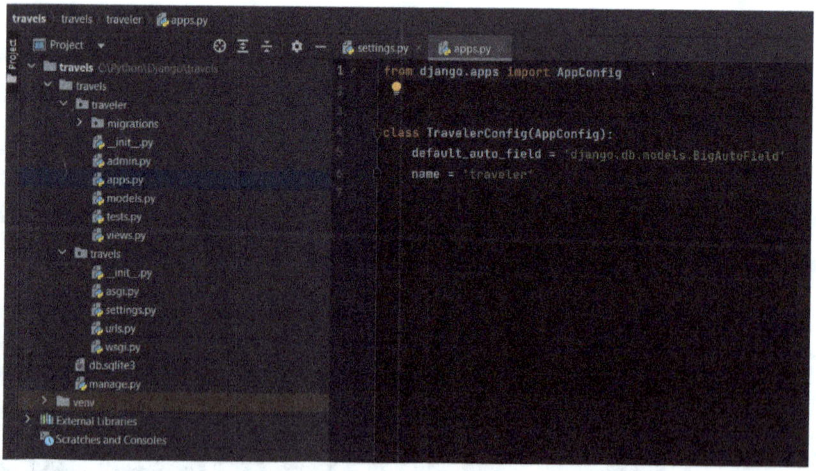

We will see the following code:

from django.apps import AppConfig

class TravelerConfig(AppConfig):

default_auto_field = 'django.db.models.BigAutoField'

name = 'traveler'

Returning to the "**settings.py**" file and making a slight modification to the entry:

INSTALLED_APPS = [

'django.contrib.admin',

'django.contrib.auth',

'django.contrib.contenttypes',

'django.contrib.sessions',

'django.contrib.messages',

'django.contrib.staticfiles',

'traveler.apps.TravelerConfig'

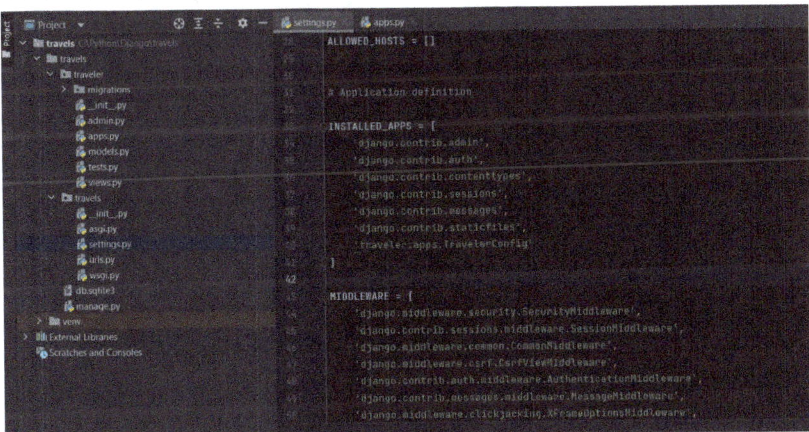

At this stage, the application is created and registered.

Next, let's create a handler for the main page of the website. To do this, we need to define the view for this page.

Presentation Views

(Creation of the main page handler)

In **Django**, views can be implemented either as functions or as classes. Let's start by using a function, as it's the simplest implementation to understand. We define all views in the **views.py** file.

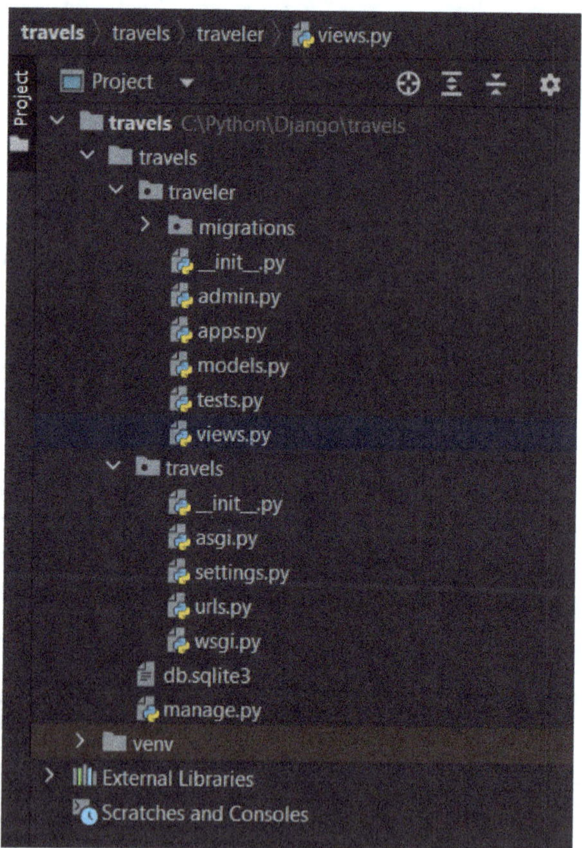

Let's define the first view function for the main page.

```
def index(request):

    return HttpResponse("Application page traveler.")
```

The function name "**index**" is chosen arbitrarily, but typically, for the main page, it's customary to use this name.

Next, (**request**) essentially refers to an **HttpRequest** object that contains information about the request, session, cookies, etc. So, using the request variable, we have access to all the information within the current request context.

As an output, this function should create an instance of the HttpResponse class.

The content of the main page will be the string ("**Application page content**.").

However, in order to use this, you need to import the **HttpResponse** class.

from django.http import HttpResponse

from django.shortcuts import render

def index(request):

 return HttpResponse("Application page traveler.")

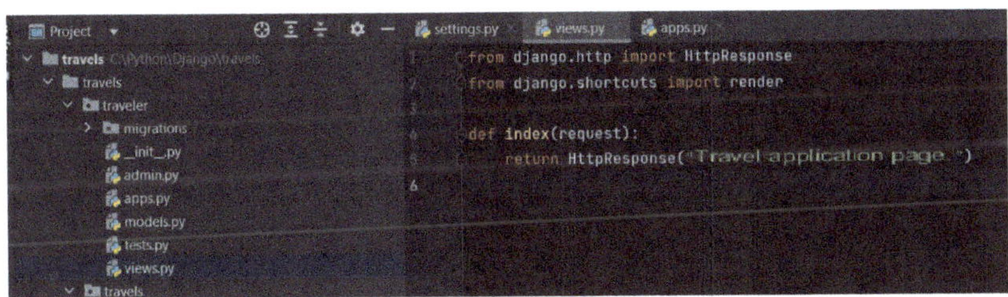

In the simplest case, the **view** function is created.

Now, you need to associate this function with the appropriate **URL address**.

To do this, in the "**travels**" configuration package, you should open the **"urls.py"** file and add to the list

urlpatterns = [

 path('admin/', admin.site.urls),

]

we add another route.

As we can see, there's already one route in it. This is the access to the admin panel of our site.

In a similar manner, we add another route.

```python
urlpatterns = [
    path('admin/', admin.site.urls),
    path('traveler/', index),
]
```

We insert the path function, define the pattern **'traveler/'**, and then provide a link to the **view** function that will be triggered upon the request to **'traveler/'**.

We also need to import the index function.

```python
from django.contrib import admin
from django.urls import path
from traveler.views import index

urlpatterns = [
    path('admin/', admin.site.urls),
    path('traveler/', index),
]
```

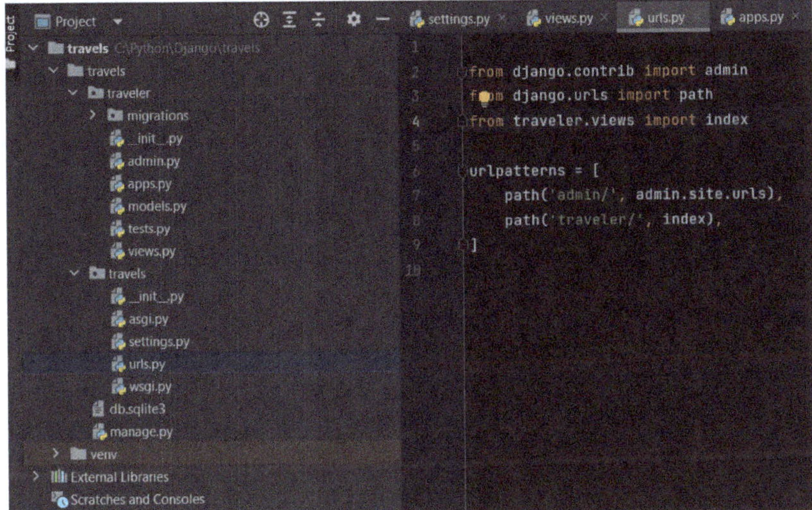

The question arises: what will be the page where the index view function will be triggered?

In reality, it will look like this:

http://127.0.0.1:8000/traveler/

That is, the prefix **traveler/** will be added to the domain of our site.

The route

http://127.0.0.1:8000/traveler/

will activate the index function.

If an error occurs, you need to mark our traveler directory as the main directory. To do this, click on the directory with the right mouse button, then click on "**Mark Directory as**" and select "**Sources Root**". After that, the error should disappear.

After doing this, we will test the functionality of our page by entering the following **URL** in the browser:

http://127.0.0.1:8000/traveler/

But before that, you need to start our web server using the command **python manage.py runserver**.

However, first navigate to the travels directory using the **cd travels** command.

We navigate to the page http://127.0.0.1:8000/traveler/

← → C   ⓘ 127.0.0.1:8000/traveler/

Traveler app page.

Everything is working!

Using the same approach, we can define as many view functions and **URL** routes as needed.

Also, please note that if you enter the address in the browser's **URL** bar

http://127.0.0.1:8000/

then you will see a page like this

← → C   ⓘ 127.0.0.1:8000

Page not found (404)

       Request Method: GET
         Request URL: http://127.0.0.1:8000/

Using the URLconf defined in `travels.urls`, Django tried these URL patterns, in this order:

1. admin/
2. traveler/

The empty path didn't match any of these.

You're seeing this error because you have DEBUG = True in your Django settings file. Change that to False, and Django will display a standard 404 page

In order to get everything working again, you need to change the line in the **urls.py** file to

```
urlpatterns = [

  path('admin/', admin.site.urls),
```

```
    path('', index),
]
```

So, instead of path(**'traveler/', index),** insert a blank line.

Refresh the browser page, and you will see the familiar page.

However, this approach, where the application routes are directly defined in the project's configuration file, violates the principle of application independence.

If you ever want to move this application to another project, you would need to copy these routes as well. This is not very convenient.

How can this be resolved?

Django allows you to pass a list of **URL** addresses for the application and their associated view functions as the second parameter, instead of just a view function.

This is done using the include function, which we import, and instead of all the routes we defined, we just write one line..

```
from django.contrib import admin
from django.urls import path, include
from traveler.views import index


urlpatterns = [
    path('admin/', admin.site.urls),
    path('traveler/', include('traveler.urls')),
]
```

```
from django.contrib import admin
from django.urls import path, include
from traveler.views import index

urlpatterns = [
    path('admin/', admin.site.urls),
    path('traveler/', include(traveler.urls)),
]
```

A certain prefix is still specified, in our case **traveler/,** and then the include function is called. We pass the path to the file that will contain the routes of our application to this function. Currently, there is no **urls.py** file in the traveler application. So, we'll create one.

The contents of this file will be as follows:.

from django.urls import path

*from .views import **

urlpatterns = [

  path('', index)

]

First, we import the path function to create our routes. Then, we import all our view functions using from **.views import *.** We define the standard urlpatterns collection. Within this list, we define all the routes for the current application.

The index view handler will correspond to the following route:

http://127.0.0.1:8000/traveler

The prefix traveler will be attached to the domain because we specified it in the **urls.py** file of the overall project configuration.

To do this, we use the path(**'travels/', include(traveler.urls**)) line, which is located in the travels directory.

This file should be created in the traveler application directory.

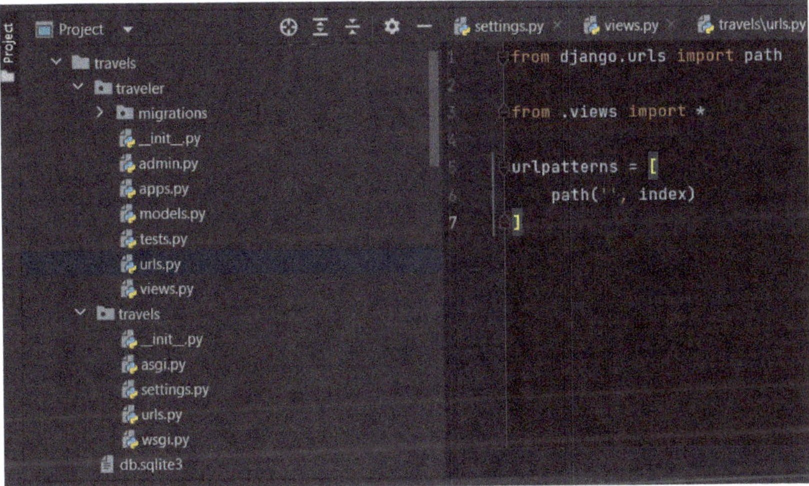

Copy and paste the route http://127.0.0.1:8000/traveler

into the browser. You will see the familiar page

In this simple way, you can create view functions and define routes.

Continuing with the topic of routing, let's make a few adjustments. Open the urls.py file in the **travels** configuration package. In the urlpatterns list, remove the **traveler/** prefix, which is associated with the route of our **traveler.urls** application, and leave it as an empty string. Now, all routes related to this application will be based directly on the domain name.

```python
from django.contrib import admin
from django.urls import path, include
from traveler.views import index


urlpatterns = [
    path('admin/', admin.site.urls),
    path('', include('traveler.urls')),
]
```

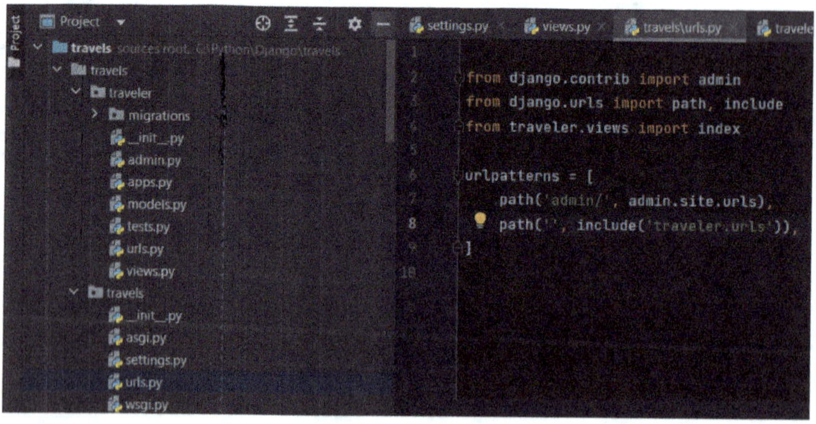

For example, let's open the **urls.py** file of our application

```python
from django.urls import path
from .views import *
urlpatterns = [
    path('', index),
]
```

In it, **path('', index)** will correspond to the main page

http://127.0.0.1:8000/

For clarity, let's define one more route.

This is done in a similar manner.

```
from django.urls import path
from .views import *
urlpatterns = [
    path('', index),
    path('cats/', categories),
]
```

Also, we specify the view function that will handle this route and render the page. We also need to import it. To avoid listing the functions to import every time with commas, we use *.

The template **path('cats/', categories)** will correspond to the address http://127.0.0.1:8000/cats/

But that's not enough, as we remember. Next, we open the views.py file and add the view function.

```
def index(request):
    return HttpResponse("Application page traveler.")


def categories(request):
    return HttpResponse("Articles by categories.")
```

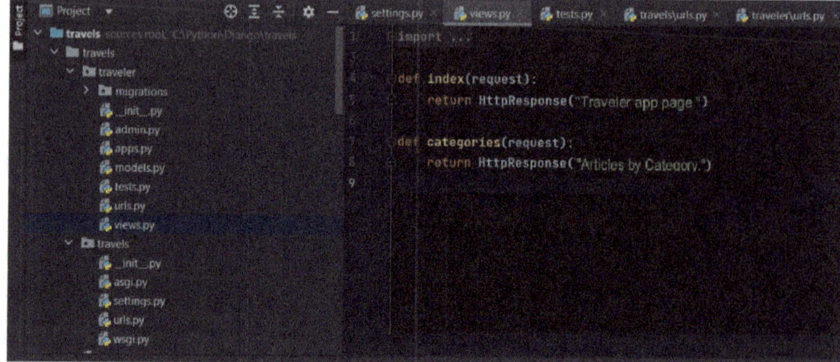

We launch the web server and navigate to the page

http://127.0.0.1:8000/cats/

Articles by category

As we can see, everything is working.

Let's continue our example with routing.

We will display our categories based on their index.

For example,

http://127.0.0.1:8000/cats/1/

http://127.0.0.1:8000/cats/2/ and so on.

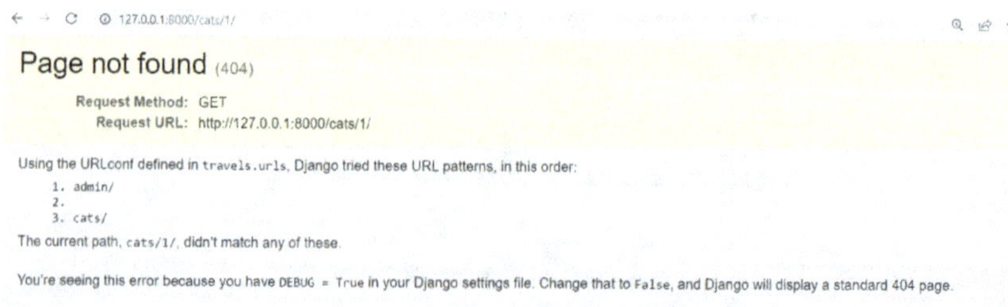

 Currently, we don't have such a route. Let's fix that.

To do this, in the part where our category is being generated, we will add a numerical parameter.

```
from django.urls import path

from .views import *

urlpatterns = [

    path('', index),

    path('cats/<int: order_id/>', categories),

]
```

We enclose the parameter in angle brackets **<>,** specifying the data type as an integer, i.e., int. Next, we give a name to this parameter, let's call it **order_id**. In this case, the categories function will be associated with a route that has the prefix **'cats/...'** and is connected to a number, for example,

http://127.0.0.1:8000/cats/1/.

Now, how do we capture this numerical parameter in the categories function!

In the **views.py** file of the **"traveler"** application, we will locate the categories function and specify this parameter. Let's also display this **order_id** number on the page.

```
def index(request):

    return HttpResponse("Application page traveler.")


def categories(request, order_id):

    return HttpResponse(f"<h1> Articles by categories.</h1><p>{order_id}</p>")
```

```python
from django.urls import path

from .views import *

urlpatterns = [
    path('', index),
    path('cats/<int:order_id>/', categories),
]
```

Let's restart the server.

Enter the route in the browser's address bar, for example, http://127.0.0.1:8000/cats/2/

And we will see the displayed page.

← → C ⓘ 127.0.0.1:8000/cats/2/

Articles by category

2

 If you enter

http://127.0.0.1:8000/cats/

without a number, you will see a **404 page**

Page not found (404)

Request Method: GET
Request URL: http://127.0.0.1:8000/cats/

Using the URLconf defined in `travels.urls`, Django tried these URL patterns, in this order:

1. admin/
2.
3. cats/<int:order_id>/

The current path, `cats/`, didn't match any of these.

You're seeing this error because you have `DEBUG = True` in your Django settings file. Change that to `False`, and Django will display a standard 404 page.

Or if you enter http://127.0.0.1:8000/cats/ek/

, i.e., a non-numeric value, you will also get a **404 error**, as the correspondence won't be met.

In addition to the int type, Django supports other types that we can specify here:

str – any non-empty string, excluding the **'/' character**;

int – any positive integer, including **'0'**;

slug – can use any Latin letters, including hyphens and underscores;

uuid – digits, lowercase Latin letters, hyphens;

path – any non-empty string, including the **'/' character**.

As an example, let's replace int with slug and see how it affects our template.

from django.urls import path

*from .views import **

urlpatterns = [

  path('', index),

  *path('cats/<**slug**:order_id>/', categories),*

]

Let's go to the browser and see how it works

Articles by category

1

Yes, if you append a letter to the number, it will still work. This is because we are using the slug type, which allows for a combination of letters and numbers.

Articles by category

1a

⚠ Exactly, Cyrillic letters will not work in this case because they are considered invalid characters within the slug type in **Django's URL** routing system. Only Latin letters, numbers, hyphens, and underscores are allowed in slug patterns.

Page not found (404)

```
Request Method:  GET
   Request URL:  http://127.0.0.1:8000/cats/1%D1%8B
```

Using the URLconf defined in `travels.urls`, Django tried these URL patterns, in this order:

```
1. admin/
2.
3. cats/<slug:order_id>/
```

The current path, `cats/1ы`, didn't match any of these.

You're seeing this error because you have DEBUG = True in your Django settings file. Change that to False, and Django will display a standard 404 page.

Indeed, if you ask the reasonable question of why we need this! After all, numbers are simpler. The thing is that words are better indexed by search engines and better understood by users.

Having demonstrated how it works as a demonstration, I'll revert to how it was.

Working with regular expressions.

The function re_path()

If for some reason the above-mentioned patterns are not sufficient, in **Django**, you can use a special function called re_path(). It allows you to do the same thing but with the use of regular expressions. For example, you can define a **URL** where you can specify the year as four digits. Then you can describe the route using this function as follows.

from django.urls import path, **re_path**

*from .views import **

urlpatterns = [

  path('', index),

  path('cats/<int:order_id>/', categories),

  re_path(r'^archive/(?P<year>[0-9]{4})/', archive),

]

We import this function and add one line in which we placed the prefix and the archive handler function, specifying in the regular expression that the year should consist of four digits

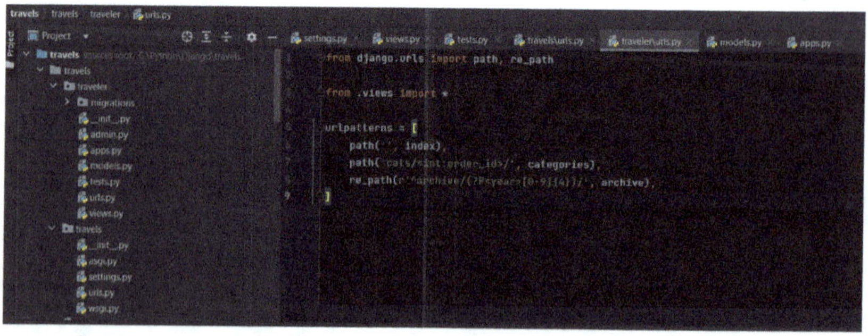

Next, let's go to the **views.py** file and accordingly define this function.

from django.http import HttpResponse

from django.shortcuts import render

def index(request):

return HttpResponse("The page of the application traveler.")

def categories(request, order_id):

return HttpResponse(f"<h1> Articles by categories.</h1><p>{order_id}</p>")

def archive (request, year):

return HttpResponse(f"<h1> Yearly archive</h1><p>{year}</p>")

This function takes two parameters, one of which is **year**.

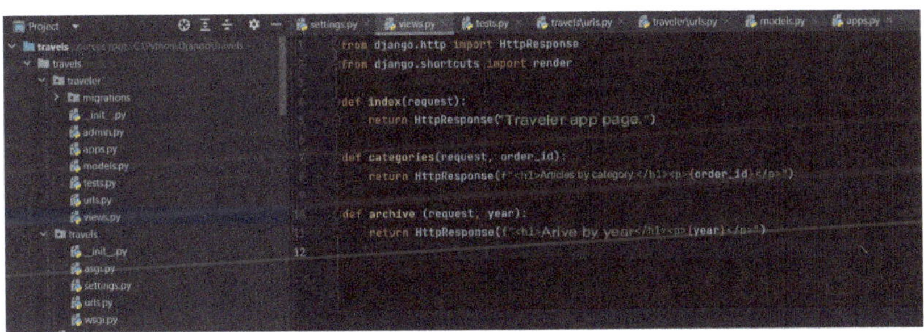

Let's check how this will work. Go to the browser and enter the following **URL** string

http://127.0.0.1:8000/archive/2022/

Archive by years

2022

It's working fine!

If we specify 3 or 2 digits, we will encounter an error because the pattern does not match. As we remember, we should have 4 digits.

Processing GET and POST requests

The structure of a **URL** can contain the following parameters:

http://127.0.0.1:8000/?name=Akademgorodok&order_id=smartphon

? - a special character.

name=Akademgorodok - key-value pair.

& - delimiter character.

order_id=smartphon - key-value pair.

The entire string ?name=Akademgorodok&order_id=smartphon is an example of a **GET** request.

To extract a key from a **GET** request, you use the first (request) parameter in the view function.

def categories(request, order_id)

Through it, we can access the special request.GET dictionary where all this data is stored.

Let's look at a specific example of how **GET** requests work and how to catch them.

Open the views.py file and add two lines to the categories function.

```
def categories(request, order_id):
    if(request.GET):
        print(request.GET)
    return HttpResponse(f"<h1> Articles by Categories.</h1><p>{order_id}</p>")
```

Before printing the dictionary to the console, let's check the condition to see if this dictionary exists in the string. And if it is present there, then we will output it to the console of our terminal. To do this, let's put the following line in the browser

http://127.0.0.1:8000/?name=Akademgorodok&order_id=smartphon

← → C ⓘ 127.0.0.1:8000/?name=Akademgorodok&order_id=smartphon

Application Page traveler.

The page has loaded. Let's access our terminal now.

Django version 4.1.1, using settings 'travels.settings'

Starting development server at http://127.0.0.1:8000/

Quit the server with CTRL-BREAK.

*[18/Sep/2022 16:48:43] "**GET /?name=Akademgorodok&order_id=smartphon** HTTP/1.1" 200 47*

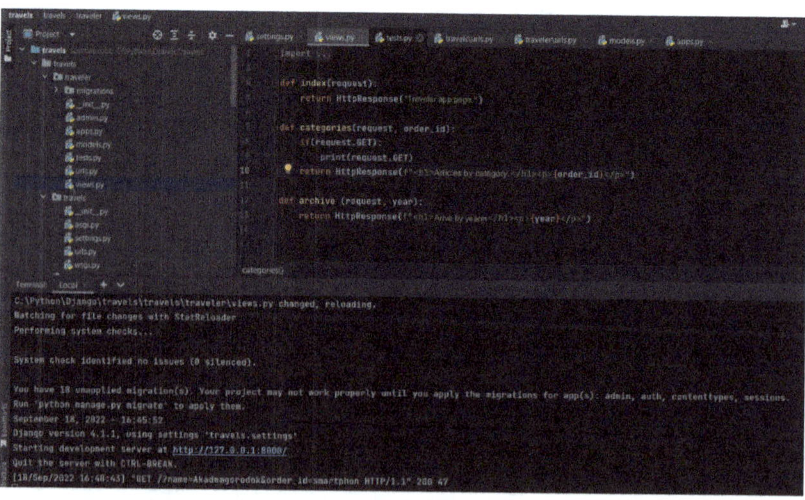

If we remove the **GET** request from our browser and record
http://127.0.0.1:8000/cats/1/

← → C ⓘ 127.0.0.1:8000/cats/1/

Articles by category

1

We will receive

[18/Sep/2022 16:52:23] "GET / HTTP/1.1" 200 47

[18/Sep/2022 16:53:58] "GET /cats/2/ HTTP/1.1" 200 56

[18/Sep/2022 16:54:02] "GET /cats/1/ HTTP/1.1" 200 56

As we can see, there is no dictionary anymore.

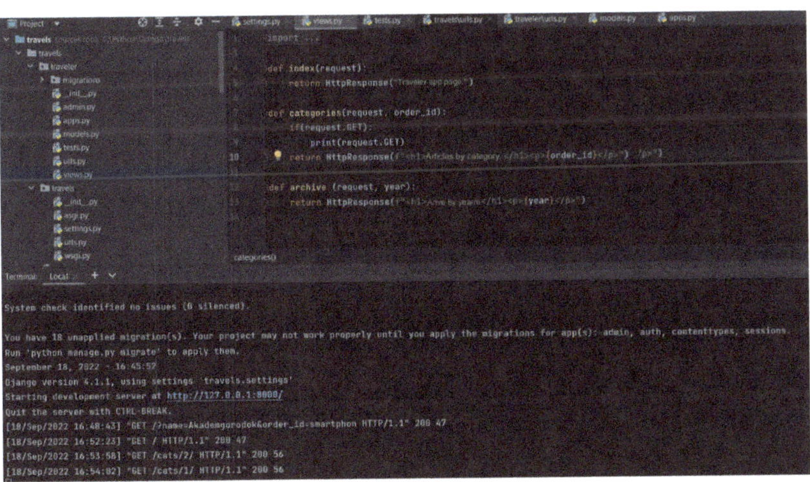

You can work in a similar way with a **POST** request.

```
def categories(request, order_id):
    if(request.POST):
```

```python
print(request.POST)

return HttpResponse(f"<h1> Articles by categories.</h1><p>{order_id}</p>")
```

Usually, a **POST** request works in conjunction with forms when we use it to submit data such as a username and password.

Exception handling when making requests to a server.

⚠ If you enter a string with a non-existent address, for example,
http://127.0.0.1:8000/cats/hjhsdjhsdj

We will receive a page **404**

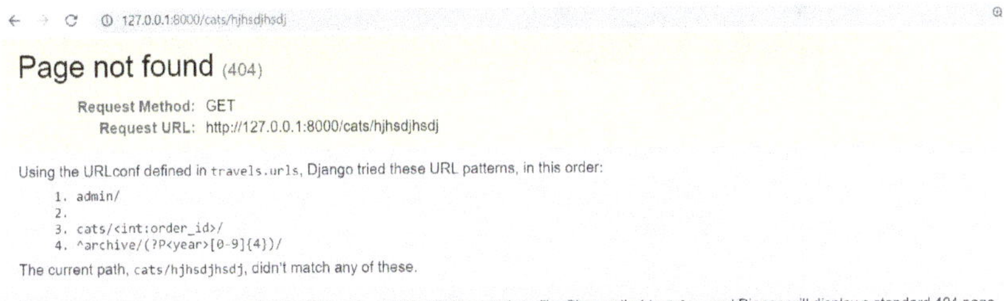

We see such a page exclusively during debugging, i.e., when the value is

DEBUG = True

You can change this value in the "**settings.py**" file in the "**travels**" folder.

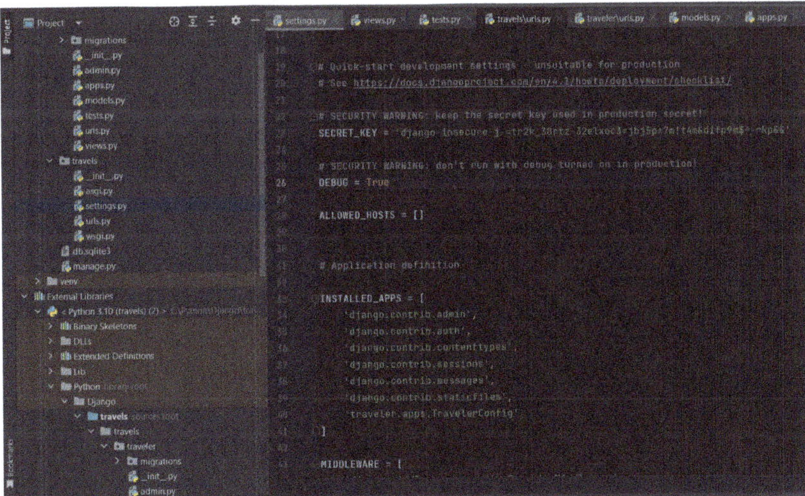

In non-debug mode, i.e., when **DEBUG = False** (in production mode), you will receive the following message in the console.

```
Not Found: /favicon.ico
[20/Sep/2022 11:48:23] "GET /favicon.ico HTTP/1.1" 404 2612
C:\Python\Django\travels\travels\travels\settings.py changed, reloading.
CommandError: You must set settings.ALLOWED_HOSTS if DEBUG is False.
(venv) PS C:\Python\Django\travels\travels>
```

This means that you don't have any allowed hosts specified. To fix this, you can specify the hostname in the same file by adding it to the line **ALLOWED_HOSTS = ['http://127.0.0.1']**

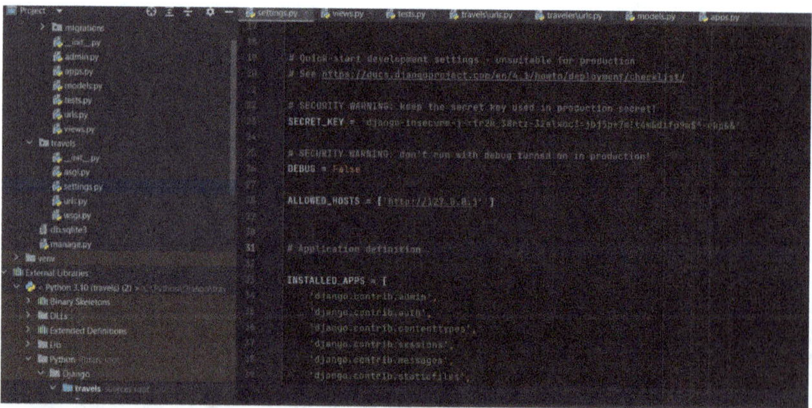

And then, restart the server as well as our webpage. As a result, you will see...

Bad Request (400)

Let's make a more user-friendly page in this case. In this situation, a 400 error means that the server couldn't understand the request.

To do this, open the "**urls.py**" file in the same configuration package where the "**settings.py**" file is located. In this file, you can define a special handler for this page.

Add the following line at the very end: **handler400 = pageNotFound**

And don't forget to import the necessary function.

from traveler.views import pageNotFound

from django.contrib import admin

from django.urls import path, include

from traveler.views import index

from traveler.views import pageNotFound

urlpatterns = [

  path('admin/', admin.site.urls),

  path('', include('traveler.urls')),

]

handler400 = pageNotFound

```
travels sources root  C:\Python\Django\travels       1
  travels                                            2  from django.contrib import admin
    traveler                                         3  from django.urls import path, include
      migrations                                     4  from traveler.views import index
      _init_.py                                      5  from traveler.views import pageNotFound
      admin.py                                       6
      apps.py                                        7  urlpatterns = [
      models.py                                      8      path('admin/', admin.site.urls),
      tests.py                                       9      path('', include('traveler.urls')),
      urls.py                                       10  ]
      views.py                                      11
    travels                                         12  handler400 = pageNotFound
      _init_.py
      asgi.py
      settings.py
      urls.py
      wsgi.py
```

Currently, we don't have the **pageNotFound function**. So, let's define it in the "**views.py**" file within the "**traveler**" package.

```
...

def archive (request, year):

    return HttpResponse(f"<h1> Archive by years </h1><p>{year}</p>")


def pageNotFound(request, exception):

    return HttpResponseNotFound('<h1> Page not found </h1>')
```

To use the **HttpResponseNotFound class**, you need to import it

```
from django.http import HttpResponse, HttpResponseNotFound
from django.shortcuts import render


def index(request):

    return HttpResponse("Application page traveler.")


def categories(request, order_id):

    return HttpResponse(f"<h1> Articles by categories.</h1><p>{order_id}</p>")


def archive (request, year):

     return HttpResponse(f"<h1> Yearly archive</h1><p>{year}</p>")


def pageNotFound(request, exception):

    return HttpResponseNotFound('<h1> Page not found</h1>')
```

```python
from django.http import HttpResponse, HttpResponseNotFound
from django.shortcuts import render


def index(request):
    return HttpResponse("The traveler app page.")


def categories(request, order_id):
    return HttpResponse(f"<h1>Articles by category</h1><p>{order_id}</p>")


def archive (request, year):
    return HttpResponse(f"<h1>Arive by yearm</h1><p>{year}</p>")


def pageNotFound(request, exception):
    return HttpResponseNotFound('<h1>Page not found</h1>')
```

You have obtained a more user-friendly page now.

In a similar manner, you can override handlers for other exceptions as well.

For example:

Handler500 – server error

Handler403 – access denied

All of these handlers come into play when **DEBUG = False** is set.

You can find more detailed information about exception handling by following this link: **Django Exceptions** Documentation.

In the future, if you can't access these links due to obsolescence or any other reason, it's always advisable to search for documentation on the official **Django** website using their search feature.

Creating 301 and 302 redirects.

301 – The page has been moved to another permanent URL

302 – The page has been moved to another temporary URL

Such redirects are often used in website development.

For this purpose, the **django.shortcuts.redirect** function is used.

Open the **views.py** file of our project and add the following line.

```python
from django.http import HttpResponse
from django.shortcuts import render, redirect


def index(request):
    return HttpResponse("Application page traveler.")


def categories(request, order_id):
    return HttpResponse(f"<h1> Articles by categories.</h1><p>{order_id}</p>")


def archive (request, year):
    if int(year) > 2022:
        return redirect('/')
    return HttpResponse(f"<h1>Yearly archive </h1><p>{year}</p>")
```

```python
from django.http import HttpResponse
from django.shortcuts import render, redirect


def index(request):
    return HttpResponse("Traveler app page.")


def categories(request, order_id):
    return HttpResponse(f"<h1>Articles by category</h1><p>{order_id}</p>")


def archive (request, year):
    if int(year) > 2022:
        return redirect('/')
    return HttpResponse(f"<h1>Archive by year</h1><p>{year}</p>")
```

If the year in the browser's address bar is greater than 2022, it will be redirected to the main page. To accomplish this, we will restart the server using the command we already know:

python manage.py runserver

When you refresh the browser page, you will see a page like this.

traveler app page

In the console, you will also see that a redirect with a status code of **302** was triggered

```
[22/Sep/2022 12:06:01] "GET /archive/2032 HTTP/1.1" 301 0
[22/Sep/2022 12:06:01] "GET /archive/2032/ HTTP/1.1" 302 0
[22/Sep/2022 12:06:01] "GET / HTTP/1.1" 200 47
Not Found: /favicon.ico
[22/Sep/2022 12:06:03] "GET /favicon.ico HTTP/1.1" 404 2612
```

As we remember, this is a temporary redirect.

To make it a permanent redirect, we will change the line to:

```
...

def archive (request, year):

  if int(year) > 2022:

    return redirect('/', permanent=True)

  return HttpResponse(f"<h1>Yearly archive </h1><p>{year}</p>")
```

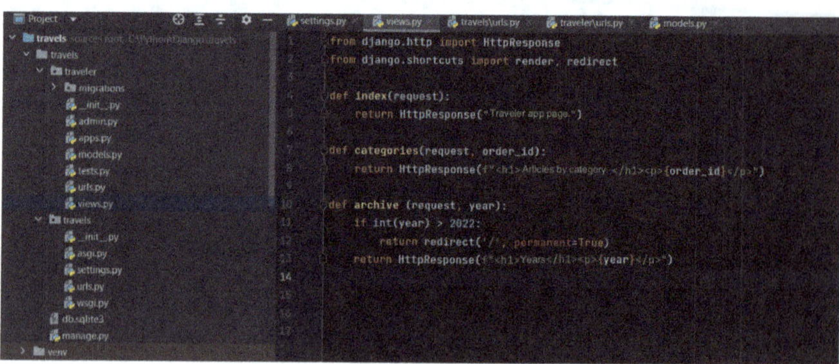

We return to the browser and refresh the page

```
Terminal:    Local  ×   +  ∨

Quit the server with CTRL-BREAK.
[22/Sep/2022 12:12:50] "GET / HTTP/1.1" 200 47
[22/Sep/2022 12:13:23] "GET /archive/2012/ HTTP/1.1" 200 46
[22/Sep/2022 12:13:30] "GET /archive/2030/ HTTP/1.1" 301 0
[22/Sep/2022 12:13:30] "GET / HTTP/1.1" 200 47
```

And we find in the console that a **301** redirect has been triggered.

It's important to mention one more thing. Explicitly hardcoding the **URL** we are redirecting to is considered bad practice. If the destination page's address changes for any reason, we would have to manually update the **URL** everywhere the function is used, which can be inconvenient and error-prone. It's not recommended to do it this way.

To avoid this practice, we specify the name of the **URL** in the redirect function instead of its explicit address. For example, for the main page, let's define the name as **'home'**. Next, we need to make these changes in the **URL** route. Open the 'urls.py' file of your application, find the route for the main page, and add the following line to it

```python
urlpatterns = [
    path('', index, name='home'),
    path('cats/<int:order_id>/', categories),
    re_path(r'^archive/(?P<year>[0-9]{4})/', archive),
]
```

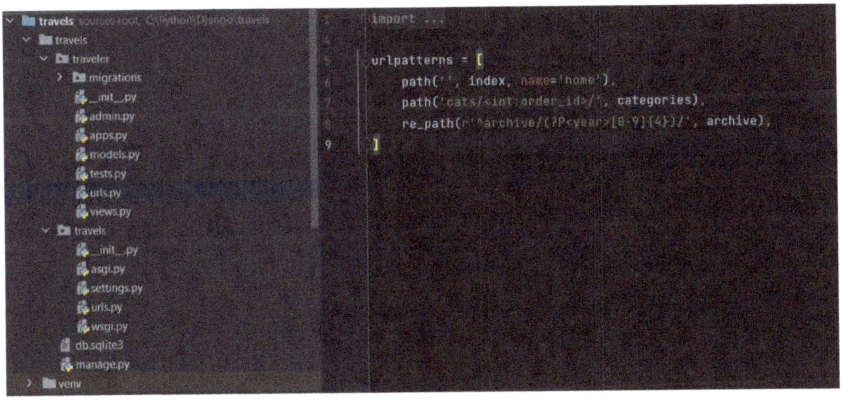

If you refresh the page and enter http://127.0.0.1:8000/archive/2045/

, you will be redirected to the main page.

Try entering a year that you haven't entered before to ensure that the browser doesn't use cached data.

traveler app page

Data Models. Migrations.

Data models are responsible for storing and manipulating a website's data. Standard database management systems are often used for this purpose. These include **SQLite, MySQL, PostgreSQL, Oracle,** and others.

For simplicity and clarity, you can use any database management system. However, during the development process or when deploying the website on a production server, there may be a need to change the system. This can be easily accomplished through what is known as **Object-Relational Mapping (ORM)**.

In other words, a **WSGI** application can interact with any type of database through the **Django ORM's** API interface. And the code at the WSGI application level remains universal.

By default, **Django** is configured to work with **SQLite**. In the context of our project, we will leave it as is. You can view the current database configuration in the configuration package, in the settings.py file, within the **'DATABASES'** dictionary.

```
DATABASES = {

  'default': {

    'ENGINE': 'django.db.backends.sqlite3',

    'NAME': BASE_DIR / 'db.sqlite3',

  }

}
```

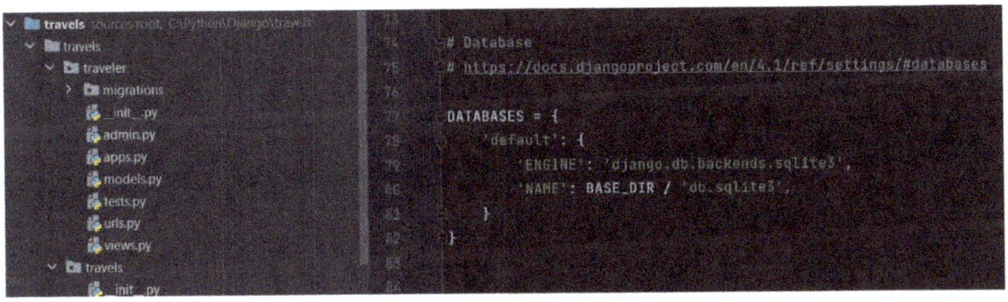

Connecting to other databases is done within the same dictionary. The key is to have the appropriate driver for interaction with them.

Let's add the first model to our program, which will describe the **"traveler"** table for storing information.

I've chosen the following database model structure. Yours may be different. Since our website is related to tourism, it's practical to name our models based on the context.

Let's name the first model "**dir_travel**," which corresponds to the chosen location that is likely to interest website users.

dir_travel

id: Integer, primary key

title: Varchar

content: Text

photo: Image

time_create: DateTime

time_update: DateTime

is_puplished: Boolean

Let me provide a translation of the explanation and instructions you provided:

We should clarify this structure a bit. Here,

"**id**" is the primary key, which accepts unique numerical values.

Essentially, it serves as the identifier for a record.

"**title**" is the article's title as a string with a specified number of characters.

"**content**" is the text.

"**photo**" is a field for linking to the primary photo of the post.

"**time_create**" and "**time_update**" represent the time of article creation and the time of its last update.

"**is_published**" is a boolean value that can be either True or False, depending on whether the post is published or not.

To create a table in our database with this structure, it's sufficient to define a class with these fields and then perform a migration.

So, let's define a class for this model. To do this, go to your project and open the **models.py** file. In this file, we will store all our models.

This file is currently empty and contains only the line "**from django.db import models**," which imports the models package. This package contains basic model classes that can be used as a basis for creating your own models.

Let's create a "**Dir_travel**" table that will contain information about tourist locations.

from django.db import models

```python
class Dir_travel(models.Model):

    title = models.CharField(max_length=255)

    content = models.TextField(blank=True)

    photo = models.ImageField(upload_to="photos/%Y/%m/%d/")

    time_create = models.DateTimeField(auto_now_add=True)

    time_update = models.DateTimeField(auto_now=True)

    is_puplished = models.BooleanField(default=True)
```

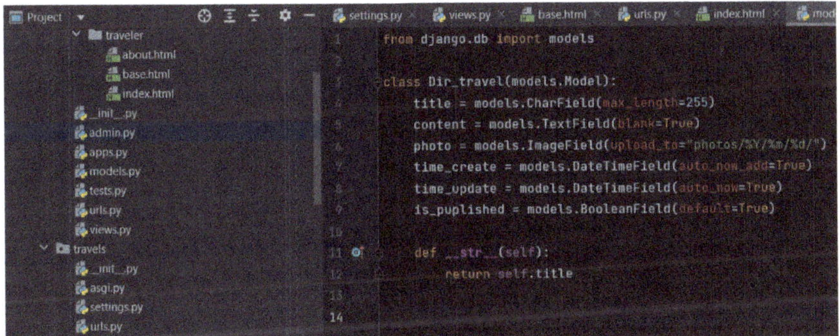

The class name is created by us.

Next, we inherit this class from the base class **models.Model**.

There is no 'id' field defined in this class anywhere. The reason is that this field is already automatically defined in the base **Model class**. This field is standard and exists in all **model classes**. To avoid specifying it redundantly in each class, developers have included it in the base class.

Next, we define the 'title' field as a reference to an instance of **CharField(max_length=255)**, which defines a text field with a maximum length of **255** characters.

You can find more detailed information about field types by following the link
https://django.fun/ru/docs/django/4.0/ref/models/fields/

Next, we define the **'content' field** as a reference to an instance of **TextField(blank=True),** which contains more extensive textual information. It has the **blank=True** parameter, which means that this field can be left empty.

The **'photo'** field stores a reference to our photograph. This field is defined through the **class ImageField(upload_to="photos/%Y/%m/%d/"),** and it has the **upload_to** parameter. This parameter specifies the directory and subdirectory where we will upload our images. We can define these directories using a template like **"photos/%Y/%m/%d/"**.

"photos/%Y/%m/%d/" - The current directory is **"photos,"** followed by **%Y for the year, %m for the month, and %d for the day**. As a result, our photos will be evenly distributed into folders, with new photos being uploaded to their respective folders each day. This structure makes sense in high-traffic projects.

The fields **'time_create' and 'time_update'** represent the creation time and the time of article editing, respectively.

We define these fields using the **DateTimeField(auto_now=True) class**, and this parameter means that if it is set to True, the **'time_create'** field will take the current time at the moment of adding a new record and will not change afterward.

When we specify **auto_now=True**, the **'time_update'** field will change every time we make any changes to that record.

When we add a new record, the **'is_published'** field will, by default, take the value **True**.

The sequence of these fields in the table by default will be the same as in this class.

To make this model work, you need to configure some settings for the **'photo'** field. This field will store only the path to the database table. In order for **Django** to perform automatic file uploads and generate a path to it, you need to define and configure the following constants: **MEDIA_ROOT and MEDIA_URL.**

You can find detailed information on how to configure these parameters in the official Django documentation https://docs.djangoproject.com/en/4.1/topics/files/

So, let's open the settings.py file in the configuration package, and at the very bottom of this file, add descriptions for these two constants:

MEDIA_ROOT = os.path.join(BASE_DIR, 'media')

MEDIA_URL = '/media/'

MEDIA_ROOT will point to the 'media' folder located in the current directory of our **project, BASE_DIR** (which determines the current directory of our project). A subdirectory **'media'** will be added to this working folder, where all our uploaded files will be located. To make everything work, it's necessary to import the os module.

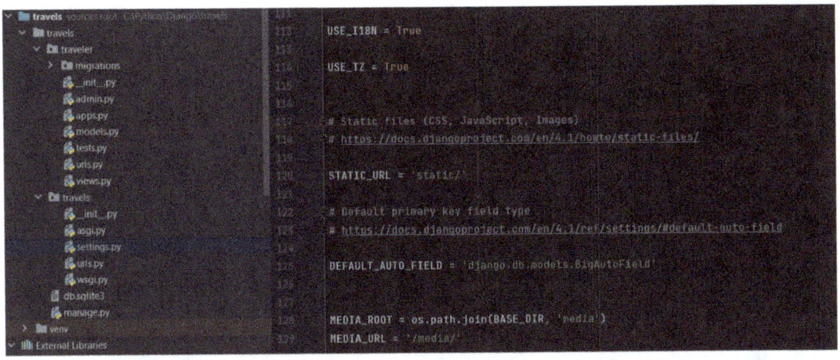

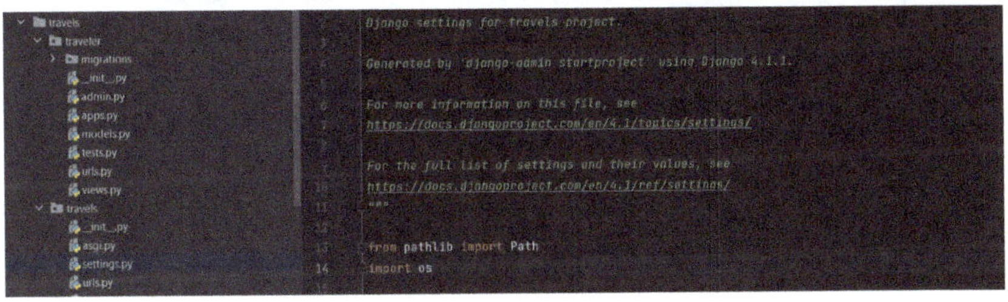

The constant **MEDIA_URL** will add the prefix '**/media/**' to the **URLs** of graphic files. And one more thing! **During** the debugging process, we need to simulate the operation of a real server to retrieve previously uploaded files and pass them to our application. To do this, in the configuration package, open the urls.py file, and after the urlpatterns collection, add the following

if settings.DEBUG:

  urlpatterns += static(settings.MEDIA_URL, document_root=settings.MEDIA_ROOT)

In debug mode, we add to the routes

urlpatterns = [

  path('admin/', admin.site.urls),

  path('', include('traveler.urls')),

]

In debug mode, we add another route. To make this work, we import the **static module** and **settings**

```python
from django.contrib import admin
from django.urls import path, include
from traveler.views import index


from django.conf.urls.static import static
from travels import settings


urlpatterns = [
    path('admin/', admin.site.urls),
    path('', include('traveler.urls')),
]

if settings.DEBUG:
    urlpatterns += static(settings.MEDIA_URL, document_root=settings.MEDIA_ROOT)
```

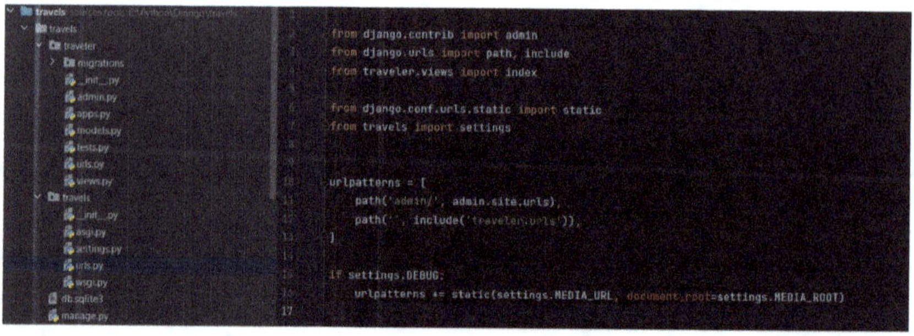

Now we can create a **database** table based on the created model. For this purpose, there is a mechanism called "**migrations**" for databases.

Migrations are **Python modules** that contain sets of **ORM-level** commands. When you execute a migration file, it automatically creates new tables or modifies existing ones in the database, as well as their relationships.

Each new migration file is placed in the "**migrations**" folder of our application.

The structure of tables in our database is created based on these migration files.

We go to our terminal and to the command line **(venv) PS C:\Python\Django\travels\travels>**

We add **python manage.py makemigrations**

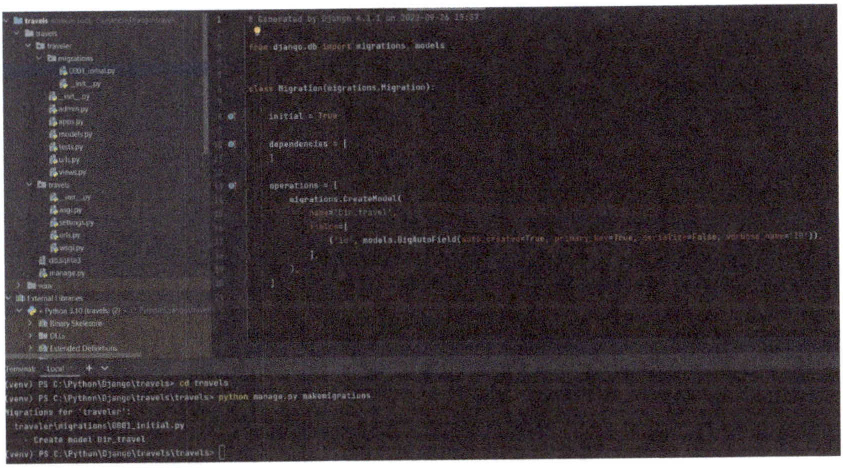

So, we have our first migration. To work with graphic files, it's better to install the **Pillow** package right away using the command **python -m pip install Pillow**

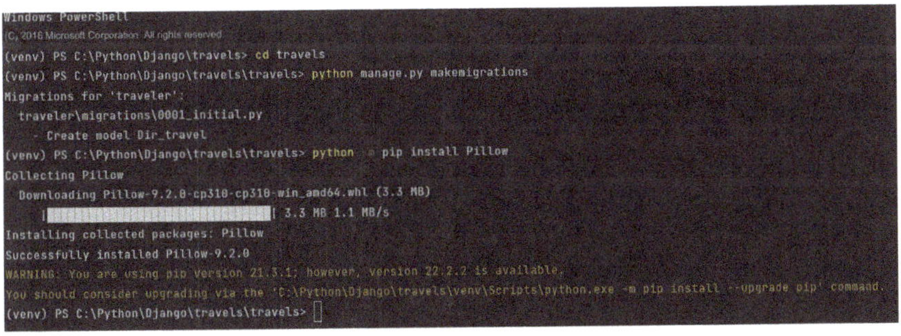

And at the same time, let's update the package manager **pip**

python -m pip install --upgrade pip

And as you can see, we now have a migration file

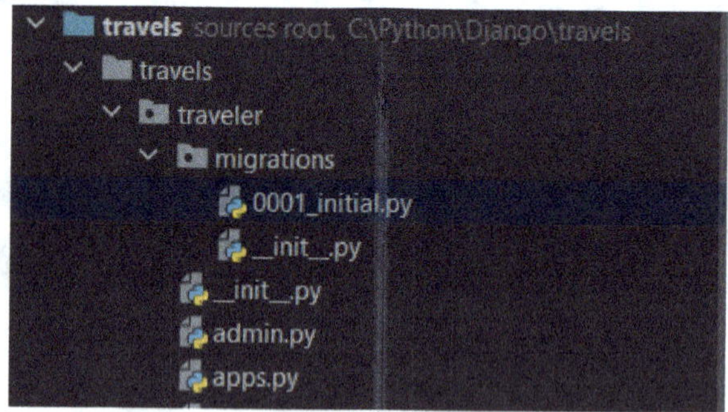

We'll create the table directly in the database by running the command

python manage.py migrate

The migration process in our terminal console looks like this

```
(venv) PS C:\Python\Django\travels\travels> python manage.py migrate
Operations to perform:
  Apply all migrations: admin, auth, contenttypes, sessions, traveler
Running migrations:
  Applying contenttypes.0001_initial... OK
  Applying auth.0001_initial... OK
  Applying admin.0001_initial... OK
  Applying admin.0002_logentry_remove_auto_add... OK
  Applying admin.0003_logentry_add_action_flag_choices... OK
  Applying contenttypes.0002_remove_content_type_name... OK
  Applying auth.0002_alter_permission_name_max_length... OK
  Applying auth.0003_alter_user_email_max_length... OK
  Applying auth.0004_alter_user_username_opts... OK
  Applying auth.0005_alter_user_last_login_null... OK
  Applying auth.0006_require_contenttypes_0002... OK
  Applying auth.0007_alter_validators_add_error_messages... OK
  Applying auth.0008_alter_user_username_max_length... OK
  Applying auth.0009_alter_user_last_name_max_length... OK
  Applying auth.0010_alter_group_name_max_length... OK
  Applying auth.0011_update_proxy_permissions... OK
  Applying auth.0012_alter_user_first_name_max_length... OK
  Applying sessions.0001_initial... OK
  Applying traveler.0001_initial... OK
(venv) PS C:\Python\Django\travels\travels>
```

Templates

We will discuss where to store templates and how to connect them in this section. You can find more detailed information about templates by visiting the official **Django** website https://django.fun/ru/docs/django/4.0/topics/templates/

Let's assume that as our main page, we want to use a template that is stored in a file **index.html**

To begin, let's import the built-in **Django** template engine. Next, go to our project and open the **views.py** file. This is the file where we will place all our templates.

```python
from django.shortcuts import render, redirect


def index(request):
    return HttpResponse("The traveler app page")


def categories(request, order_id):
    return HttpResponse(f"<h1>Category Articles</h1><p>{order_id}</p>")


def archive (request, year):
    if int(year) > 2022:
        return redirect('home', permanent=True)
    return HttpResponse(f"<h1>Arive by year</h1><p>{year}</p>")
```

As we can see, the render function is already imported here. This function is the built-in template engine in **Django**, and it processes our templates.

Next, to make the index function display the desired template instead of the **HttpResponse** class, we'll use the render function. We'll pass the **HttpRequest** object as the first parameter and specify the path to the template as the second parameter, leaving it empty for now.

Now, where should we place our template files for our application? They should be located in the "**templates**" folder of our "**traveler**" application. However, there's an important detail to consider. When building the entire project and deploying it on a live server, all templates from different applications are placed in a single "**templates**" folder, but this folder is shared across the entire project. If there are two identical files in different applications, the first one encountered will be used. This can create some difficulties.

To avoid this, within the "**templates**" folder of our application, "**traveler**," we'll create another subfolder with the name of our application, "**traveler.**" Inside this subfolder, we'll place our template files

Let's create a template file **index.html**

Please note the file extension of this file.

```
travels  sources root  C:\Python\Django\travels
  travels
    traveler
      migrations
        0001_initial.py
        __init__.py
      templates
        traveler
          index.html
      __init__.py
      admin.py
```

```html
1   <!DOCTYPE html>
2   <html lang="en">
3   <head>
4       <meta charset="UTF-8">
5       <title>Main page </title>
6   </head>
7   <body>
8   <h2>Main page </h2>
9   </body>
10  </html>
```

Pay attention to the **UTF-8** encoding. **Python** itself works with this encoding, so using other encodings may lead to issues.

We've created our first, very simple template. Now, let's go back to the **views.py** file and specify the path to our template in the index function.

from django.shortcuts import render, redirect

def index(request):

return render(request, 'traveler/index.html')

The thing is, **Django** by default looks for all templates in the **"templates"** folder, and anything within that folder needs to be specified by us.

Let's start our server and check the functionality of our modified application.

Main page

In this way, we've separated the code of our application from the actual templates.

In the future, we can change the template code without altering anything in the application itself. This is the essence of templates: to separate the application's logic from its presentation.

As an example, let's add another template that contains information about the website and name it **about.html.**

```
<!DOCTYPE html>

<html lang="en">

<head>

  <meta charset="UTF-8">

  <title> About the website</title>

</head>

<body>

<h1> About the website</h1>

</body>

</html>
```

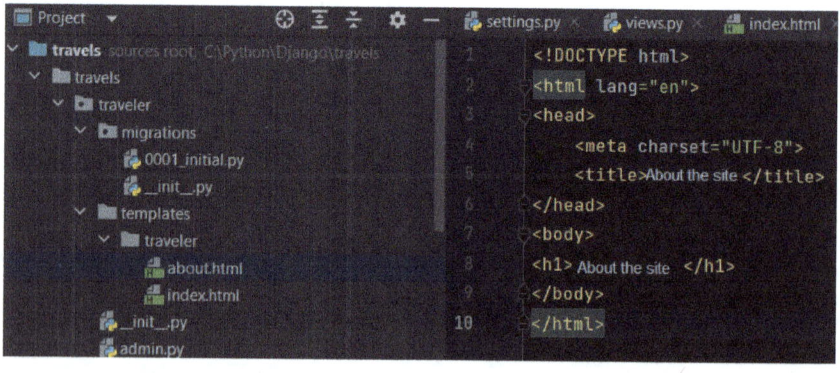

In the **views.py** file, we will define the corresponding view function for this template.

```
def about(request):
  return render(request, 'traveler/about.html')
```

```python
from django.http import HttpResponse
from django.shortcuts import render, redirect


def index(request):
    return render(request, 'traveler/index.html')


def about(request):
    return render(request, 'traveler/about.html')


def categories(request, order_id):
    return HttpResponse(f"<h1>Category Articles </h1><p>{order_id}</p>")


def archive (request, year):
    if int(year) > 2022:
        return redirect('home', permanent=True)
    return HttpResponse(f"<h1>Archive by year</h1><p>{year}</p>")
```

We will also define a route for this view function. Open the **urls.py** file in the application and add the following

```python
urlpatterns = [

    path('', index, name='home'),

    path('about/', about, name='about'),]
```

```python
import ...


urlpatterns = [
    path('', index, name='home'),
    path('about/', about, name='about'),
]
```

Let's start the web server (using the command **python manage.py runserver** within your virtual environment), and then enter the following **URL** in your browser's address bar: **http://127.0.0.1:8000/about/**

About the site

We got the expected result.

In the simplest form, this is how you can add templates to your application.

If you look at the **index.html** and **about.html** files, they are just **HTML** pages. In these files, you can include constructs to display information, for example, from a database.

As an example, let's make it so that a specific title is displayed for each page. Instead of **<title> Main Page </title>, we'll use <title>{{ title }}</title> in the index.html file.** We'll do the same in the about.html file.

```
travels  sources root  C:\Python\Django\travels
  travels
    traveler
      migrations
        0001_initial.py
        __init__.py
      templates
        traveler
          about.html
          index.html
      __init__.py
      admin.py
```

```html
1   <!DOCTYPE html>
2   <html lang="en">
3   <head>
4       <meta charset="UTF-8">
5       <title>{{ title }}</title>
6   </head>
7   <body>
8   <h1>О сайте</h1>
9   </body>
10  </html>
```

Where will this variable come from?

If we go to the **views.py** file, we can pass parameters to these templates. Parameters are passed as the third argument in the form of a dictionary, where we specify the key and value.

```python
def index(request):
    return render(request, 'traveler/index.html', {'title':' Main Page '})


def about(request):
    return render(request, 'traveler/about.html', {'title': "About the Website'})
```

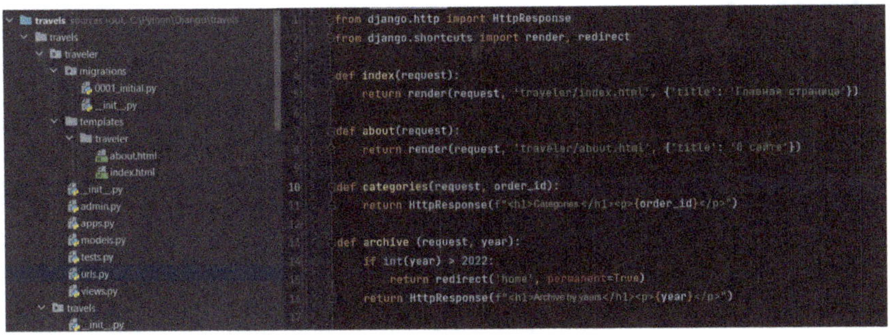

```
from django.http import HttpResponse
from django.shortcuts import render, redirect


def index(request):
    return render(request, 'traveler/index.html', {'title': 'Главная страница'})


def about(request):
    return render(request, 'traveler/about.html', {'title': 'О сайте'})


def categories(request, order_id):
    return HttpResponse(f"<h1>Categories</h1><p>{order_id}</p>")


def archive (request, year):
    if int(year) > 2022:
        return redirect('home', permanent=True)
    return HttpResponse(f"<h1>Archive by years</h1><p>{year}</p>")
```

Or we can make it more complex. For example, a list of the main menu

menu = ["About the website", "Add an article", "Feedback", "Log in"]

```
from django.http import HttpResponse
from django.shortcuts import render, redirect


menu = ["O site", "Add article", "Feedback", "Login"]
```

We want to display this list - the menu list, for example, on the main page.

You can do this as follows.

In the **views.py** file of our application, instead of the line

def index(request):

  return render(request, 'traveler/index.html', {'title': Main page})

пропишем

def index(request):

  return render(request, 'traveler/index.html', {'menu': menu, 'title': Main page})

or more precisely, we'll add.

'menu': menu. The first parameter - directly the menu and will have a link to the list that we defined earlier, and the second

'title': 'Main page' – link to the home page.

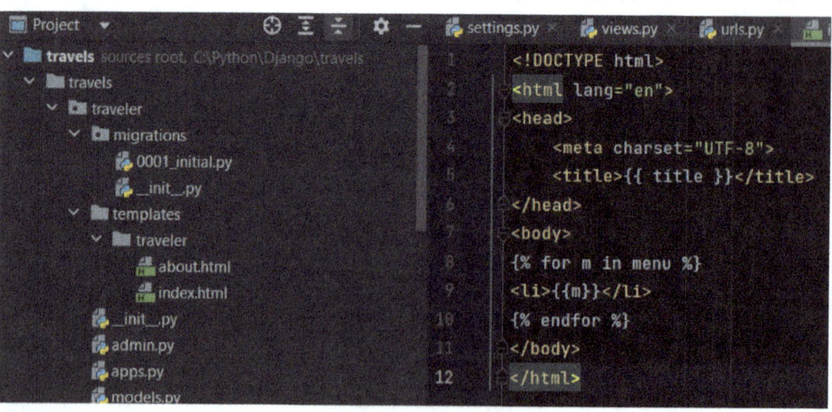

Now, in the **index.html** template, we will use the menu parameter and display this list. To do this, go to the **index.html** file and in the **<body></body>** section, display this list

```html
<!DOCTYPE html>
<html lang="en">
<head>
  <meta charset="UTF-8">
  <title>{{ title }}</title>
</head>
<body>
{% for m in menu %}
<li>{{m}}</li>
{% endfor %}
</body>
</html>
```

We used the 'for' tag to iterate through the menu parameters to display the value of 'm,' i.e., the strings from **menu = ["About the website", "Add an article", "Feedback", "Log in"]** as a list.

We will start the **runserver**, open the browser, and refresh the main page.

We will do the same for the page **about.html**

If you take a closer look, you'll notice that **index.html** and **about.html** essentially have the same content, meaning the **DRY** principle (**Don't Repeat Yourself**) is being violated here. To address this issue, a common approach is to create a base template for the overall site's pages, which is then extended by individual page templates.

We will create a base template for the site and name it **base.html**.

```
<!DOCTYPE html>

<html lang="en">

<head>

  <meta charset="UTF-8">
```

```html
<title>{{ title }}</title>
</head>
<body>
{% block mainmenu %}
<ul>
{% for m in menu %}
<li>{{m}}</li>
{% endfor %}
</ul>
{% endblock mainmenu %}


{% block content %}
{% endblock %}
</body>
</html>
```

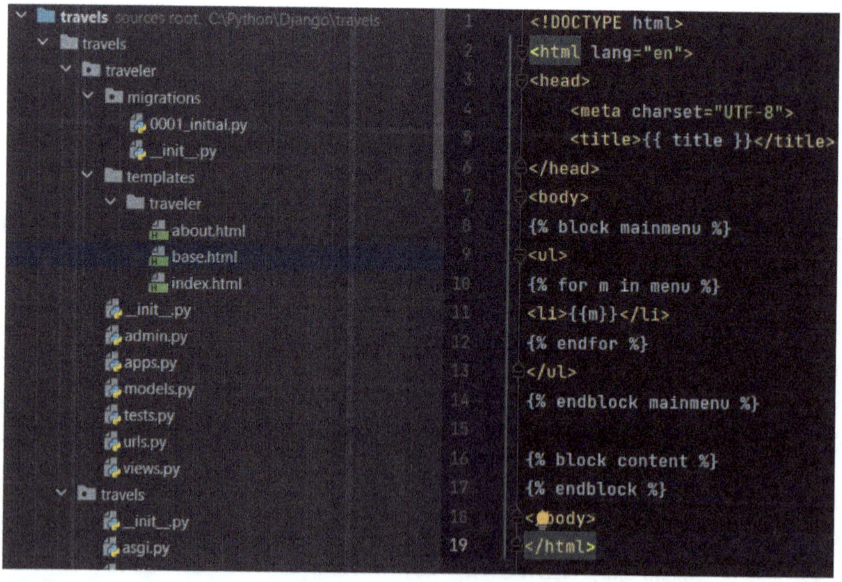

```
travels  sources root  C:\Python\Django\travels
  travels
    traveler
      migrations
        0001_initial.py
        __init__.py
      templates
        traveler
          about.html
          base.html
          index.html
      __init__.py
      admin.py
      apps.py
      models.py
      tests.py
      urls.py
      views.py
    travels
      __init__.py
      asgi.py
```

```html
1   <!DOCTYPE html>
2   <html lang="en">
3   <head>
4       <meta charset="UTF-8">
5       <title>{{ title }}</title>
6   </head>
7   <body>
8   {% block mainmenu %}
9   <ul>
10  {% for m in menu %}
11  <li>{{m}}</li>
12  {% endfor %}
13  </ul>
14  {% endblock mainmenu %}
15
16  {% block content %}
17  {% endblock %}
18  <body>
19  </html>
```

Next, in the **index.html** file, instead of

```
<!DOCTYPE html>
<html lang="en">
<head>
  <meta charset="UTF-8">
  <title>{{ title }}</title>
</head>
<body>
{% for m in menu %}
<li>{{m}}</li>
{% endfor %}
</body>
</html>
```

We will specify it as follows

```
{% extends 'traveler/base.html' %}

{% block content %}
<h1>{{title}}</h1>
<p>The content of the page</p>
{% endblock %}
```

{% extends 'traveler/base.html' %} - we are extending the base template, **base.html**, and within the content block **{% block content %} {% endblock %}**, we include the following information.

```
<h1>{{title}}</h1>
<p>The content of the page</p>
```

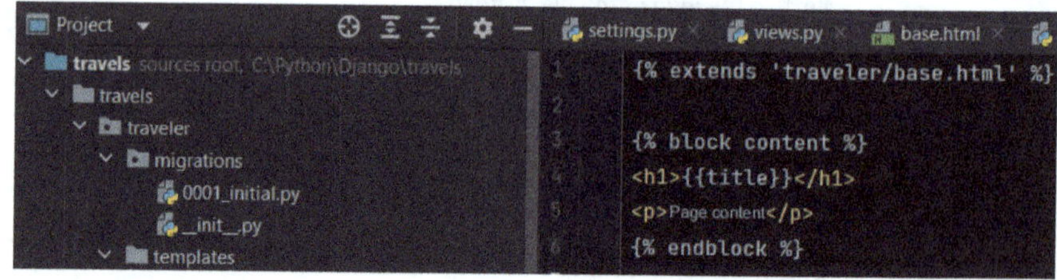

We will do the same for **about.html**. We reload our page and obtain...

- About the site
- Add article
- Feedback
- To come in

About the site

Page content

In this way, by using template inheritance or extending a base template, we eliminate code duplication, which is the recommended practice.

Let's proceed with reading data from the **'traveler'** table and displaying a list of articles on the main page of our site. First, we'll go to the **views.py** file and import our models.

```python
from django.http import HttpResponse
from django.shortcuts import render, redirect


from .models import *
```

...we access the **models.py** file with our models and import all models. Instead of specifying each model individually, we can import all models using '*****'.

Next, in the index function, we will add the line **posts = Dir_travel.objects.all()** - which selects all the records in the **Dir_travel** table and stores the references to these records in the '**posts**' variable, which we will then pass to the template.

```python
def index(request):

   posts = Dir_travel.objects.all()

   return render(request, 'traveler/index.html', { 'posts': posts, 'menu': menu, 'title': Main page '})
```

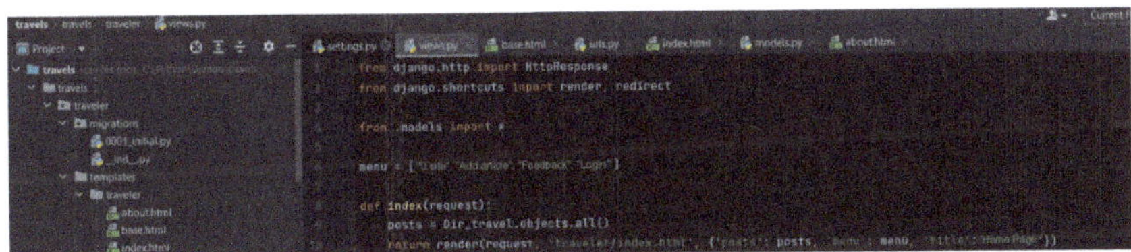

Open the **index.html** file, and instead of the paragraph **<p>Page content</p>**, we will create a list of our articles.

```html
{% extends 'traveler/base.html' %}


{% block content %}
<h1>{{title}}</h1>
<ul>
   {% for p in posts %}
   <li>
     <h2>
       {{p.title}}
     </h2>
     <h2>
       {{p.content}}
     </h2>
```

```
        <hr>
      </li>
      {% endfor %}
    </ul>


{% endblock %}
```

In this code, we iterate through all objects of our model using a loop and display only the **'title'** and **'content'**. To test the functionality of this code, start the web server using the known command **'python manage.py runserver'** and refresh the page http://127.0.0.1:8000/

Nothing surprising – we don't have any records yet. We only have the model, but the table is empty.

Creating an Admin Panel

To launch the admin panel, you need to enter into the browser

http://127.0.0.1:8000/admin/

After that, a page will appear

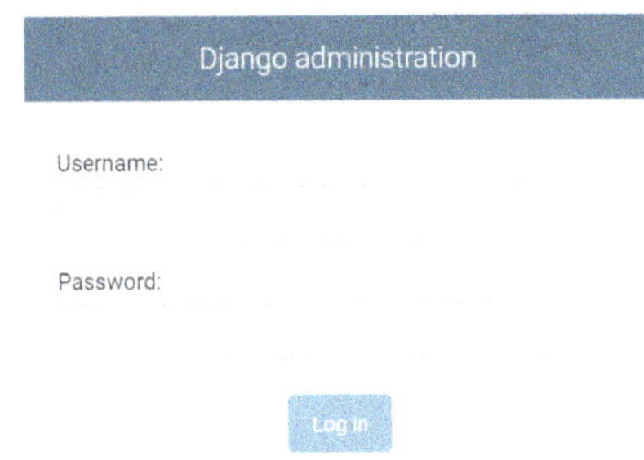

The admin panel is currently displayed in English. If you want to change the language, then go to the configuration package **"travels"** and open the **"settings.py"** file. In it, find the variable **"LANGUAGE_CODE = 'en-us'."** By default, it is set to English. You can leave it as is, but if necessary, you can change the language, for example, to Russian..

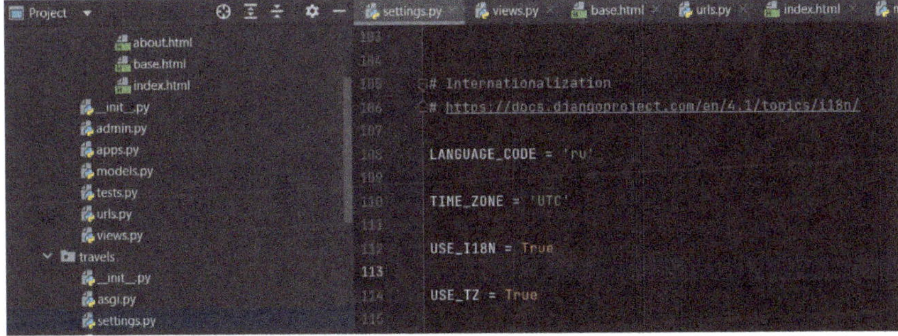

The web server is restarted, you refresh the page, and you will see the admin panel in Russian. Additionally, the entire Django framework will be localized in Russian. The same procedure can be followed to change the language to other languages as well.

This admin panel allows you to handle all standard tasks. This includes creating users with different permissions, displaying all of our applications, adding, modifying, deleting records, and more.

So, to log in, you need to enter a username and password, but we don't have them yet. First, it is necessary to create a **superuser**, also known as the site administrator.

To do this, go to the project's terminal and execute the command

Python manage.py createsuperuser

```
(venv) PS C:\Python\Django\travels\travels> Python manage.py createsuperuser
Username (leave blank to use 'user'):
```

Let's enter the username. For example, "**root**."

```
Username (leave blank to use 'user'): root
E-mail address :
```

An email address, for example root@gmail.com

```
Username (leave blank to use 'user'): root ): root
E-mail address : root@gmail.com
Password:
Password (again):
```

Next, we come up with a password and enter it again. For educational purposes, we use simple and easy-to-remember names, email addresses, and passwords. However, when deploying on a production server, it's important to create non-standard and complex usernames and passwords, as well as use a valid email address for receiving administrative information.

```
Superuser created successfully.
(venv) PS C:\Python\Django\travels\travels>
```

The superuser has been created. Now we can enter the username and password in the admin panel.

Django administration

Username:

```
root
```

Password:

```
••••
```

To come in

And we log into the admin panel... Don't forget to restart the server!

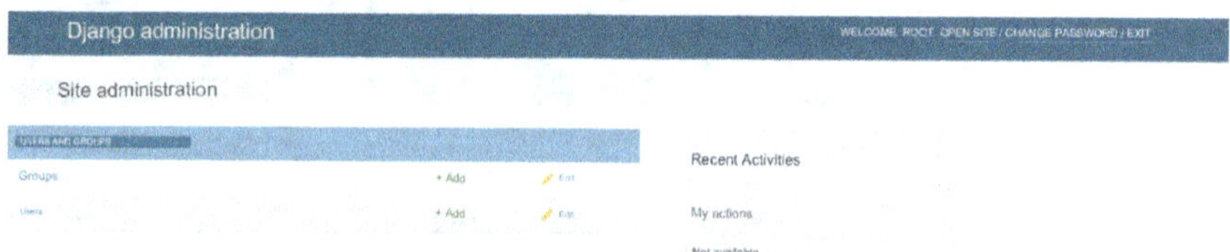

On the main page, we see two registered applications - these are "Groups" and "Users." We can create new users and assign them specific roles.

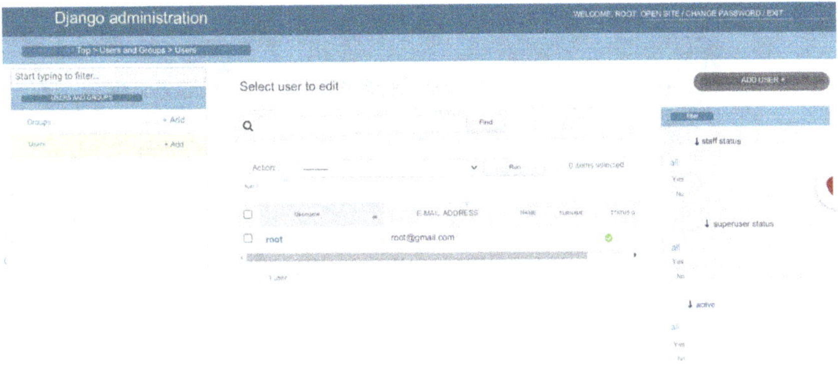

Forming groups for users

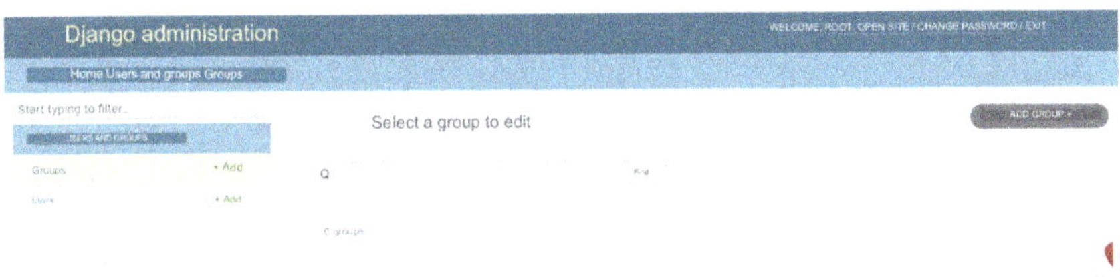

However, our "**Dir_travel**" application is not listed here because it needs to be registered with this admin panel. To do this, open the project's "**admin.py**" file and specify the registration for our application. In this file, our model should be accessible, so we import it (import all models at once).

*from .models import **

Next, let's add the following line

admin.site.register(Dir_travel)

The entire code:

from django.contrib import admin

*from .models import **

admin.site.register(Dir_travel)

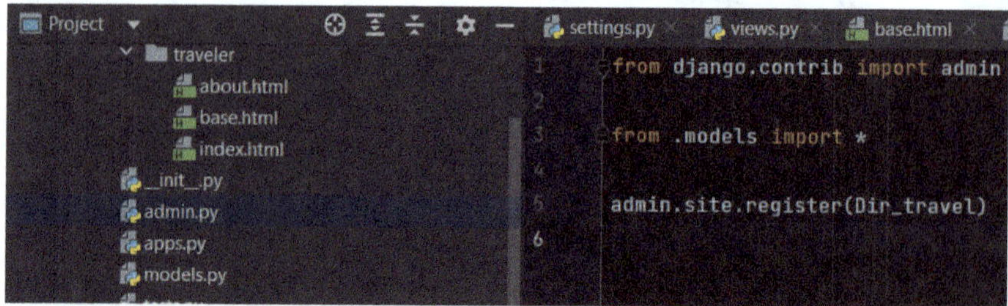

Let's refresh the page in the browser

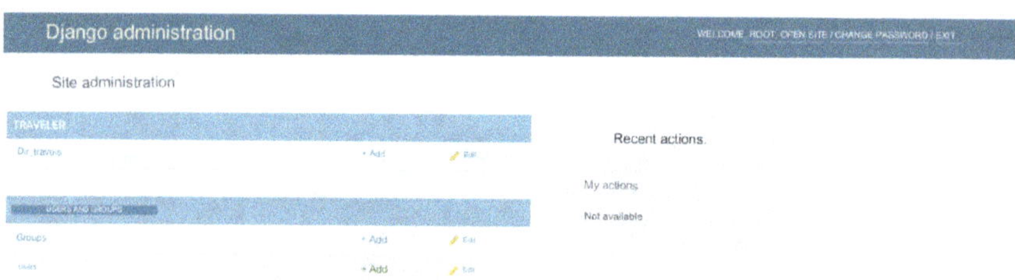

And we can see that our model has appeared. If you click on the model's tab, you'll see that we have no articles. Let's create a few articles. Click on the "**Add**" button and fill in the fields

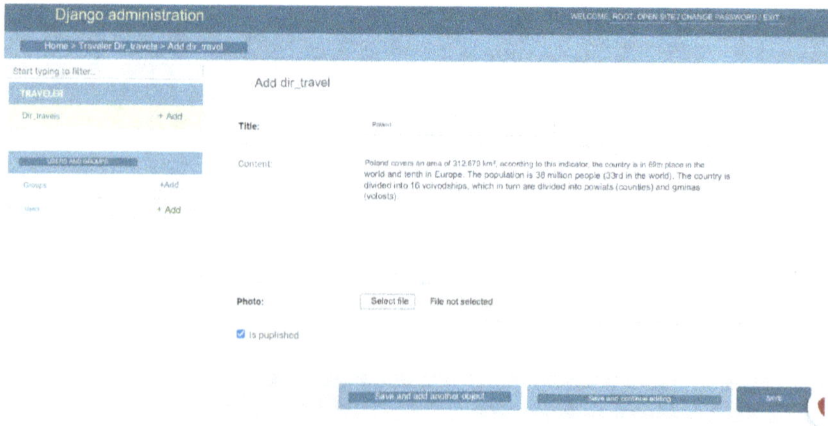

And click **"Save."**

 **Django** It suggests that we haven't filled in all the fields

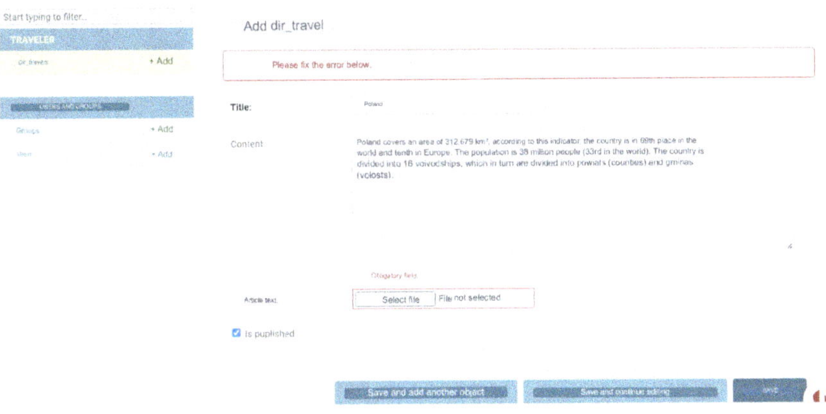

Let's select a file with a photo

OperationalError at /admin/traveler/dir_travel/add/

table traveler_dir_travel has no column named title

Request Method:	POST
Request URL:	http://127.0.0.1:8000/admin/traveler/dir_travel/add/
Django Version:	4.1.1
Exception Type:	OperationalError
Exception Value:	table traveler_dir_travel has no column named title
Exception Location:	C:\Python\Django\travels\venv\lib\site-packages\django\db\backends\sqlite3\base.py, line 357, in execute
Raised during:	django.contrib.admin.options.add_view
Python Executable:	C:\Python\Django\travels\venv\Scripts\python.exe
Python Version:	3.10.7
Python Path:	['C:\\Python\\Django\\travels\\travels', 'C:\\Python\\python310.zip', 'C:\\Python\\DLLs', 'C:\\Python\\lib', 'C:\\Python', 'C:\\Python\\Django\\travels\\venv', 'C:\\Python\\Django\\travels\\venv\\lib\\site-packages']
Server time:	Wed, 12 Oct 2022 11:23:09 +0000

 What is the cause of this error?

You can spend a long time figuring out where the mistake was made. In my case, I simply deleted the database file **db.sqlite3** and the migration **file 0001_initial.py**, and then re-entered the commands in the console

python manage.py makemigrations

then

python manage.py migrate

You also need to re-create the superuser using the command

Python manage.py createsuperuser

Let's access the admin panel and create our first post by filling in all the fields. The result will look as follows:

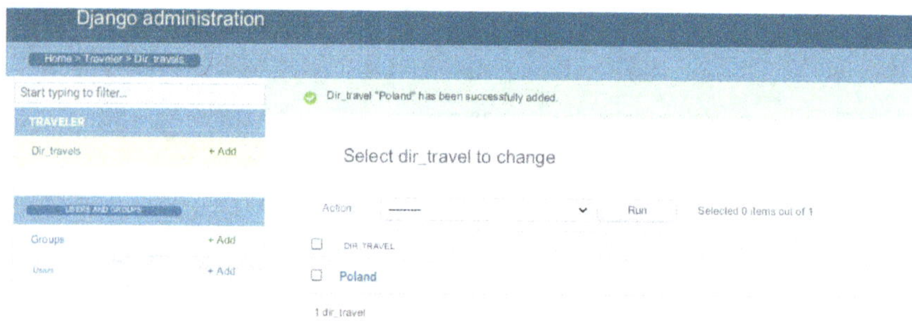

Poland,[b] officially the Republic of Poland,[c] is a country in Central Europe. It is divided into 16 administrative provinces called voivodeships, covering an area of 312,696 km2 (120,733 sq mi). Poland has a population of over 38 million and is the fifth-most populous member state of the European Union.[12] Warsaw is the nation's capital and largest metropolis. Other major cities include Kraków, Wrocław, Łódź, Poznań, Gdańsk, and Szczecin. Poland has a temperate transitional climate. Its territory extends from the Baltic Sea in the north to the Sudeten and Carpathian Mountains in the south. The country is bordered by Lithuania and Russia to the northeast,[d] Belarus and Ukraine to the east, Slovakia and the Czech Republic to the south, and Germany to the west. Poland also shares maritime boundaries with Denmark and Sweden.

We will display the photos on the page later. Similarly, we will create a few more posts.

Main page

- Poland

Poland,[b] officially the Republic of Poland,[c] is a country in Central Europe. It is divided into 16 administrative provinces called voivodeships, covering an area of 312,696 km2 (120,733 sq mi). Poland has a population of over 38 million and is the fifth-most populous member state of the European Union.[12] Warsaw is the nation's capital and largest metropolis. Other major cities include Kraków, Wrocław, Łódź, Poznań, Gdańsk, and Szczecin. Poland has a temperate transitional climate. Its territory extends from the Baltic Sea in the north to the Sudeten and Carpathian Mountains in the south. The country is bordered by Lithuania and Russia to the northeast,[d] Belarus and Ukraine to the east, Slovakia and the Czech Republic to the south, and Germany to the west. Poland also shares maritime boundaries with Denmark and Sweden.

- Ukraine

Ukraine (Ukrainian: Україна, romanized: Ukraïna, pronounced [ʊkrɐˈjinɐ] (listen)) is a country in Eastern Europe. It is the second-largest European country after Russia, which it borders to the east and northeast.[a][11] Ukraine covers approximately 600,000 square kilometres (230,000 sq mi).[b] Prior to the ongoing Russo-Ukrainian War, it was the eighth-most populous country in Europe, with a population of around 41 million people.[c][6] It is also bordered by Belarus to the north; by Poland, Slovakia, and Hungary to the west; and by Romania and Moldova[d] to the southwest; with a coastline along the Black Sea and the Sea of Azov to the south and southeast.[e] Kyiv is the nation's capital and largest city. The country's national language is Ukrainian, and most people are also fluent in Russian.[14]

- Germany

Germany (German: Deutschland, pronounced [ˈdɔʏtʃlant] (listen)), officially the Federal Republic of Germany,[f] is a country in Central Europe. It is the second most populous country in Europe after Russia, and the most populous member state of the European Union. Germany is situated between the Baltic and North seas to the north, and the Alps to the south; it covers an area of 357,022 square kilometres (137,847 sq mi), with a population of almost 84 million within its 16 constituent states. Germany borders Denmark to the north, Poland and the Czech Republic to the east, Austria and Switzerland to the south, and France, Luxembourg, Belgium, and the Netherlands to the west. The nation's capital and largest city by population is Berlin and its financial centre is Frankfurt; the largest urban area is the Ruhr.

So, we have a **Dir_travel** model. Let's configure our admin panel to make it more user-friendly. The first thing we'll do is change the name **Dir_travel** to **'All Countries.'** How to do this? We go to the **models.py** file and in the **Dir_travel** class, we add an inner class Meta

class Meta:

verbose_name = "Все страны"

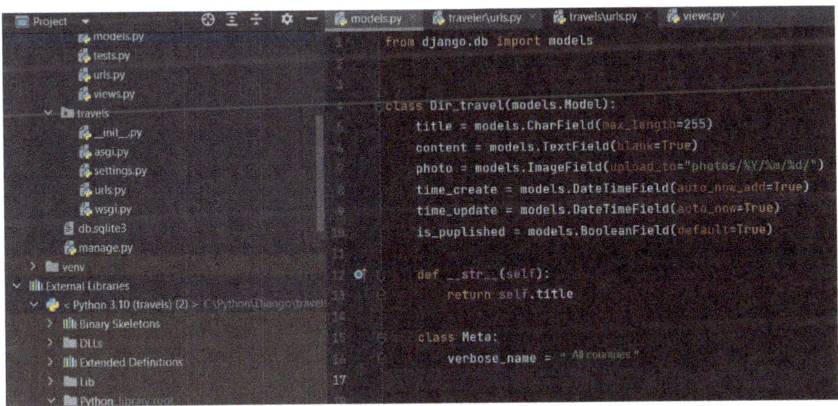

*This is a special class used by the admin panel to configure the **Dir_travel** model. Let's go to the admin panel and refresh/update it.*

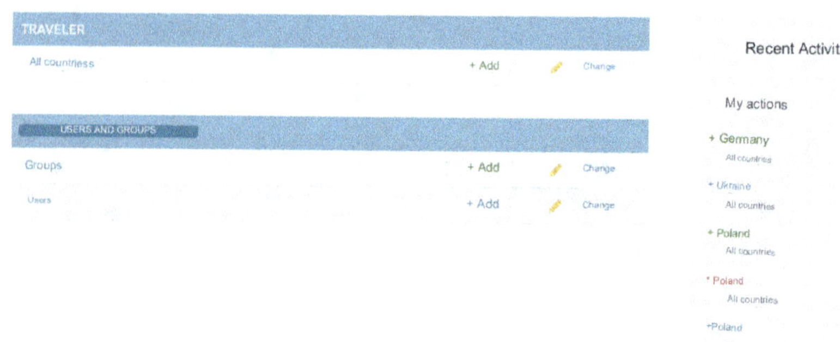

The letter 's' is added automatically by **Django** to convert the singular form into the plural form. This can be corrected by specifying the second attribute

class Meta:

verbose_name = " All Countries"

verbose_name_plural = "All Countries"

We refresh the browser page, and as we can see, the letter 's' is gone.

Next, let's create sorting of records by their creation time.

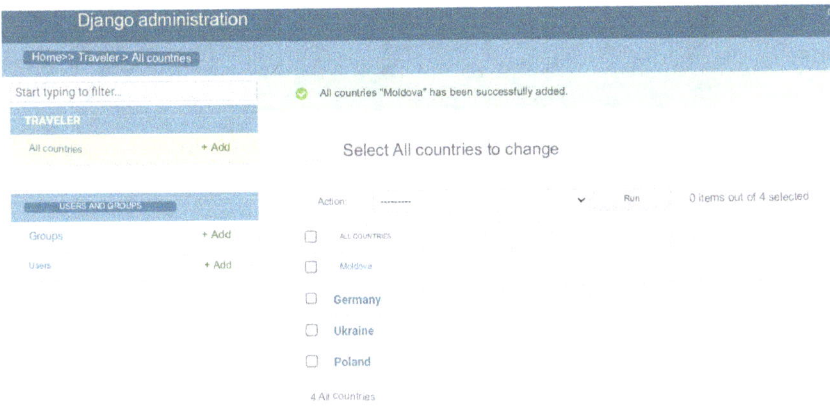

In the same **Meta** subclass, we add another attribute and specify the fields by which sorting will occur. You can specify multiple fields, and sorting will be performed from left to right.

```
class Meta:
    verbose_name = "All Countries"
    verbose_name_plural = "All Countries"
    ordering = ['time_create', 'title']
```

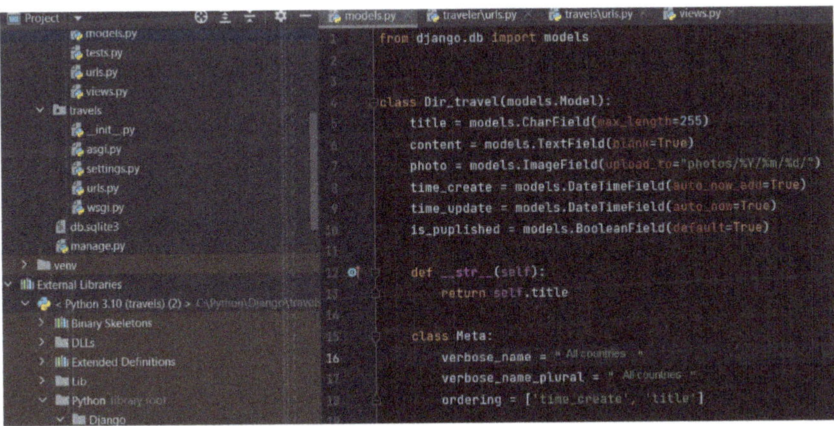

Let's go to the admin panel and refresh the page

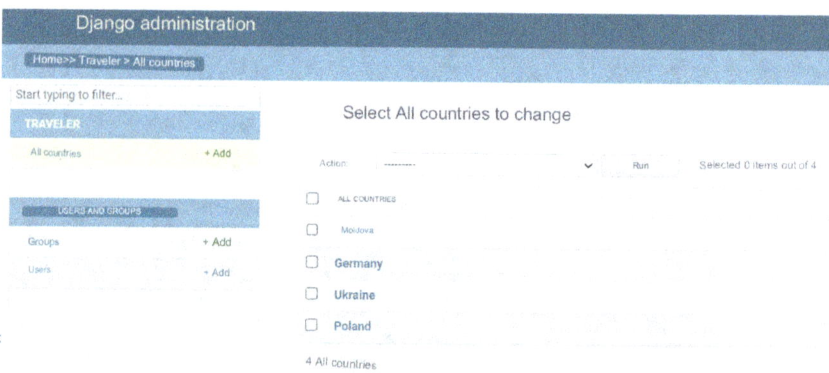

We will see that the order has changed. We can reverse the order by adding a '-' sign. For example

ordering = ['-time_create', 'title']

And, if we refresh, we will get reverse sorting.

This sorting is applied not only to the admin panel but also to our web page. Let's go back to the admin panel and continue making improvements. We will change the name **'TRAVELER'** to **'My travels.'** To do this, open the apps.py file and add the following code in the **TravelerConfig class**

verbose_name = " TRAVELER"

class TravelerConfig(AppConfig):

  default_auto_field = 'django.db.models.BigAutoField'

  name = 'traveler'

  verbose_name = "TRAVELER"

This class is used for configuring the entire application.

Let's go to the admin panel and refresh.

Django administration

Site administration

USERS AND GROUPS

Groups · + Add · Change

Users · + Add · Change

TRIPS

All countries · + Add · Change

This change will work if we register our application in the settings.py file in exactly this way:

'traveler.apps.TravelerConfig'

If you register it simply as **'traveler'**, it won't work. Keep that in mind.

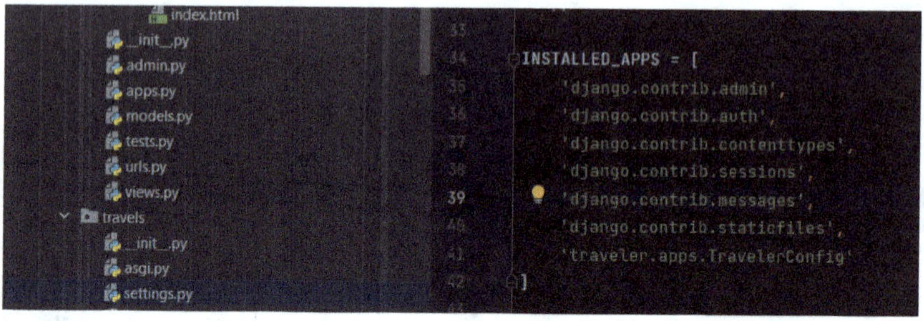

```
index.html
__init__.py
admin.py
apps.py
models.py
tests.py
urls.py
views.py
travels
    __init__.py
    asgi.py
    settings.py
```

```python
INSTALLED_APPS = [
    'django.contrib.admin',
    'django.contrib.auth',
    'django.contrib.contenttypes',
    'django.contrib.sessions',
    'django.contrib.messages',
    'django.contrib.staticfiles',
    'traveler.apps.TravelerConfig'
]
```

Next, let's add more fields in the list of articles, not just the title (such as publication time, publication flag, etc.). Open the **admin.py** file and add the following:

from django.contrib import admin

*from .models import ***

class Dir_travelAdmin(admin.ModelAdmin):

  list_display = ('id', 'title', 'time_create', 'photo')

  list_display_links = ('id', 'title')

  search fields = ('title', 'content')

Please note that if in the line **'search_fields = ('title', 'content')'** we were searching by a single field, such as **'title,'** then we would need to write **'search_fields = ('title',)'**. That is, after **'title,'** it's essential to add a comma, as we are passing a tuple. Without the comma, it would no longer be a tuple but a string

admin.site.register(Dir_travel)

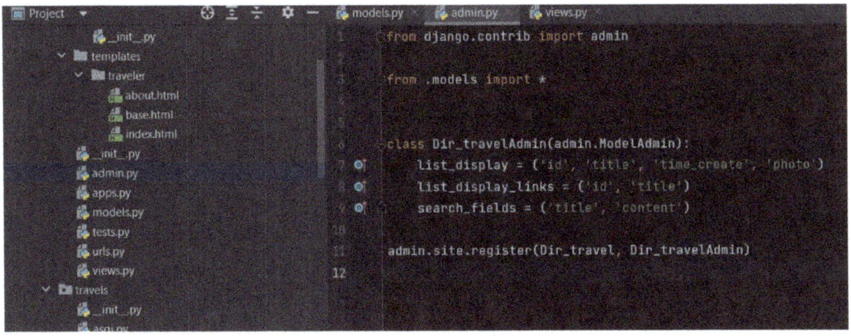

```
from django.contrib import admin

from .models import *


class Dir_travelAdmin(admin.ModelAdmin):
    list_display = ('id', 'title', 'time_create', 'photo')
    list_display_links = ('id', 'title')
    search_fields = ('title', 'content')


admin.site.register(Dir_travel, Dir_travelAdmin)
```

list_display" contains a list of all the fields we want to see in our admin panel.

"**list_display_links**" contains the fields on which we can click to go to the corresponding article for editing.

"**search_fields**" specifies the fields by which we can search for specific information.

And now, we specify this class as the second parameter when registering it

admin.site.register(Dir_travel, Dir_travelAdmin)

Let's go to the browser and refresh the admin panel. Now, let's translate the headings into Russian. To do this, open models.py and add a few lines in the **Dir_travel** class

class Dir_travel(models.Model):

   *title = models.CharField(max_length=255, **verbose_name = "Heading"**)*

   *content = models.TextField(blank=True, **verbose_name = "Article text"**)*

   *photo = models.ImageField(upload_to="photos/%Y/%m/%d/", **verbose_name = "Photo"**)*

   *time_create = models.DateTimeField(auto_now_add=True, **verbose_name = "Time of creation"**)*

   *time_update = models.DateTimeField(auto_now=True, **verbose_name = "Change time"**)*

   is_puplished = models.BooleanField(default=True)

```python
from django.db import models


class Dir_travel(models.Model):
    title = models.CharField(max_length=255, verbose_name = "")
    content = models.TextField(blank=True, verbose_name = "")
    photo = models.ImageField(upload_to="photos/%Y/%m/%d/", verbose_name =
    time_create = models.DateTimeField(auto_now_add=True, verbose_name
    time_update = models.DateTimeField(auto_now=True, verbose_name = "
    is_published = models.BooleanField(default=True)

    def __str__(self):
```

Let's go to the browser and update.

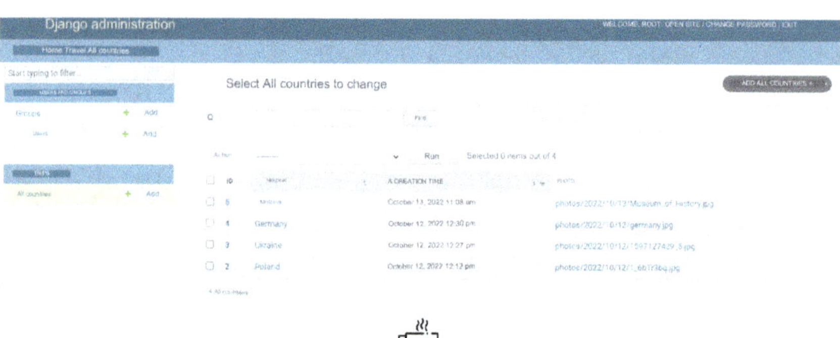

Connecting static files

Let's consider the possibility of connecting static files, such as CSS, JavaScript, and so on. Our application can operate in two modes: debugging mode on a test web server and production mode on a real server. In debugging mode, **Django** looks for static files in all subdirectories named **"static"** in our applications. If there are multiple such directories, static files will be searched in all of them. Non-standard paths for static files can also be defined, where static files will be searched.

In production mode, the real server will take all static files from the **"static"** folder located in the project's root directory. How does this folder with all these files appear? To achieve this, a special command is executed when preparing the project for production:

Copy code

python manage.py collectstatic

After running this command, all static files scattered across different **"static"** directories located at various paths are collected into a common **"static"** folder for the entire project.

To ensure that all this functionality works correctly, you need to define the following three constants in the configuration package:

STATIC_URL - the URL prefix for static files.

STATIC_ROOT - the path to the common static folder used by the real web server.

STATICFILES_DIRS - a list of additional paths to static files used for collection and debugging mode.

So, in the configuration package, open the settings.py file and add all these constants at the bottom.

STATIC_URL = '/static/'

STATIC_ROOT = os.path.join(BASE_DIR, 'static')

STATICFILES_DIRS = []

The first constant is already in place, and the last one is empty for us because there are no non-standard paths.

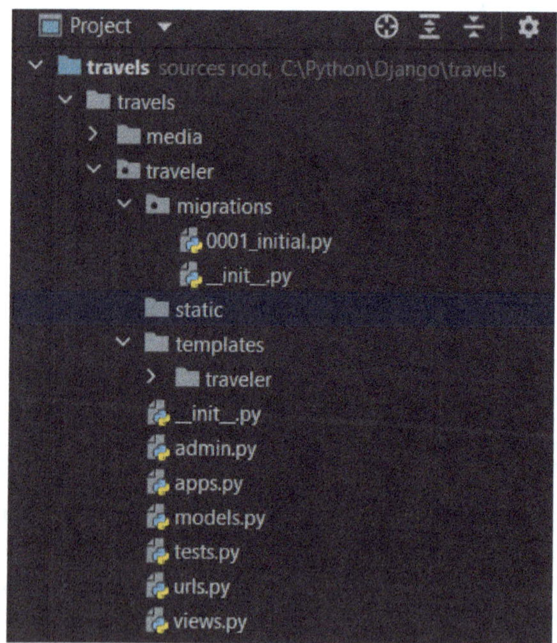

Next, let's create a "**static**" folder in our "**traveler**" application.

In the same folder, create a directory named "**traveler**" for templates to avoid naming conflicts.

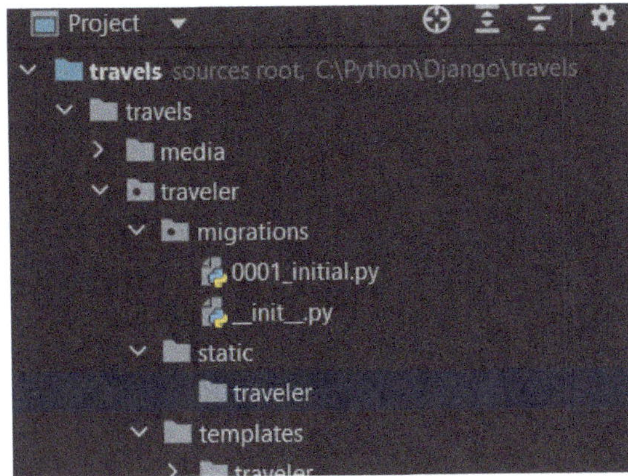

In this subdirectory, create the following directories:

"**css**" for storing cascading style sheets (**CSS**).

"**js**" for storing JavaScript files.

"**images**" for storing image files.

Within the "**css**" directory, create a file named "**styles.css**" to hold the style rules for page formatting. We won't go into detail about writing the style rules here, as it's a separate topic, but you can simply copy and paste a pre-made template.

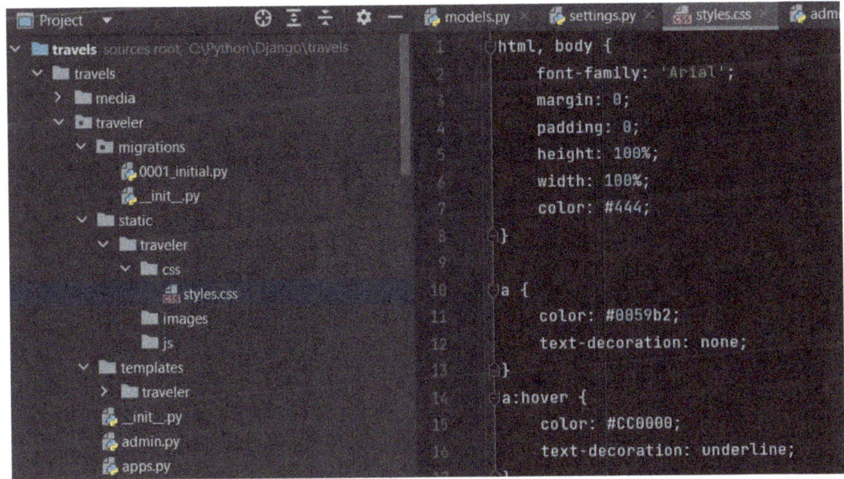

Using the same analogy, I prepared and uploaded image templates to the "**images**" directory.

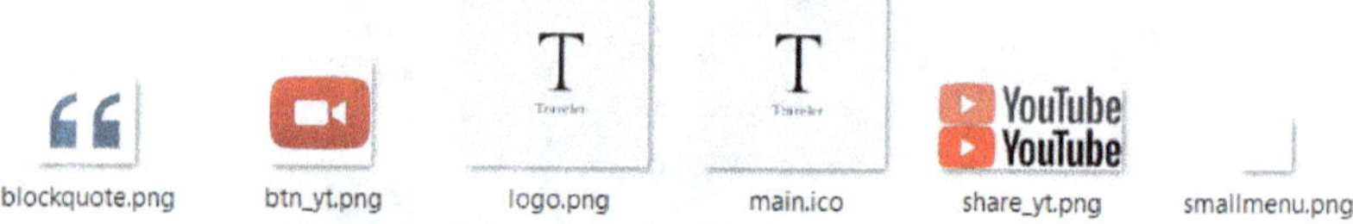

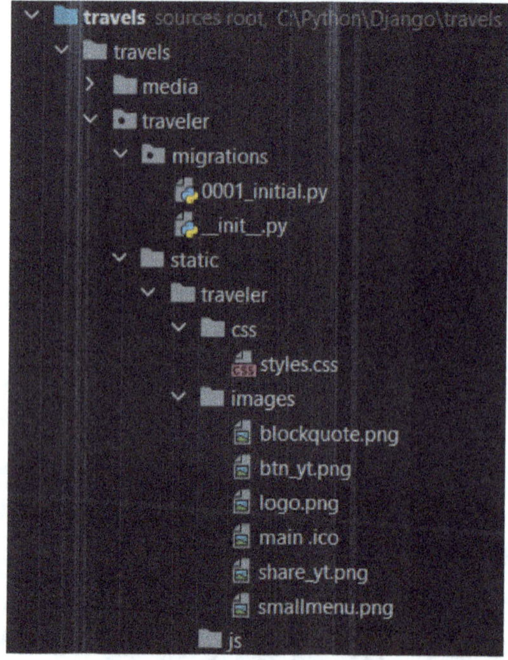

Next, open the base template, **base.html**, and at the very beginning of the template, add the tag **{% load static %}**.

The load tag loads the static tag, through which we will connect external files. Then, in the **<head></head>** section, we will link the styling file:

<link type="text/css" href="{% static 'traveler/css/styles.css' %}" rel="stylesheet/>. Here, we specify the path to the **styles.css** file. **Django** will automatically find the styles directory, and then we specify the path ourselves. Let's see how it will look. First, start our server and enter the standard URL in your browser:

http://127.0.0.1:8000/.

Main page

☐ Moldova

Moldova (Romanian: Republica Moldova), is a landlocked country in Eastern Europe.[17] It is bordered by Romania to the west and Ukraine to the north, east Russian puppet state of Transnistria lies across the Dniester on the country's eastern border with Ukraine. Moldova's capital and largest city is Chișinău.

. Germany

Germany (German: Deutschland, pronounced [dɔʏtʃlant] (listen)), officially the Federal Republic of Germany,[f] is a country in Central Europe. It is the secon after Russia, and the most populous member state of the European Union. Germany is situated between the Baltic and North seas to the north, and the Alps 357,022 square kilometres (137,847 sq mi), with a population of almost 84 million within its 16 constituent states. Germany borders Denmark to the north, Po east, Austria and Switzerland to the south, and France, Luxembourg, Belgium, and the Netherlands to the west. The nation's capital and largest city by popul Frankfurt; the largest urban area is the Ruhr.

. Ukraine

Ukraine (Ukrainian: Україна, romanized: Ukraïna, pronounced [ukre jinɐ] (listen)) is a country in Eastern Europe. It is the second-largest European country af and northeast.[a][11] Ukraine covers approximately 600,000 square kilometres (230,000 sq mi).[b] Prior to the ongoing Russo-Ukrainian War, it was the eighth with a population of around 41 million people.[c][6] It is also bordered by Belarus to the north; by Poland, Slovakia, and Hungary to the west; and by Romani with a coastline along the Black Sea and the Sea of Azov to the south and southeast.[e] Kyiv is the nation's capital and largest city. The country's national lan are also fluent in Russian.[14]

. Poland

Poland,[b] officially the Republic of Poland,[c] is a country in Central Europe. It is divided into 16 administrative provinces called voivodeships, covering an i Poland has a population of over 38 million and is the fifth-most populous member state of the European Union.[12] Warsaw is the nation's capital and larges! Kraków, Wrocław, Łódź, Poznań, Gdańsk, and Szczecin. Poland has a temperate transitional climate. Its territory extends from the Baltic Sea in the north to t in the south. The country is bordered by Lithuania and Russia to the northeast,[d] Belarus and Ukraine to the east, Slovakia and the Czech Republic to the so also shares maritime boundaries with Denmark and Sweden.

If you look at the code of the loaded page, you will find that the **CSS** stylesheet file is included

```html
1
2  <!DOCTYPE html>
3  <html lang="en">
4  <head>
5      <meta charset="UTF-8">
6      <title>Главная страница</title>
7      <link type="text/css" href="/static/traveler/css/styles.css" rel="stylesheet" />
8  </head>
9  <body>
```

Clicking on **href="/static/traveler/css/styles.css"**, the next thing you will see is the code for our stylesheet

```css
html, body {
        font-family: 'Arial';
        margin: 0;
        padding: 0;
        height: 100%;
        width: 100%;
        color: #444;
}

a {
        color: #0059b2;
        text-decoration: none;
}
a:hover {
        color: #CC0000;
        text-decoration: underline;
}

img {max-width: 600px; height: auto;}

img.img-article-left {
        max-width: 300px;
        height: auto;
        float: left;
        padding: 0 10px 10px 0;
}

img.img-article-left.thumb {
        max-width: 150px;
        height: auto;
}
```

In this way, we have connected the stylesheet to the base template using the **{% static %}** tag.

Next, to style our pages with the help of the stylesheet and graphic files, we will make some modifications to the **index.html**, **base.html**, and **about.html** files

Base.html

```html
{% load static %}

<!DOCTYPE html>

<html>

<head>

        <title>{{title}}</title>

        <link type="text/css" href="{% static 'traveler/css/styles.css' %}" rel="stylesheet" />

        <meta http-equiv="Content-Type" content="text/html; charset=utf-8">

        <link rel="shortcut icon" href="{% static 'traveler/images/main.ico' %}" type="image/x-icon"/>

        <meta name="viewport" content="width=device-width, initial-scale=1.0">

</head>
```

```
<body>
<table class="table-page" border=0 cellpadding="0" cellspacing="0">
<tr><td valign=top>
{% block mainmenu %}


  <div class="header">
    <ul id="mainmenu" class="mainmenu">
    <li class="logo"><a href="#"><div class="logo"></div></a></li>
{% for m in menu %}
  {% if not forloop.last %}
    <li><a href="#">{{m.title}}</a></li>
  {% else %}
    <li class="last"><a href="#">{{m.title}}</a></li>
  {% endif %}
{% endfor %}
    </ul>
    <div class="clear"></div>
  </div>
{% endblock mainmenu %}


<table class="table-content" border="0" cellpadding="0" cellspacing="0">
<tr>
<!--Sidebar слева -->
  <td valign="top" class="left-chapters">
  <ul id="leftchapters">
    <li class="selected">All countries</li>
    <li><a href="#"></a>Ukraine</li>
    <li><a href="#"></a>Poland</li>
    <li><a href="#"></a>Moldova</li>
    <li><a href="#"></a>Germany</li>
    <li><a href="#"></a>Spain</li>
    <li class="share">
```

```
    <p>Our channel</p>
    <a class="share-yt" href="#"> </a>
    </li>
  </ul>
  </td>
<!-- End Sidebar -->
<td valign="top" class="content">
  <!-- bread crumbs -->
  {% block breadcrumbs %}
  {% endblock %}

<!-- Content block -->
  <div class="content-text">
{% block content %}
{% endblock %}
  </div>
<!-- End of content block -->
</td></tr></table>
</td></tr>
<!-- Footer -->
<tr><td valign="top">
  <div id="footer">
    <p>traveler</p>
  </div>
</td></tr></table>
<!-- End Footer -->
</body>
</html>
```

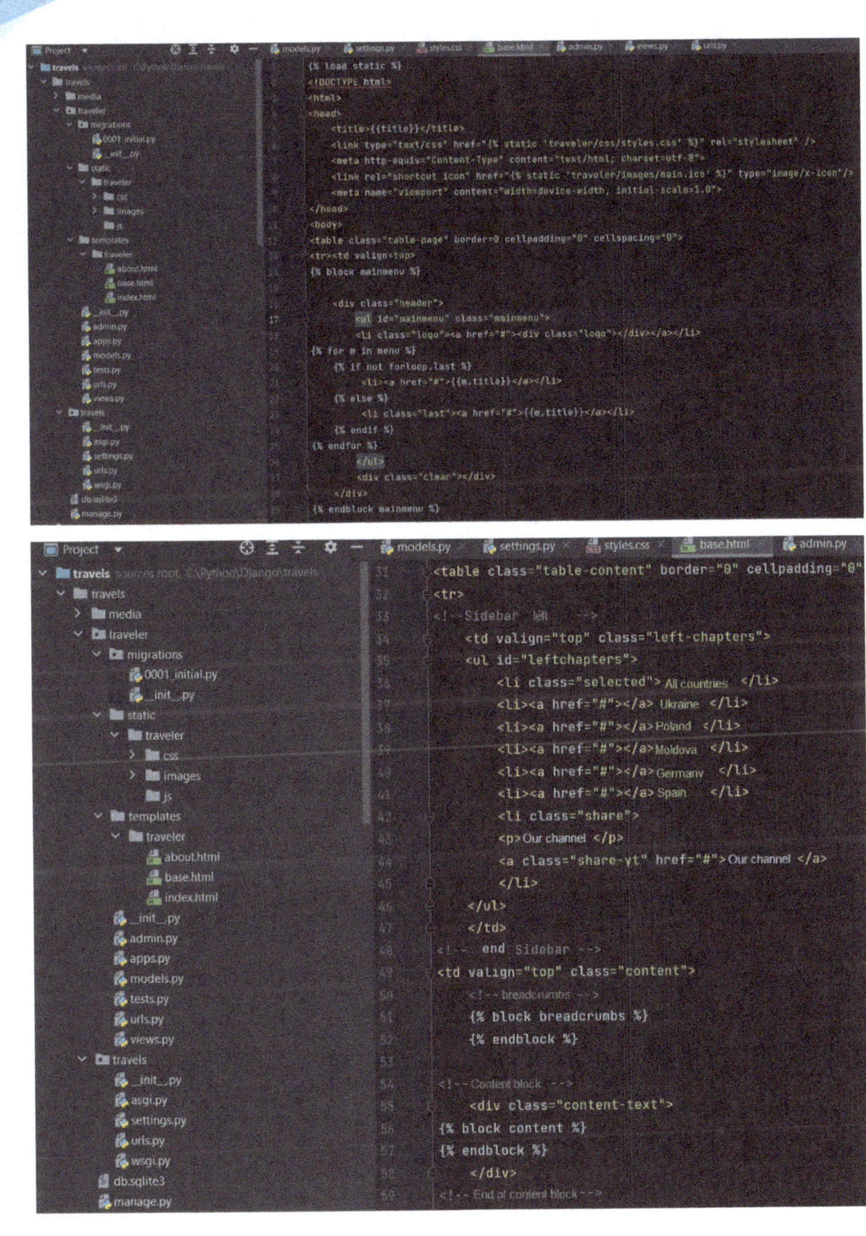

```
53
54      <!-- Content block -->
55          <div class="content-text">
56      {% block content %}
57      {% endblock %}
58          </div>
59      <!-- End of content block -->
60      </td></tr></table>
61      </td></tr>
62      <!-- Footer -->
63      <tr><td valign="top">
64          <div id="footer">
65              <p>traveler</p>
66          </div>
67      </td></tr></table>
68      <!-- End Footer -->
69      </body>
70      </html>
```

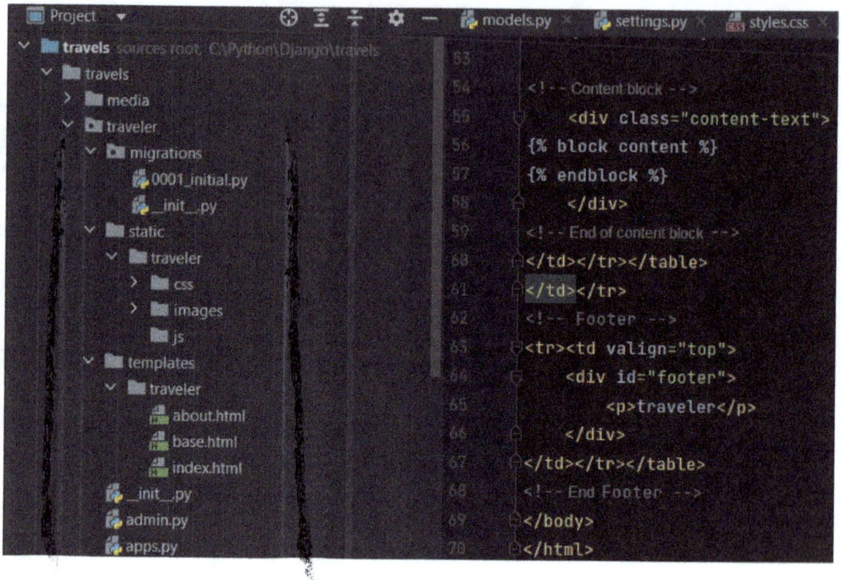

Connecting the file **styles.css**

```
<link type="text/css" href="{% static 'traveler/css/styles.css' %}" rel="stylesheet" />
```

Additionally, we connect an icon

```
<link rel="shortcut icon" href="{% static 'traveler/images/main.ico' %}" type="image/x-icon"/>
```

Next comes the main menu block

```
{% block mainmenu %}

  <div class="header">

    <ul id="mainmenu" class="mainmenu">

    <li class="logo"><a href="#"><div class="logo"></div></a></li>
{% for m in menu %}
  {% if not forloop.last %}
    <li><a href="#">{{m.title}}</a></li>
  {% else %}
```

```
        <li class="last"><a href="#">{{m.title}}</a></li>
    {% endif %}
{% endfor %}
    </ul>
    <div class="clear"></div>
</div>
{% endblock mainmenu %}
```

Here we use a loop

```
{% for m in menu %}
    {% if not forloop.last %}
        <li><a href="#">{{m.title}}</a></li>
    {% else %}
        <li class="last"><a href="#">{{m.title}}</a></li>
    {% endif %}
{% endfor %}
```

To iterate through our main menu, which we pass from the **views.py** file and looks like..

```
menu = ["About the site", "Add an article", "Feedback", "Log in"]
```

Here, only the names are being passed for now.

Next...

```
    {% if not forloop.last %}
        <li><a href="#">{{m.title}}</a></li>
    {% else %}
        <li class="last"><a href="#">{{m.title}}</a></li>
```

We display these names and pass a link. Instead of a link, we currently have a placeholder '#'. We'll fill it in a bit later.

Next comes the category selection menu

```html
<table class="table-content" border="0" cellpadding="0" cellspacing="0">
<tr>
<!--Sidebar слева -->
  <td valign="top" class="left-chapters">
  <ul id="leftchapters">
    <li class="selected">All countries</li>
    <li><a href="#"></a>Ukraine</li>
    <li><a href="#"></a>Poland</li>
    <li><a href="#"></a>Moldova</li>
    <li><a href="#"></a>Germany</li>
    <li><a href="#"></a>Spain</li>
```

Below is the content block

```html
<!-- Content block -->
  <div class="content-text">
{% block content %}
{% endblock %}
  </div>
<!-- End of the content block -->
```

Displayed at the very bottom Footer

```html
<!-- Footer -->
<tr><td valign="top">
  <div id="footer">
    <p>traveler</p>
  </div>
</td></tr></table>
```

<!-- End Footer -->

Next, based on this basic template, a base page template is created. We change almost nothing, only creating some styling.

{% extends 'traveler/base.html' %}

{% block content %}

<ul class="list-articles">

  {% for p in posts %}

  <li><h2>{{p.title}}</h2>

  <p>{{p.content}}</p>

  <div class="clear"></div>

  <p class="link-read-post"><a href="#">Read the post</a></p>

  </li>

  {% endfor %}

</ul>

{% endblock %}

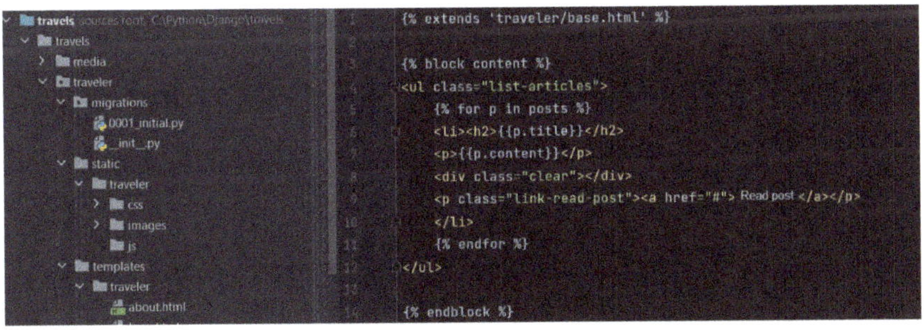

We're not changing the **about.html** template for now. Now let's see how the main page will look. Refresh the page in your browser.

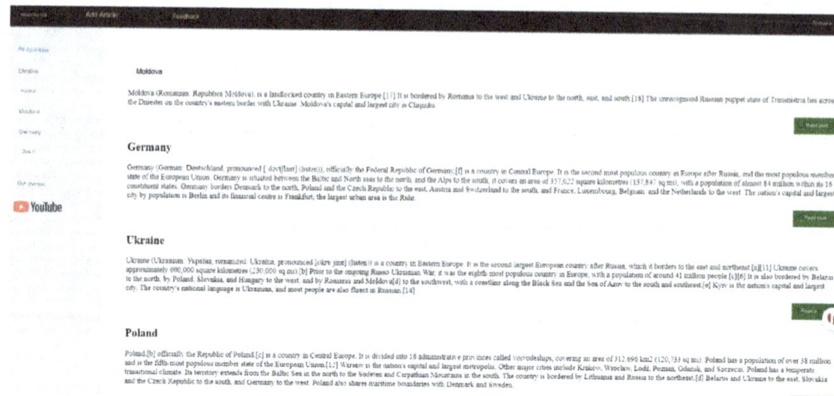

Let's try to format the content output on the website in such a way that the text below the header is not displayed in full, as shown in the screenshot,

Moldova

Moldova (Romanian: Republica Moldova), is a landlocked country in Eastern Europe.[17] It is bordered by Romania to the west and Ukraine to the north, east, and south.[18] The unrecognised Russian puppet state of Transnistria lies across the Dniester on the country's eastern border with Ukraine. Moldova's capital and largest city is Chişinău.

Read post

Germany

Germany (German: Deutschland, pronounced [ˈdɔʏtʃlant] (listen)), officially the Federal Republic of Germany,[f] is a country in Central Europe. It is the second most populous country in Europe after Russia, and the most populous member state of the European Union. Germany is situated between the Baltic and North seas to the north, and the Alps to the south; it covers an area of 357,022 square kilometres (137,847 sq mi), with a population of almost 84 million within its 16 constituent states. Germany borders Denmark to the north, Poland and the Czech Republic to the east, Austria and Switzerland to the south, and France, Luxembourg, Belgium, and the Netherlands to the west. The nation's capital and largest city by population is Berlin and its financial centre is Frankfurt; the largest urban area is the Ruhr.

Read post

.and only a small fragment was displayed, for example, the first 10 words. To achieve this in **Django** when working with content, there are special filters. You can view a list of all filters by following the link

https://django.fun/ru/docs/django/4.1/ref/templates/builtins/#ref-templates-builtins-filters

To do this, let's go to the index.html file and use the filter...

truncatewords

Truncates a string after a certain number of words.

Argument: The number of words to truncate after. ango

For example:

```
{{ value|truncatewords:2 }}
```

If value is "Joel is a slug", then the output will be "Joel is ...".

New lines in the string will be removed.

Let's change our code a little

```
{% extends 'traveler/base.html' %}
{% block content %}
<ul class="list-articles">
  {% for p in posts %}
  <li><h2>{{p.title}}</h2>
  <p>{{p.content|truncatewords:10}}</p>
  <div class="clear"></div>
  <p class="link-read-post"><a href="#">Read the post</a></p>
  </li>
  {% endfor %}
</ul>
{% endblock %}
```

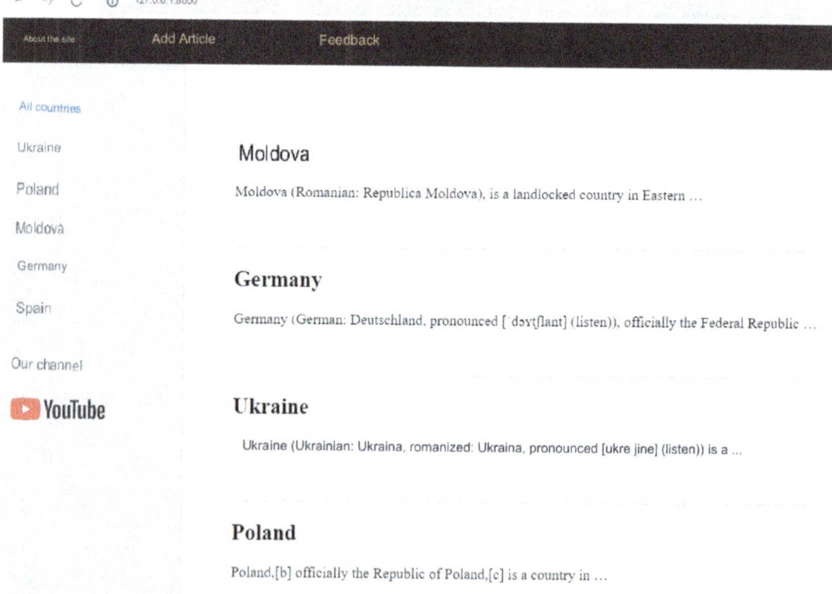

And now let's see how this filter will affect the content display. Let's refresh our page

As we can see, only a portion of the post is displayed. We can briefly review the post, and if we need to delve into the information, we click the **'Read the post'** button. For now, it doesn't lead to anything, as the button is inactive.

Filters can be composite, meaning they can be applied simultaneously to the same content. For example, let's transform the string into all uppercase letters. In this case, it doesn't make sense and is only required for demonstration

Let's use the filter **upper**

```
<p>{{p.content|truncatewords:10|upper}}</p>
```

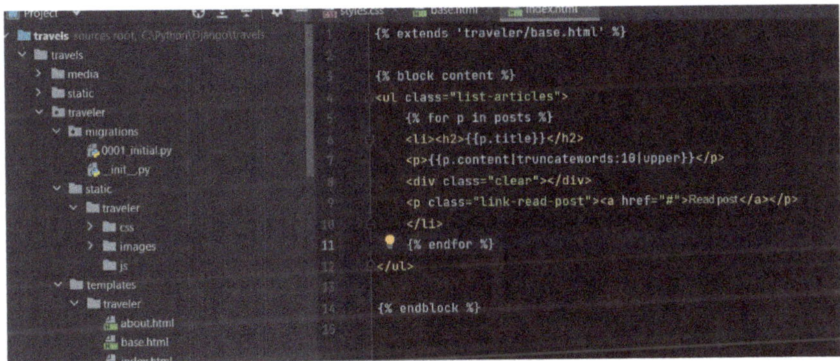

Let's refresh the page

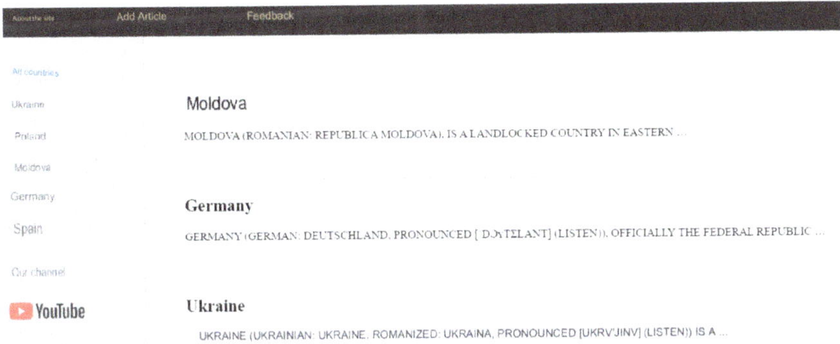

In conclusion of this topic, I want to highlight one important feature. Let's go to the admin panel at

http://127.0.0.1:8000/admin/

and wrap a fragment of content in the **<h3></h3>** tag. Then, save it and go back to the main page

Change All countries

Moldova

Title: Moldova

Article text:

```
<h3>Moldova (Romanian: Republica Moldova)</h3>, is a landlocked country in Eastern Europe [17] It is
bordered by Romania to the west and Ukraine to the north, east, and south.[18] The unrecognised Russian
puppet state of Transnistria lies across the Dniester on the country's eastern border with Ukraine.
Moldova's capital and largest city is Chişinău.
```

Photo: At the moment: photos/2022/10/13/Museum_of_History.jpg

Change: Choose File File not selected

☑ Is puplished

Delete

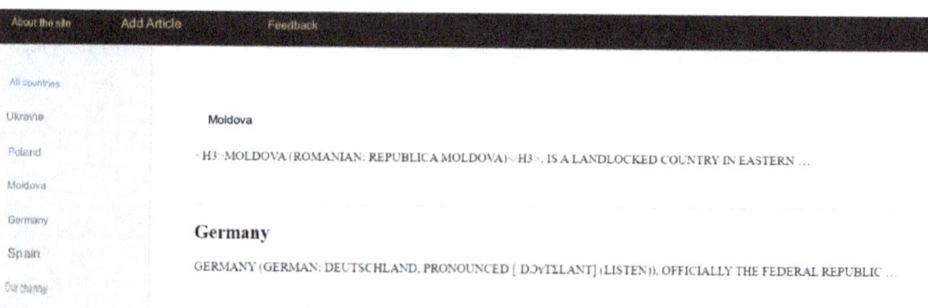

As we can see, the **<h3></h3>** tag is displayed as text. If we view the **HTML** page's source code, we'll see the following

```
67  <ul class="list-articles">
68
69      <li><h2>Moldova</h2>
70      <p>&lt;H3&gt;MOLDOVA (ROMANIAN: REPUBLICA MOLDOVA)&lt;/H3&gt;, IS A LANDLOCKED COUNTRY IN EASTERN ...</p>
71      <div class="clear"></div>
72      <p class="link-read-post"><a href="#">read post</a></p>
73      li>
74
75      <li><h2>Germany</h2>
76      <p>GERMANY (GERMAN: DEUTSCHLAND, PRONOUNCED ['DƆYTƩLANT] (LISTEN)), OFFICIALLY THE FEDERAL REPUBLIC ...</p>
77      <div class="clear"></div>
78      <p class="link-read-post"><a href="#">read post</a></p>
79        </li>
```

`<p><H3>MOLDOVA (ROMANIAN: REPUBLICA MOLDOVA)</H3> -`

This is called tag escaping. **Django** does this intentionally! If any tags are inserted as content, they won't execute. This includes the script tag, which can contain malicious code and create an extra vulnerability for the website. To prevent this, **Django** escapes such tags.

Nevertheless, there are times when there's a need for tags to function as tags and not be escaped. To achieve this in **Django**, there is a tag called

`{% autoescape <on|off> %}` контент`{% endautoescape %}`

On – All tags are escaped

Off – Escaping is disabled.

Let's apply it to our template.

```
<li><h2>{{p.title}}</h2>
    {% autoescape off %}
    <p>{{p.content|truncatewords:10|upper}}</p>
    {% endautoescape %}
    <div class="clear"></div>
```

```
{% extends 'traveler/base.html' %}

{% block content %}
<ul class="list-articles">
    {% for p in posts %}
    <li><h2>{{p.title}}</h2>
    {% autoescape off %}
    <p>{{p.content|truncatewords:10|upper}}</p>
    {% endautoescape %}
    <div class="clear"></div>
    <p class="link-read-post"><a href="#">Read post</a></p>
    </li>
    {% endfor %}
</ul>

{% endblock %}
```

Let's refresh our page

About the site   Add Article   Feedback

All countries

Ukraine

Poland

Moldova

Germany

Spain

Our channel

Moldova

MOLDOVA (ROMANIAN: REPUBLICA MOLDOVA)

. IS A LANDLOCKED COUNTRY IN EASTERN …

Germany

GERMANY (GERMAN: DEUTSCHLAND, PRONOUNCED [ˈDɔʏTƐLANT] (LIST.
REPUBLIC …

Generating URL addresses in templates.

Previously, in almost all links, we used to create a placeholder like this:

Let's create full-fledged links to pages. To do this in Django, you can use a special tag:

{% url '<URL address or route name>' [link parameters] %}

[link parameters] - an optional parameter.

So, let's define a route to the main page. Go to your project, open the base.html template file.

The first thing you can do is to add a slash to the line like this:

```html
<li class="logo"><a href="/"><div class="logo" ></div></a></li>
```

```html
10    </head>
11    <body>
12    <table class="table-page" border=0 cellpadding="0" cellspacing="0">
13    <tr><td valign=top>
14    {% block mainmenu %}
15
16        <div class="header">
17            <ul id="mainmenu" class="mainmenu">
18                <li class="logo"><a href="/"><div class="logo" ></div></a></li>
19    {% for m in menu %}
```

And this will work. If you start our server and click on the logo (currently represented by an empty square, which we'll fix later), you'll be taken to the same main page.

Creating links in this way is not the best solution because the **URL** of the main page doesn't necessarily have to match the name of the main page. If it changes, you'd have to make changes in all the templates. It's more practical to use route names.

If you open the **urls.py** file, you'll see the names of our routes

```python
urlpatterns = [
    path('', index, name='home'),
    path('about/', about, name='about'),
]
```

Сейчас нас интересует имя **home**.

Let's change the previous line to:

```html
<li class="logo"><a href="{% url 'home' %}"><div class="logo" ></div></a></li>
```

```
13    <tr><td valign=top>
14    {% block mainmenu %}
15
16        <div class="header">
17            <ul id="mainmenu" class="mainmenu">
18                <li class="logo"><a href="{% url 'home' %}"><div class="logo" ></div></a></li>
19    {% for m in menu %}
20        {% if not forloop.last %}
```

We'll save this, go to the browser, refresh the page, and see that the link to the main page is indeed preserved.

Next, what we'll do is add links to menu items on the website.

To do this, in the project where the menu item is created, open the **views.py** file, and replace the line...

```python
4    from .models import *
5
6    menu = ["About", "Add article", "Feedback", "To come in"]
```

on

```python
menu = [{'title': 'About the site', 'url_name': 'about'},
{'title': 'Add an article', 'url_name': 'add_page'},
{'title': 'Contact us', 'url_name': 'contact'},
{'title': 'Login', 'url_name': 'login'}
]
```

```python
6    menu = [{'title': "About", 'url_name': 'about'},
7            {'title': "Add article", 'url_name': 'add_page'},
8            {'title': "Feedback", 'url_name': 'contact'},
9            {'title': "To come in", 'url_name': 'login'}
10    ]
```

So, we replaced the old list with a new list of dictionaries, each containing two keys: '**title**' and '**url_name**'.

Next, let's go to the urls.py file and add three more routes

```python
urlpatterns = [
    path('', index, name='home'),
    path('about/', about, name='about'),
    path('addpage/', addpage, name='add_page'),
    path('contact/', addpage, name='contact'),
    path('login/', login, name='login'),
]
```

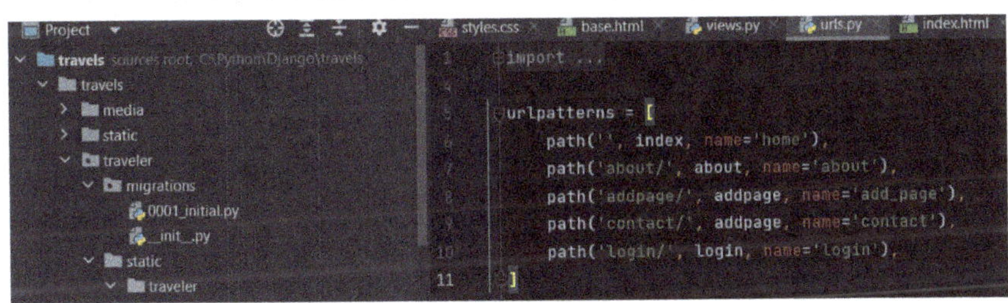

Let's add three more view functions, initially as placeholder functions. We'll go back to **views.py** and remove the categories and archive functions, replacing them with:

```python
def addpage(request):
    return HttpResponse("Adding an article")


def contact(request):
    return HttpResponse("Feedback")


def login(request):
    return HttpResponse("Authorization")
```

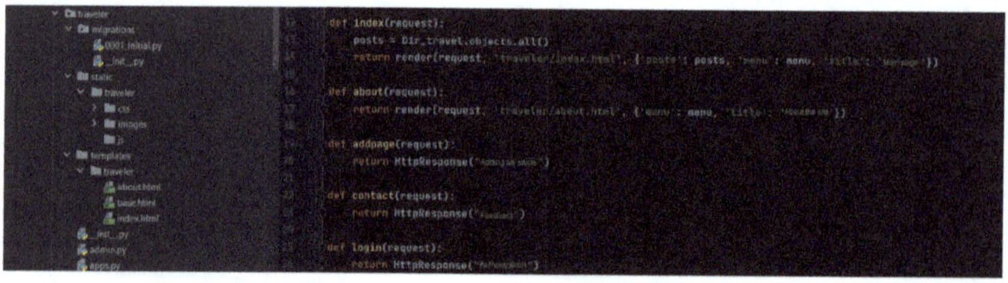

Let's make some slight modifications to the **index** function right away. If we take a closer look at this function...

```python
def index(request):
    posts = Dir_travel.objects.all()
    return render(request, 'traveler/index.html', {'posts': posts, 'menu': menu, 'title': ' Home page})
```

Intuitively, we might want to shorten the bottom line of the index function ourselves. This is a commendable desire since shorter lines are more readable and generally easier to understand. Let's create a special dictionary within this function where we list all the parameters we'll be passing.

```python
def index(request):
    posts = Dir_travel.objects.all()
    context = {
        'posts': posts,
        'menu': menu,
        'title': 'Home page'
    }
    return render(request, 'traveler/index.html', context=context)
```

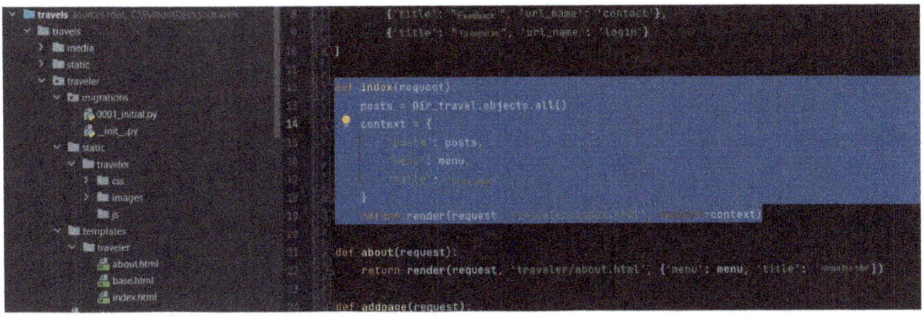

Now, let's incorporate our modified menu into the **base.html** file. Let's focus on our menu block, and instead of placeholders, include the **URLs.**

```
{% block mainmenu %}


  <div class="header">
    <ul id="mainmenu" class="mainmenu">
            <li class="logo"><a href="{% url 'home' %}"><div class="logo" ></div></a></li>
{% for m in menu %}
  {% if not forloop.last %}
    <li><a href="{% url m.url_name %}">{{m.title}}</a></li>
  {% else %}
    <li class="last"><a href="{% url m.url_name %}">{{m.title}}</a></li>
  {% endif %}
{% endfor %}
    </ul>
    <div class="clear"></div>
  </div>
{% endblock mainmenu %}
```

```html
</head>
<body>
<table class="table-page" border=0 cellpadding="0" cellspacing="0">
<tr><td valign=top>
{% block mainmenu %}

    <div class="header">
        <ul id="mainmenu" class="mainmenu">
        <li class="logo"><a href="{% url 'home' %}"><div class="logo" ></div></a></li>
{% for m in menu %}
    {% if not forloop.last %}
        <li><a href="{% url m.url_name %}">{{m.title}}</a></li>
    {% else %}
        <li class="last"><a href="{% url m.url_name %}">{{m.title}}</a></li>
    {% endif %}
{% endfor %}
        </ul>
        <div class="clear"></div>
    </div>
{% endblock mainmenu %}

<table class="table-content" border="0" cellpadding="0" cellspacing="0">
<tr>
```

So, in each iteration of the loop, we take the **"m"** - an element from the menu dictionary, extract its **url_name**. Then, this name is retrieved from **urls.py** within the urlpatterns collection and is used to substitute the specific route.

Let's return to the browser, refresh the main page, and click on "**About the site**" to navigate to the page shown below in the screenshot

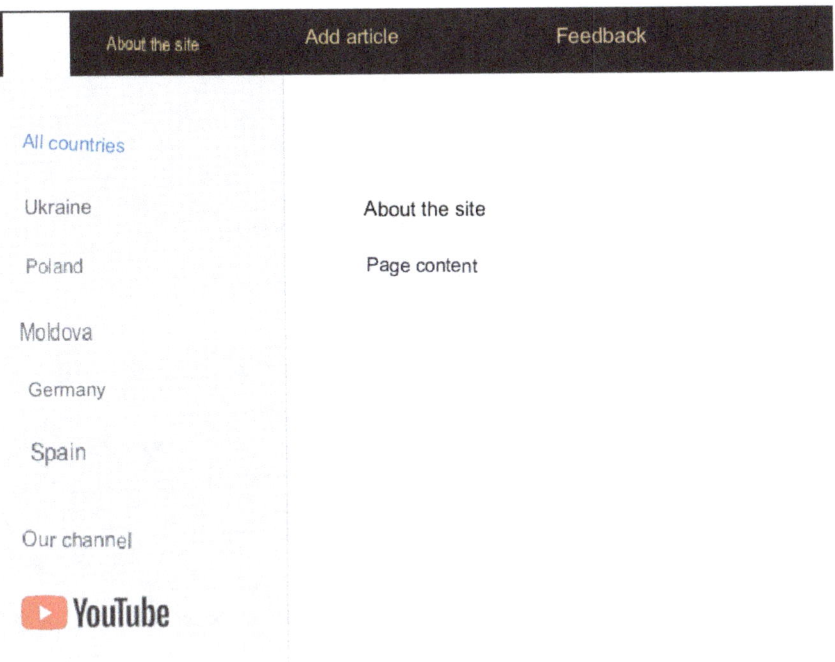

Далее, нажмём "**Добавить статью**"

Adding an article

We remember that we created placeholder functions. We'll add more functionality later!

The same approach applies to " **Feedback** " and " **To come in.**" Now, we need to define links for our list of articles and understand how to create dynamic links at the template level.

Let's open the urls.py file and define another route.

```python
urlpatterns = [
    path('', index, name='home'),
    path('about/', about, name='about'),
    path('addpage/', addpage, name='add_page'),
    path('contact/', addpage, name='contact'),
    path('login/', login, name='login'),
    path('post/<int:post_the>/', show_post, name='post'),
]
```

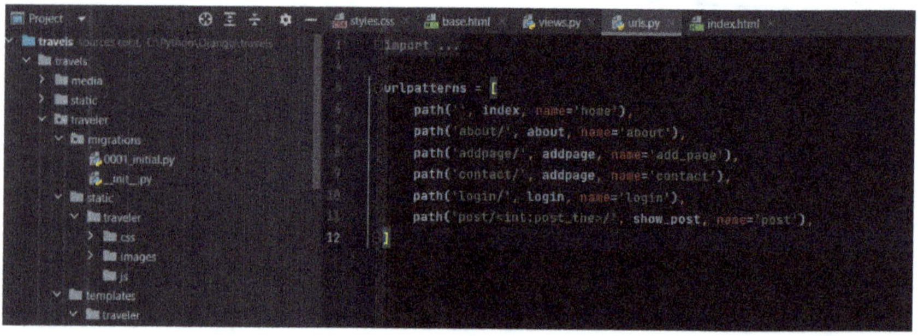

We have a specific article that will open through such a route

path('post/<int:post_the>/', show_post, name='post'),

> **int:post_the –** The identifier of the specific route

> **name='post' –** The name of the route

Typically, in real projects, instead of **'post_the,'** a string, also known as a slug, is used. The slug is written in Latin characters and reflects the context of the article. Such links are better ranked by search engines and are more understandable for users. We will fix this a bit later. Right now, our task is to figure out how to generate dynamic **URL** links at the template level.

Next, we will define the **'show_post'** function.

Let's open the **'views.py'** file.

We'll define it as a placeholder function. We'll format it later.

```python
def show_post(request, post_the):
    return HttpResponse(f" Displaying the article with id = {post_the}")
```

```
def login(request):
    return HttpResponse("Authorization")

def show_post(request, post_the):
    return HttpResponse("... ... ..." + post_the)
```

We just need to properly set up these links in **index.html**. There are two ways to do this. Let's go through the first one.

```
<p class="link-read-post"><a href="{% url 'post' p.pk %}"> Read the post </a></p>
```

```
{% extends 'traveler/base.html' %}

{% block content %}
<ul class="list-articles">
    {% for p in posts %}
    <li><h2>{{p.title}}</h2>
    {% autoescape off %}
    <p>{{p.content|truncatewords:10|upper}}</p>
    {% endautoescape %}
    <div class="clear"></div>
    <p class="link-read-post"><a href="{% url 'post' p.pk %}">Read post</a></p>
    </li>
    {% endfor %}
</ul>

{% endblock %}
```

post – The name of our link

p.pk – (pk) – The identifier of our record; (p) – an instance of our model **Dir_travel,** that has an attribute **pk**, which **Django** uses by default as the record identifier.

Meaning the **'url'** tag will take the address using the name **'post'** and instead of **'post_the,'** it will substitute this record identifier, forming the corresponding link. Let's update the page and see how it all looks. Click on the **'Read the post'** button. If everything was done correctly and without errors, you will get the page

Display article with $id = 5$

Let's experiment with the other posts.

Display article with $id = 4$

Display article with $id = 2$

But there's another way. The method described above has one drawback. If the format of our address changes from **'post_the'** to, for example, using a slug, we will have to change the **'p.pk'** parameter in the 'index.html' file. In this case, we'd need to pass not the identifier but the slug, which is not very convenient. We may have dynamic addresses in various places and templates, and it's easy to forget to update something. Let's use the second method. We can define a method in the class of our model in the **'models.py'** file that will generate the desired route for us.

```python
from django.db import models
from django.urls import reverse


class Dir_travel(models.Model):
    title = models.CharField(max_length=255, verbose_name = " Heading ")
    content = models.TextField(blank=True, verbose_name = " Article text ")
    photo = models.ImageField(upload_to="photos/%Y/%m/%d/", verbose_name = " Photo ")
    time_create = models.DateTimeField(auto_now_add=True, verbose_name = " Time of creation ")
    time_update = models.DateTimeField(auto_now=True, verbose_name = " Change time ")
    is_puplished = models.BooleanField(default=True)

    def __str__(self):
        return self.title


    def get_absolute_url(self):
        return reverse('post', kwargs={'post_the': self.pk})
```

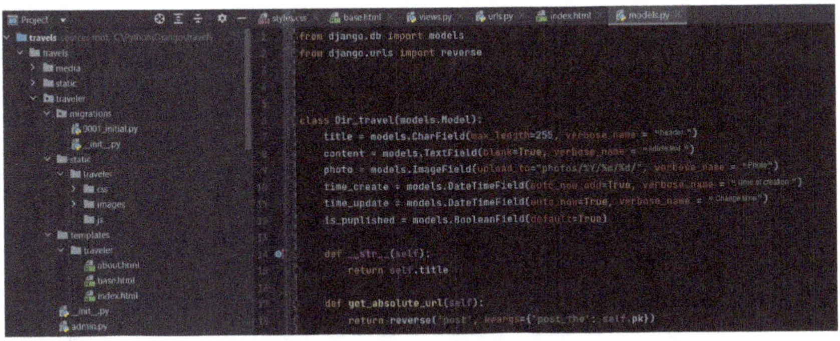

```python
from django.db import models
from django.urls import reverse


class Dir_travel(models.Model):
    title = models.CharField(max_length=255, verbose_name = "header")
    content = models.TextField(blank=True, verbose_name = "detailed")
    photo = models.ImageField(upload_to="photos/%Y/%m/%d/", verbose_name = "Photo")
    time_create = models.DateTimeField(auto_now_add=True, verbose_name = "Time of creation")
    time_update = models.DateTimeField(auto_now=True, verbose_name = "Change time")
    is_puplished = models.BooleanField(default=True)

    def __str__(self):
        return self.title

    def get_absolute_url(self):
        return reverse('post', kwargs={'post_the': self.pk})
```

We have defined a method in this class

def get_absolute_url(self):

  return reverse('post', kwargs={'post_the': self.pk})

that will generate the necessary route to a specific record for us.

The **'self'** reference is a reference to an instance of the **'Dir_travel'** class. Consequently, with this reference, we can access any attribute of the current record. In this case, we are accessing the **'pk'** attribute and, using the **'reverse'** function (which needs to be imported), we will generate a route with the name **'post'** according to the template specified in the **'urls.py'** file

```python
path('post/<int:post_the>/', show_post, name='post'),
```

To do this, we additionally pass the **'post_the'** parameter with the identifier of the current record, which is **'self.pk.'** This identifier will be inserted into the template

```python
path('post/<int:post_the>/', show_post, name='post'),
```

and the necessary link will be generated, which will be returned by the function

def get_absolute_url(self):

Next, you need to change the line in the **'index.html'** file

```html
<p class="link-read-post"><a href="{% p.get_absolute_url %}"> Read post </a></p>
```

Just keep in mind that you should write the function without parentheses, as we won't be calling it, and the template engine will take care of that.

```
{% extends 'traveler/base.html' %}

{% block content %}
<ul class="list-articles">
    {% for p in posts %}
    <li><h2>{{p.title}}</h2>
    {% autoescape off %}
    <p>{{p.content|truncatewords:10|upper}}</p>
    {% endautoescape %}
    <div class="clear"></div>
    <p class="link-read-post"><a href="{% p.get_absolute_url %}">Read post </a></p>
    </li>
    {% endfor %}
</ul>

{% endblock %}
```

 Let's go back to the browser, refresh the page.

← → C ⓘ 127.0.0.1:8000

TemplateSyntaxError at /

Invalid block tag on line 11: 'p.get_absolute_url', expected 'empty' or 'endfor'. Did you forget to register or load this tag?

```
Request Method:      GET
Request URL:         http://127.0.0.1:8000/
Django Version:      4.1.1
Exception Type:      TemplateSyntaxError
Exception Value:     Invalid block tag on line 11: 'p.get_absolute_url', expected 'empty' or 'endfor'. Did you forget to register or load this tag?
Exception Location:  C:\Python\Django\travels\venv\lib\site-packages\django\template\base.py, line 558, in invalid_block_tag
Raised during:       traveler.views.index
Python Executable:   C:\Python\Django\travels\venv\Scripts\python.exe
Python Version:      3.10.7
Python Path:         ['C:\\Python\\Django\\travels\\travels',
                      'C:\\Python\\python310.zip',
                      'C:\\Python\\DLLs',
                      'C:\\Python\\lib',
                      'C:\\Python',
                      'C:\\Python\\Django\\travels\\venv',
                      'C:\\Python\\Django\\travels\\venv\\lib\\site-packages']
Server time:         Mon, 31 Oct 2022 11:37:26 +0000
```

Error during template rendering

In template C:\Python\Django\travels\travels\traveler\templates\traveler\index.html, error at line 11

Invalid block tag on line 11: 'p.get_absolute_url', expected 'empty' or 'endfor'. Did you forget to register or load this tag?

```
 1  {% extends 'traveler/base.html' %}
 2
 3  {% block content %}
 4  <ul class="list-articles">
 5      {% for p in posts %}
 6      <li><h2>{{p.title}}</h2>
 7      {% autoescape off %}
 8      <p>{{p.content|truncatewords:10|upper}}</p>
 9      {% endautoescape %}
10      <div class="clear"></div>
11      <p class="link-read-post"><a href="{% p.get_absolute_url %}">Read post</a></p>
12      </li>
13      {% endfor %}
14  </ul>
15
16  {% endblock %}
17
```

And we see that an exception has occurred. We made a mistake in the line

<p class="link-read-post"><a href="{% p.get_absolute_url %}"> Read post </a></p>

The point is that you need to call it not as a tag, but as a variable.

We'll fix it

<p class="link-read-post"><a href="{{ **p.get_absolute_url** }}"> Read post </a></p>

Now everything should work. This approach is considered preferable, but only when our links are associated with records in the database.

Creating relationships between data models

Let's add another table for categories and connect it with the posts table in a way that each article is associated with the relevant category. For example, the category "**Country**" - "**Poland**" corresponds to the "**City**" - "**Warsaw**".

Dividing data into multiple tables and establishing relationships between them is called data normalization, and it's a principle worth following.

So, let's create another table, a model with categories, and connect it to the posts table.

Add another field to the **Dir_travel** table, **cat_id:** Integer, a foreign key that will be defined as a foreign key, storing the category identifier.

In the categories table, define two fields

Id: Integer, primary key

name: Varchar

The **Django** framework has three special classes for organizing relationships.

ForeignKey – For Many-to-One relationships (relationship fields).

ManyToManyField – For Many-to-Many relationships (many-to-many fields).

OneToOneField – For One-to-One relationships (one-to-one fields).

In this case, **ForeignKey** is suitable for us, as we have multiple posts associated with a specific category. **ManyToManyField** is suitable, for example, for defining tags.

To use the **ForeignKey** class, we need to specify two mandatory arguments:

ForeignKey(<reference to the primary model>, on_delete=<deletion behavior>)

Our new model, category, is the primary model, and the **Dir_travel** model is the secondary one.

on_delete is the second parameter that determines the behavior when a record is deleted from the primary model.

The **cat_id** key should reference a category. If, for some reason, a category is deleted, we need to decide what to do with the records that reference that category. There are several options.

-**models.CASCADE** – When deleting a record from the primary model (**Category**), all records from the secondary model (**Dir_travel**) linked to the deleted category are also removed.

-**models.PROTECT** – Prohibits the deletion of a record from the primary model if it is being referenced in the secondary model (throws an exception).

-**models.SET_NULL** – When deleting a record from the primary model, sets the foreign key value to NULL for the corresponding records in the secondary model.

- **models.DEFAULT** – When deleting a record from the primary model, sets the foreign key value to the default value defined in the **ForeignKey** class instead of **NULL**.

- **models.SET()**- The same thing, but sets a custom value.

- **models.DO_NOTHING** – Deletion of records in the primary model does not trigger any actions in the secondary models.

More detailed information about relationships in **Django** can be found

https://django.fun/ru/docs/django/4.1/topics/db/models/#many-to-one-relationships

Let's look at a specific example of how the **ForeignKey** class is used to establish **'Many-to-One'** relationships, as described above. To do this, let's navigate to our project, open the models.py file where we define the interactions of all models, and add another model named Category. It will inherit from the same base class, and we'll define a field 'name' for the category's name. There will also be another field **'id,'** which **Django** automatically generates.

```python
class Category(models.Model):
    name = models.CharField(max_length=100, db_index=True)


    def __str__(self):
        return self.name
```

max_length=100 – Maximum length of 100 characters

db_index=True – The field will be indexed, meaning that searches on this field will be faster.

```python
    def __str__(self):
        return self.name
```

```python
14      def __str__(self):
15          return self.title
16
17      def get_absolute_url(self):
18          return reverse('post', kwargs={'post_the': self.pk})
19
20
21
22      class Meta:
23          verbose_name = "all countries"
24          verbose_name_plural = "all countries"
25          ordering = ['-time_create', 'title']
26
27  class Category(models.Model):
28      name = models.CharField(max_length=100, db_index=True)
29
30      def __str__(self):
31          return self.name
```

This method returns the name of the category. Next, in the secondary model, we will add a foreign key.

cat = models.ForeignKey('Category', on_delete=models.PROTECT)

'Category' – We define the association with the category through a string.

on_delete=models.Protect – We prohibit deleting categories from the **Dir_travel** model if there are references. We create/modify this table in our database.

```python
class Dir_travel(models.Model):
    title = models.CharField(max_length=255, verbose_name = "header ")
    content = models.TextField(blank=True, verbose_name = "Article text ")
    photo = models.ImageField(upload_to="photos/%Y/%m/%d/", verbose_name = "Photo ")
    time_create = models.DateTimeField(auto_now_add=True, verbose_name = "Time of creation")
    time_update = models.DateTimeField(auto_now=True, verbose_name = "Change time ")
    is_puplished = models.BooleanField(default=True)
    cat = models.ForeignKey('Category', on_delete=models.PROTECT)

    def __str__(self):
        return self.title


    def get_absolute_url(self):
        return reverse('post', kwargs={'post_the': self.pk})



    class Meta:
        verbose_name = "All countries "
        verbose_name_plural = "All countries"
        ordering = ['-time_create', 'title']
```

We modify the first table, **Dir_travel**, and create the second table, **Category**, accordingly. To do this, we need to generate a new migration.

Python manage.py makemigrations

And... encountered an error.

```
(venv) PS C:\Python\Django\travels\travels> python manage.py makemigrations
It is impossible to add a non-nullable field 'cat' to dir_travel without specifying a default. This is because the database needs something to populate existing rows.
Please select a fix:
1) Provide a one-off default now (will be set on all existing rows with a null value for this column)
2) Quit and manually define a default value in models.py
```

The issue seems to be that when modifying the first table, **Dir_travel**, the 'cat' field references the Category table, which hasn't been created yet.

Temporarily, let's define this field as

cat = models.ForeignKey('Category', on_delete=models.PROTECT, null=True),

meaning that null values are allowed during creation. Press **'2'**, exit, and repeat the migration.

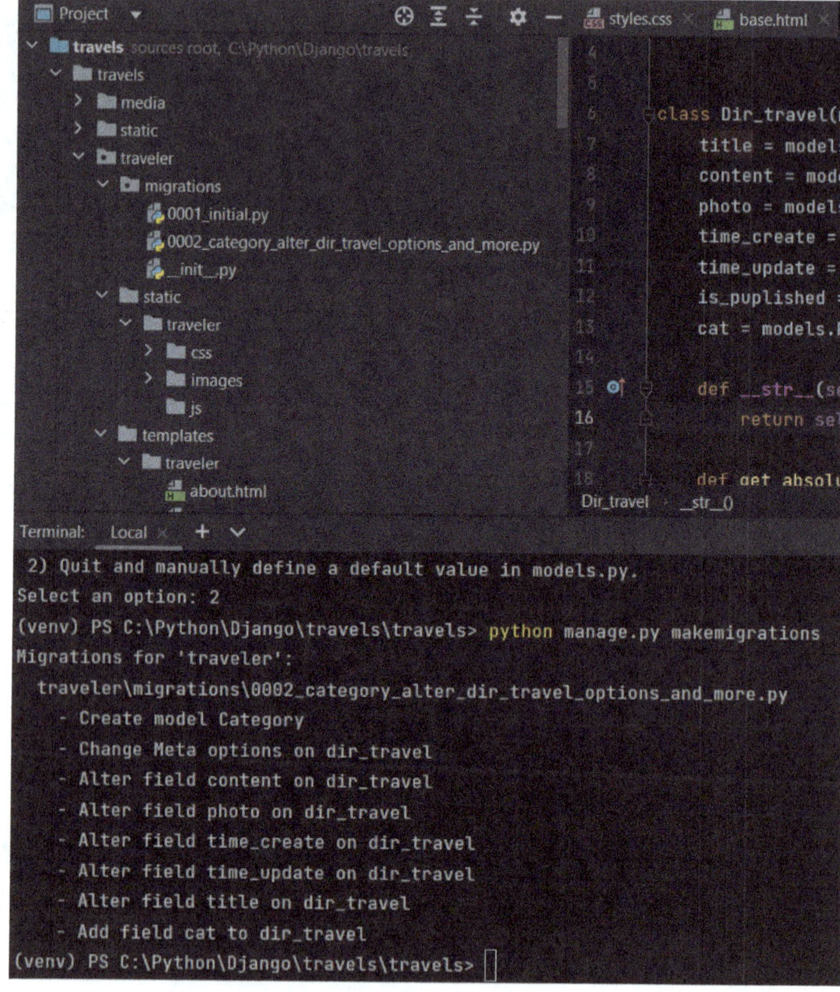

We can see that another migration file has appeared in the folder. Now, let's execute these migrations by running the command:

Python manage.py migrate

```
(venv) PS C:\Python\Django\travels\travels> python manage.py migrate
Operations to perform:
  Apply all migrations: admin, auth, contenttypes, sessions, traveler
Running migrations:
  Applying traveler.0002_category_alter_dir_travel_options_and_more... OK
(venv) PS C:\Python\Django\travels\travels>
```

So, all tables in the database have been created. It is advisable to plan all relationships in advance during the design phase and avoid making changes to existing database tables later on. Let's add two category tables. Go to the **Django** console by running the command:

python manage.py shell

Let's work with **Django's ORM** in the console to better understand the advantages of using this system. In this shell, we will first import our models

from traveler.models import *

and then proceed

Category.objects.create(name=' Europe ')

```
>>> Category.objects.create(name='Europe')
<Category: Europe >
>>>
```

Using the Category model, we access the records manager '**objects**' and call the '**create**' method. With this method, we create a new entry in the Category table, and the category will be named '**Europe**.'

Let's create additional categories

Category.objects.create(name=' Asia')

Category.objects.create(name=' Africa')

Category.objects.create(name=' North America')

Category.objects.create(name=' South America')

Then, in the table **Dir_travel**, we will set the value in the id field to **1**, meaning that all these records will correspond to **1.**

w_list = Dir_travel.objects.all()

Let's select all records from the **Dir_travel** table

w_list – A variable that refers to the list of all records in this table.

Next, we will use the update operation to change the value of the **cat_id** field to 1.

w_list.update(cat_id=1)

We see that changes have been made for four fields.

So, we have created the **Category** table and established a relationship between the tables.

Now let's display the list of categories in the **base.html** template. Open the **base.html** file, find the list of categories in the left sidebar, and make some changes according to the logic of our site, as there was a mismatch.

Let's assume that in the content block, information about a specific country will be displayed, which will be in its category indicating its continent affiliation. In the left sidebar, we will list the categories to which countries belonging to a particular continent will be included.

Instead of countries located in Europe, we will specify the names of continents.

```
<!--Sidebar слева -->

  <td valign="top" class="left-chapters">

  <ul id="leftchapters">

    <li class="selected"> Continents </li>

    <li><a href="#"></a> Europe </li>

    <li><a href="#"></a> Asia </li>

    <li><a href="#"></a> Africa </li>

    <li><a href="#"></a> North America </li>
```

```html
<li><a href="#"></a> South America </li>

<li class="share">

<p> Our channel </p>

<a class="share-yt" href="#"></a>

</li>

</ul>

</td>
<!-- End Sidebar -->
```

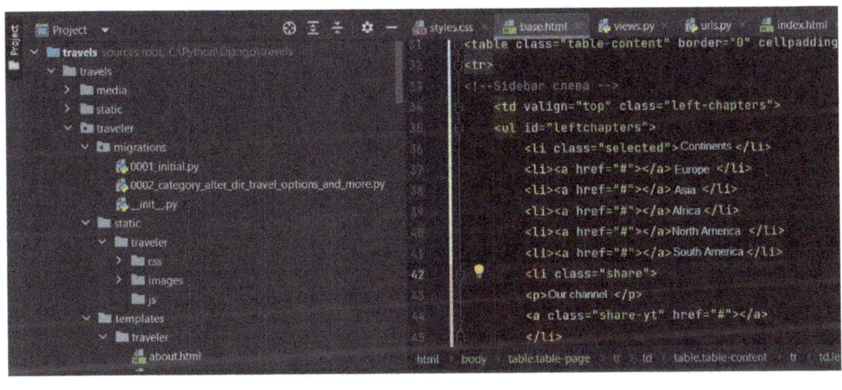

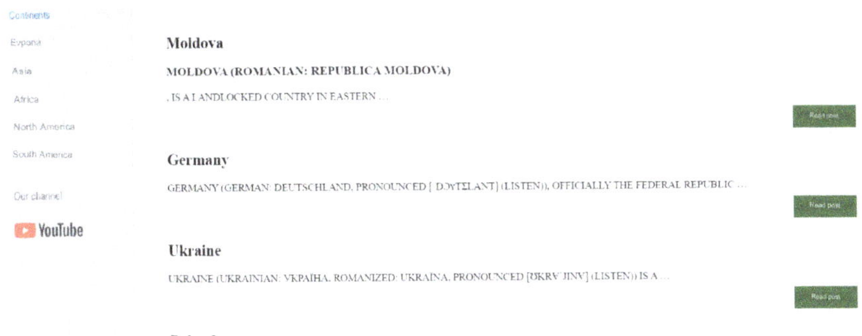

Now we will continue to change this block. Instead of the lines in the comment **<!--Left Sidebar -->**, write

```html
<!--Sidebar left -->
```

```django
<td valign="top" class="left-chapters">
  <ul id="leftchapters">
{% if cat_selected == 0 %}
    <li class="selected"> Continents </li>
{% else %}
    <li><a href="{% url 'home' %}"> Continents </a>></li>
{% endif %}


{% for c in cats %}
   {% if c.pk == cat_celected %}
      <li class="selected">{{c.name}}</li>
   {% else %}
      <li><a href="{{ c.get_absolute_url }}">{{c.name}}</a></li>
   {% endif %}
{% endfor %}


  <li class="share">
  <p> Our channel </p>
  <a class="share-yt" href="#"></a>
  </li>
 </ul>
 </td>
<!--Конец Sidebar -->
```

```
styles.css    base.html    views.py    urls.py    index.html    models.py

Project ▾
travels ~source root~ C:\Python\Django\travels
  travels
    > media
    > static
    traveler
      migrations
        0001_initial.py
        0002_category_alter_dir_travel_options_and_more.py
        __init__.py
      static
        traveler
          > css
          > images
          js
      templates
        traveler
          about.html
          base.html
          index.html
      __init__.py
      admin.py
      apps.py
      models.py
      tests.py
      urls.py

        <ul id="leftchapters">
{% if cat_selected == 0 %}
        <li class="selected">Continents </li>
{% else %}
        <li><a href="{% url 'home' %}">Continents</a></li>
{% endif %}

{% for c in cats %}
        {% if c.pk == cat_celected %}
            <li class="selected">{{c.name}}</li>
        {% else %}
            <li><a href="{{ c.get_absolute_url }}">{{c.name}}</a></li>
        {% endif %}
{% endfor %}

        <li class="share">
        <p>Наш канал</p>
        <a class="share-yt" href="#"></a>
        </li>
    </ul>
    </td>
<!-- Конец Sidebar -->
<td valign="top" class="content">
```

Let's go through this code.

Line:

<li class="selected"> Continents </li>

will be displayed always. And if

{% if cat_selected == 0 %}

we display this line not as a link but as text. If **cat_selected** is not equal to "**0**", then we display it as a link to the main page

<li><a href="{% url 'home' %}"> Continents </a>></li>.

All subsequent categories will be formed using a loop

{% for c in cats %}

    {% if c.pk == cat_celected %}

       <li class="selected">{{c.name}}</li>

    {% else %}

       <li><a href="{{ c.get_absolute_url }}">{{c.name}}</a></li>

    {% endif %}

{% endfor %}

We will pass the collection "**cats**" (this collection will consist of objects of the Category class) and iterate through it. If in this loop the primary key "**c.pk**" is equal to "**cat_selected**"

{% if c.pk == cat_celected %}

then we output the current category not as a link but as text

<li class="selected">{{c.name}}</li>

Otherwise, it will be displayed as a regular link.

<li><a href="{{ c.get_absolute_url }}">{{c.name}}</a></li>

In other words, we display it by name, and we will form the link using the method

get_absolute_url

To use this method, you need to add it to our **Category** model.

```python
class Category(models.Model):
  name = models.CharField(max_length=100, db_index=True)


  def __str__(self):
    return self.name


  def get_absolute_url(self):
    return reverse('category', kwargs={'cat_the': self.pk})
```

```python
28      class Category(models.Model):
29          name = models.CharField(max_length=100, db_index=True)
30
31          def __str__(self):
32              return self.name
33
34          def get_absolute_url(self):
35              return reverse('category', kwargs={'cat_the': self.pk})
36
```

Now, the route with the name "**category**" needs to be specified in the **urls.py** file

```python
urlpatterns = [
  path('', index, name='home'),
  path('about/', about, name='about'),
```

```python
    path('addpage/', addpage, name='add_page'),
    path('contact/', addpage, name='contact'),
    path('login/', login, name='login'),
    path('post/<int:post_the>/', show_post, name='post'),
    path('category/<int:cat_the>/', show_category, name='category'),
]
```

Let's define the function **show_category** in the **views.py** file, and for now, it will look like a placeholder function.

```python
def show_category(request, cat_the):
    return HttpResponse(f" Displaying the category c id = {cat_the}")
```

And finally! For **base.html** to work, it needs to be passed the collection "**cats**" and the variable "**cat_selected**".

Let's go to the **views.py** file and find the **index** function

```python
def index(request):
    posts = Dir_travel.objects.all()
    cats = Category.objects.all()
    context = {
        'posts': posts,
        'cats': cats,
        'menu': menu,
        'title': 'Home page',
        'cat_selected': 0,
```

```python
12    def index(request):
13        posts = Dir_travel.objects.all()
14        cats = Category.objects.all()
15        context = {
16            'posts': posts,
17            'cats': cats,
18            'menu': menu,
19            'title': 'Main page',
20            'cat_selected': 0,
21        }
22        return render(request, 'traveler/index.html', context=context)
```

Let's go to the **views.py** file, find the index function, and additionally read entries from the "**cats**" table using the command:

cats = Category.objects.all()

Pass this collection and the variable **'cat_selected'** with the value **0** to the template, so that all entries are displayed on the main page.

Now let's see how it will work. Go to the terminal and type the familiar command

Python manage.py runserver

And let's go to the link http://127.0.0.1:8000/

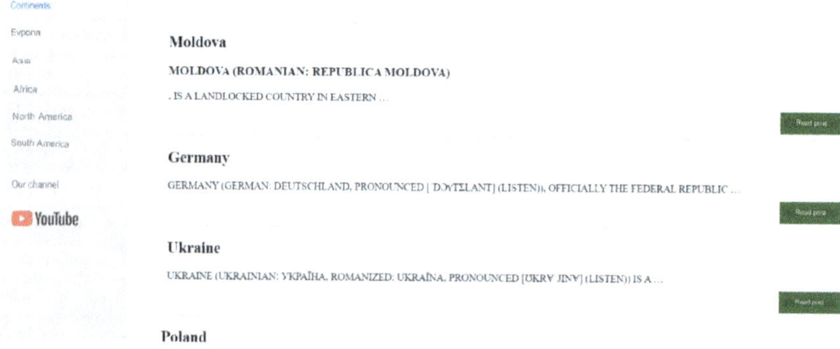

We see all our categories on the left side. If you click on each link one by one, each of them will work correctly, displaying our placeholder pages with the specified **id**.

Category display   = 2

Next, let's make different articles display in separate categories. To do this, open the **views.py** file and modify the **show_category** function. Instead of the placeholder, write the same code as in the index function. We also select posts, but not all of them, only those that correspond to the current category, i.e., where the foreign key **cat_the** matches the key we passed in the request.

```python
def show_category(request, cat_the):
    posts = Dir_travel.objects.filter(cat_the=cat_the)
    cats = Category.objects.all()
    context = {
        'posts': posts,
        'cats': cats,
        'menu': menu,
        'title': ' Display by Categories ',
        'cat_selected': cat_the,
    }
    return render(request, 'traveler/index.html', context=context)
```

```python
40  def show_category(request, cat_the):
41      posts = Dir_travel.objects.filter(cat_the=cat_the)
42      cats = Category.objects.all()
43      context = {
44          'posts': posts,
45          'cats': cats,
46          'menu': menu,
47          'title': ' Display by category ',
48          'cat_selected': cat_the,
49      }
50      return render(request, 'traveler/index.html', context=context)
```

cats = Category.objects.all() – We select all the categories that we want to display on the page.

With the help of the context, we pass the same data. Only **'title': 'Display by Categories'** and **'cat_selected'**: cat_the are changed. Now let's check how it will work. Start the server and refresh the page.

Afterward, let's navigate to the category, for example, **'Europe'**.

FieldError at /category/1/

Cannot resolve keyword 'cat_the' into field. Choices are: cat, cat_id, content, id, is_puplished, photo, time_create, time_update, title

We encountered an error. What could be the issue?! Firstly, we made a mistake in the **base.html** file, in **line 37**

```
{% if cat_selected == 0 %}

    <li class="selected"> Continents </li>

{% else %}
```

Next, let's go to the file **models.py**

In line 13, models **Dir_travel**

cat = models.ForeignKey('Category', on_delete=models.PROTECT, null=True)

Django automatically adds **'id'** to the 'cat' field with an underscore. Accordingly, let's open **urls.py** and make the correction

```
urlpatterns = [

    path('', index, name='home'),

    path('about/', about, name='about'),

    path('addpage/', addpage, name='add_page'),

    path('contact/', addpage, name='contact'),

    path('login/', login, name='login'),

    path('post/<int:post_the>/', show_post, name='post'),

    path('category/<int:cat_id>/', show_category, name='category'),

]
```

Next, in the **views.py** file, let's change **'cat_the'** to **'cat_id'**

```python
def show_category(request, cat_id):
    posts = Dir_travel.objects.filter(cat_id=cat_id)
    cats = Category.objects.all()
    context = {
        'posts': posts,
        'cats': cats,
        'menu': menu,
        'title': ' Display by Categories ',
        'cat_selected': cat_id,
    }
    return render(request, 'traveler/index.html', context=context)
```

Restart the server, refresh the page. When clicking on the **'Europe'** tab, all articles related to Europe will be displayed. Clicking on other tabs will show nothing since the lists are empty. Additionally, when clicking on the **'Europe'** tab, it is displayed not as a link but as regular text, while other tabs appear as links. All this is possible thanks to the **'cat_selected'** variable. When checking in the **base.html** template

{% if cat_selected == 0 %},

the **'Continents'** tab is displayed as text, and everything else is displayed as a link. Similarly, for countries, after the check

{% if c.pk == cat_selected %},

it is displayed either as text or a link.

Let's make a few more corrections. When using the **show_category** function, enter a non-existent category in the browser, for example,

http://127.0.0.1:8000/category/11/

After this, the function will generate an empty list, which is not good practice. It would be better if a **404** page is generated for a non-existent category. Let's do it as follows. If any category turns out to be empty, we will generate a **404** page. Go to the **views.py** file and add the following condition in the **show_category** function:

```python
def show_category(request, cat_id):
    posts = Dir_travel.objects.filter(cat_id=cat_id)
```

```python
    cats = Category.objects.all()

    if len(posts) == 0:
        raise Http404()

    context = {
        'posts': posts,
        'cats': cats,
        'menu': menu,
        'title': ' Display by Categories ',
        'cat_selected': cat_id,
    }
    return render(request, 'traveler/index.html', context=context)
```

We also need to import this function

```python
from django.http import HttpResponse
from django.shortcuts import render, redirect
from django.http import Http404
```

```python
1  from django.http import HttpResponse
2  from django.shortcuts import render, redirect
3  from django.http import Http404
```

```python
def show_category(request, cat_id):
    posts = Dir_travel.objects.filter(cat_id=cat_id)
    cats = Category.objects.all()


    if len(posts) == 0:
        raise Http404()


    context = {
        'posts': posts,
        'cats': cats,
        'menu': menu,
        'title': 'Display by category',
        'cat_selected': cat_id,
    }
    return render(request, 'traveler/index.html', context=context)
```

If the number of posts is equal to **'0'**, we will generate a **404** error. Let's check it. Click on the **'Asia'** tab, and since there are no posts yet, we will receive a **404** error.

Page not found (404)

Request Method: GET
Request URL: http://127.0.0.1:8000/category/2/
Raised by: traveler.views.show_category

In debug mode, this is sufficient for demonstration purposes. On a production server, we would redirect to a custom error page.

Let's add the following information to this list.

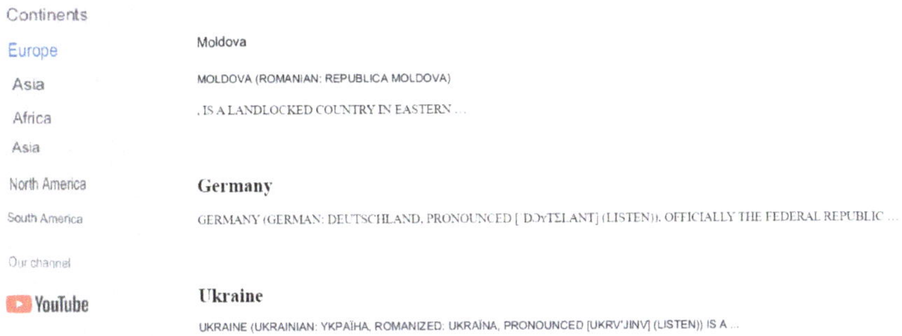

Continents

Europe

Asia

Africa

Asia

North America

South America

Our channel

YouTube

Moldova

MOLDOVA (ROMANIAN: REPUBLICA MOLDOVA)

. IS A LANDLOCKED COUNTRY IN EASTERN ...

Germany

GERMANY (GERMAN: DEUTSCHLAND, PRONOUNCED [ˈDɔʏTʃLANT] (LISTEN)), OFFICIALLY THE FEDERAL REPUBLIC ...

Ukraine

UKRAINE (UKRAINIAN: УКРАЇНА, ROMANIZED: UKRAÏNA, PRONOUNCED [UKRⱯ'JINⱯ] (LISTEN)) IS A ...

Let's add the category name and the post creation time to this list. To do this, open the **index.html** file, find where the list is being generated, and modify the lines.

```
{% extends 'traveler/base.html' %}


{% block content %}
<ul class="list-articles">
    {% for p in posts %}
      <li><div class="article-panel">
        <p class="first"> Continent: {{p.cat}}</p>
        <p class="last">Дата: {{p.time_update|date:"d-m-Y H:i:s"}}</p>
      </div>



      <h2>{{p.title}}</h2>
      {% autoescape off %}
      <p>{{p.content|truncatewords:10|upper}}</p>
      {% endautoescape %}
      <div class="clear"></div>
      <p class="link-read-post"><a href="{{ p.get_absolute_url }}"> Read the post </a></p>
      </li>
    {% endfor %}
</ul>


{% endblock %}
```

```
{% extends 'traveler/base.html' %}

{% block content %}
<ul class="list-articles">
    {% for p in posts %}
        <li><div class="article-panel">
            <p class="first">Continent: {{p.cat}}</p>
            <p class="last">date : {{p.time_update|date:"d-m-Y H:i:s"}}</p>
        </div>


        <h2>{{p.title}}</h2>
        {% autoescape off %}
        <p>{{p.content|truncatewords:10|upper}}</p>
        {% endautoescape %}
        <div class="clear"></div>
        <p class="link-read-post"><a href="{{ p.get_absolute_url }}">Read post</a></p>
        </li>
    {% endfor %}
</ul>

{% endblock %}
```

Here we display the continent using the variable **p.cat**. This attribute will return the category name since we have overridden it with the method

def __str__(self):

    return self.name

i.e., **'cat'** will refer to an instance of the **Category** class, and the method will be triggered

def __str__(self):

The date is formatted in this way

{{p.time_update|date:"d-m-Y H:i:s"}}

i.e., we access the **'time_update'** attribute and display the date using the

filter |date:"d-m-Y H:i:s" - day-month-year hours:minutes:seconds.

Let's see how it works by refreshing the page..

Continent: Europe   Date : 23-10-2022 12:07:03

Moldova

MOLDOVA (ROMANIAN: REPUBLICA MOLDOVA)

. IS A LANDLOCKED COUNTRY IN EASTERN …

Read post

Continent: Europe   Date: 12-10-2022 12:30:09

Germany

GERMANY (GERMAN: DEUTSCHLAND, PRONOUNCED [ˈDɔʏTͰΣLANT] (LISTEN)), OFFICIALLY THE FEDERAL REPUBLIC …

Read post

Admin panel. Registering the Category model

For starters, I would like to add one more field named 'Publication'.

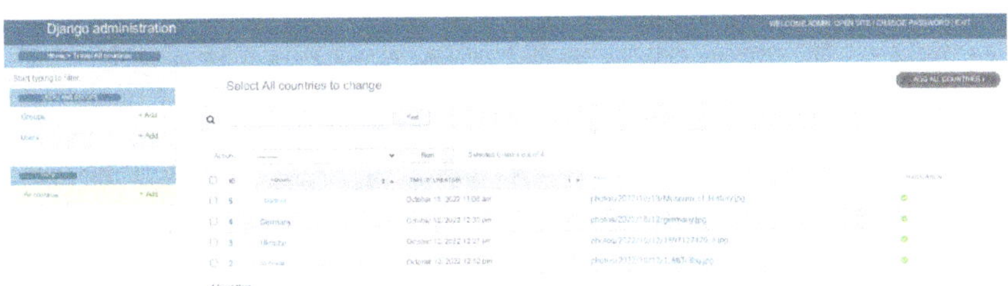

How to do it?

It's simple! Open the **admin.py** file that we've worked with before and add **'is_published'**.

```
class Dir_travelAdmin(admin.ModelAdmin):
    list_display = ('id', 'title', 'time_create', 'photo', 'is_puplished')
    list_display_links = ('id', 'title')
    search_fields = ('title', 'content')
```

```
class Dir_travelAdmin(admin.ModelAdmin):
    list_display = ('id', 'title', 'time_create', 'photo', 'is_puplished')
    list_display_links = ('id', 'title')
    search_fields = ('title', 'content')
```

To display this field in Russian within the **'Dir_travel'** class in the **models.py** file, add the line **verbose_name = "Publication"** to the **'is_published'** field.

```
class Dir_travel(models.Model):
    title = models.CharField(max_length=255, verbose_name = " Title ")
```

content = models.TextField(blank=True, verbose_name = " Article text ")

photo = models.ImageField(upload_to="photos/%Y/%m/%d/", verbose_name = " Photo ")

time_create = models.DateTimeField(auto_now_add=True, verbose_name = " Creation time ")

time_update = models.DateTimeField(auto_now=True, verbose_name = " Modification time ")

is_puplished = models.BooleanField(default=True, verbose_name = " Publication ")

cat = models.ForeignKey('Category', on_delete=models.PROTECT, null=True)

```python
class Dir_travel(models.Model):
    title = models.CharField(max_length=255, verbose_name = "header")
    content = models.TextField(blank=True, verbose_name = "Article text")
    photo = models.ImageField(upload_to="photos/%Y/%m/%d/", verbose_name = "Photo")
    time_create = models.DateTimeField(auto_now_add=True, verbose_name = "Time of creation")
    time_update = models.DateTimeField(auto_now=True, verbose_name = "Change time")
    is_puplished = models.BooleanField(default=True, verbose_name = "Publication")
    cat = models.ForeignKey('Category', on_delete=models.PROTECT, null=True)
```

Next, let's register our **Category** model.

Open the **admin.py** file and add the second class **CategoryAdmin** in it.

class CategoryAdmin(admin.ModelAdmin):

list_display = ('id', 'name')

list_display_links = ('id', 'name')

search_fields = ('name',)

```python
class CategoryAdmin(admin.ModelAdmin):
    list_display = ('id', 'name')
    list_display_links = ('id', 'name')
    search_fields = ('name',)
```

Make sure to put a comma after '**name**' in the last line as it's part of a tuple!

search_fields = ('name',)

And, in the next line, we will register the **Category** model *admin.site.register(Category, CategoryAdmin)*

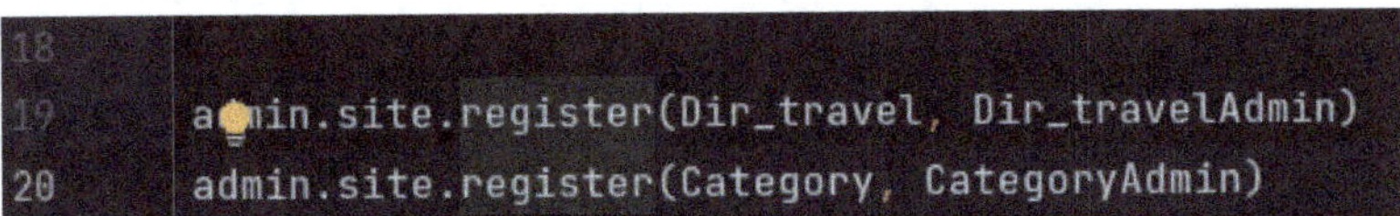

```
18
19        admin.site.register(Dir_travel, Dir_travelAdmin)
20        admin.site.register(Category, CategoryAdmin)
```

Go to the admin panel and refresh/update it!

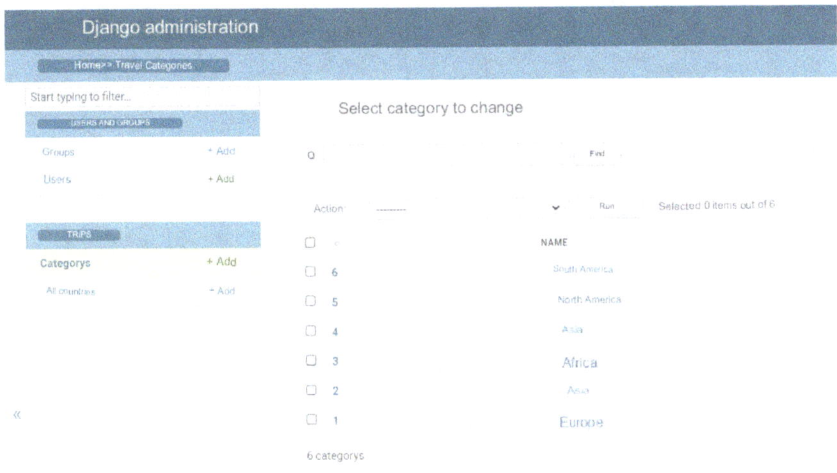

To display everything in Russian, let's add a nested class Meta within the **Category** class in the **models.py** file..

class Meta:

verbose_name = " Continent "

verbose_name_plural = " Continents "

ordering = ['id']

```python
class Category(models.Model):
    name = models.CharField(max_length=100, db_index=True)

    def __str__(self):
        return self.name


    def get_absolute_url(self):
        return reverse('category', kwargs={'cat_id': self.pk})



    class Meta:
        verbose_name = "Continent "
        verbose_name_plural = "Continents"
        ordering = ['id']
```

Instead of '**name**', let's also write the word '**Category**'

```python
class Category(models.Model):
    name = models.CharField(max_length=100, db_index=True, verbose_name = " Continent ")

    def __str__(self):
        return self.name


    def get_absolute_url(self):
        return reverse('category', kwargs={'cat_id': self.pk})
```

```python
class Category(models.Model):
    name = models.CharField(max_length=100, db_index=True, verbose_name = "Continent")

    def __str__(self):
        return self.name

    def get_absolute_url(self):
        return reverse('category', kwargs={'cat_id': self.pk})
```

Let's move to the admin panel and update

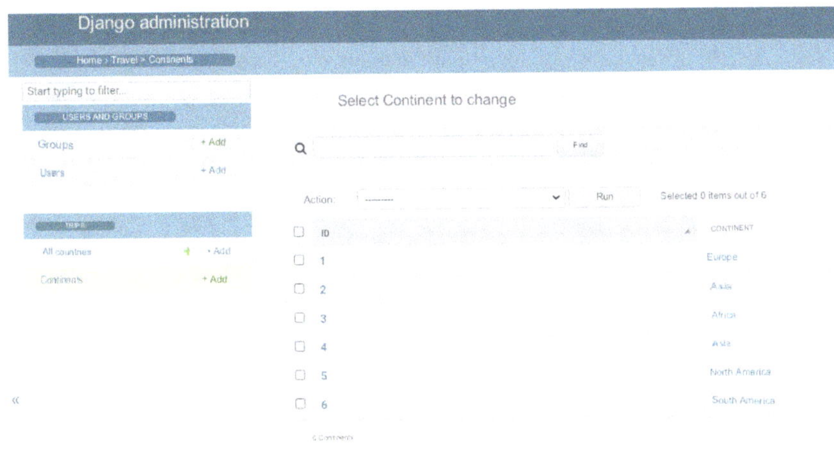

The altered meta description that we specified in both models will be entered into the database tables. Let's create another migration file using the command

python manage.py makemigrations

```
(venv) PS C:\Python\Django\travels\travels> python manage.py makemigrations
Migrations for 'traveler':
  traveler\migrations\0003_alter_category_options_alter_category_name_and_more.py
    - Change Meta options on category
    - Alter field name on category
    - Alter field is_puplished on dir_travel
(venv) PS C:\Python\Django\travels\travels>
```

Apply all these migrations to the database table

python manage.py migrate

```
(venv) PS C:\Python\Django\travels\travels> python manage.py migrate
Operations to perform:
  Apply all migrations: admin, auth, contenttypes, sessions, traveler
Running migrations:
  Applying traveler.0003_alter_category_options_alter_category_name_and_more... OK
(venv) PS C:\Python\Django\travels\travels>
```

After all these steps, we can say that the admin panel is set up and fully functional at this stage. Next, using it, we'll add a few more entries. Let's add 2-3 more countries and link them to relevant categories. I've taken the text from Wikipedia, and we'll use random photos from the internet as well.

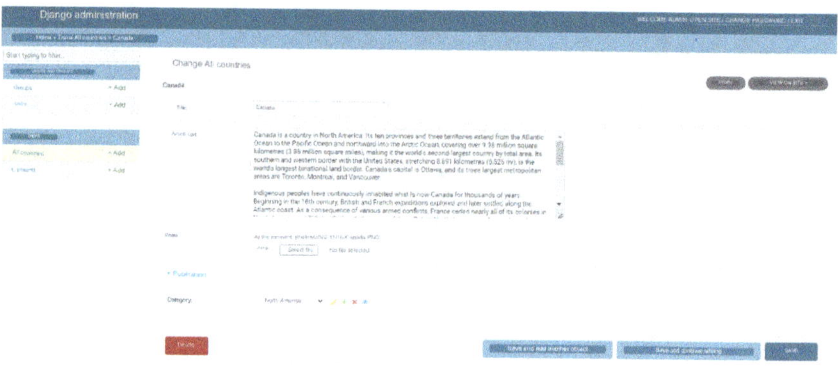

Once we exit the admin panel and refresh the page, we'll see several more entries—exactly the number that we posted through the admin panel.

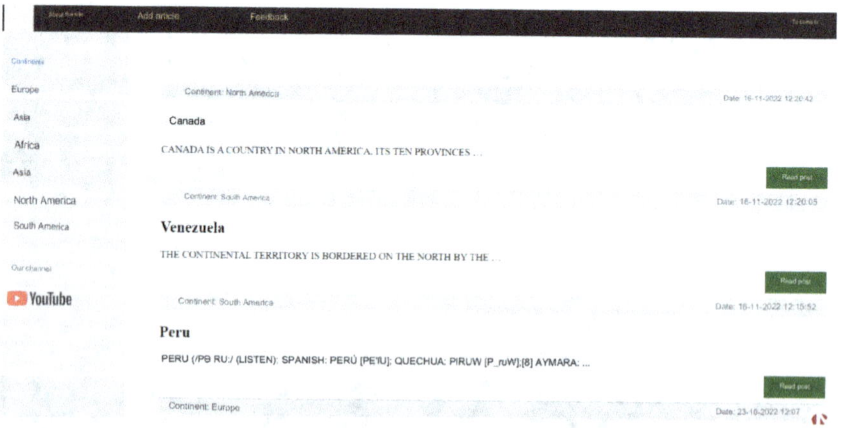

If you don't upload a photo, **Django** framework will throw an error reminding you to upload a photo because it's a mandatory field. Let's check how our photos were uploaded and the structure of their placement.

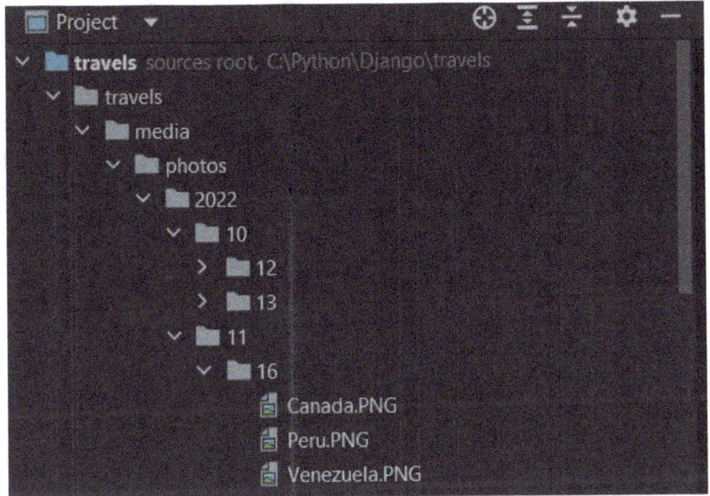

Photos were automatically uploaded to the server, as we can see. Let's add the display of the photos directly in the template.

Open the **index.html** template and place the lines

```
<li><div class="article-panel">

    <p class="first"> Continent: {{p.cat}}</p>

    <p class="last"> date: {{p.time_update|date:"d-m-Y H:i:s"}}</p>

  </div>
{% if p.photo %}

    <p><img class="img-article-left thumb" src="{{p.photo.url}}"></p>
{% endif %}


  <h2>{{p.title}}</h2>
```

```
{% block content %}
<ul class="list-articles">
    {% for p in posts %}
        <li><div class="article-panel">
            <p class="first">Continent:{{p.cat}}</p>
            <p class="last">datea:{{p.time_update|date:"d-m-Y H:i:s"}}</p>
        </div>
    {% if p.photo %}
            <p><img class="img-article-left thumb" src="{{p.photo.url}}"></p>
    {% endif %}


    <h2>{{p.title}}</h2>
    {% autoescape off %}
    <p>{{p.content|truncatewords:10|upper}}</p>
    {% endautoescape %}
```

Let's check if the '**photo**' field is empty

{% if p.photo %}

If this field isn't empty, then we display this photo using the attribute

{{p.photo.url}}

Let's check how this works. Navigate to the page and refresh it.

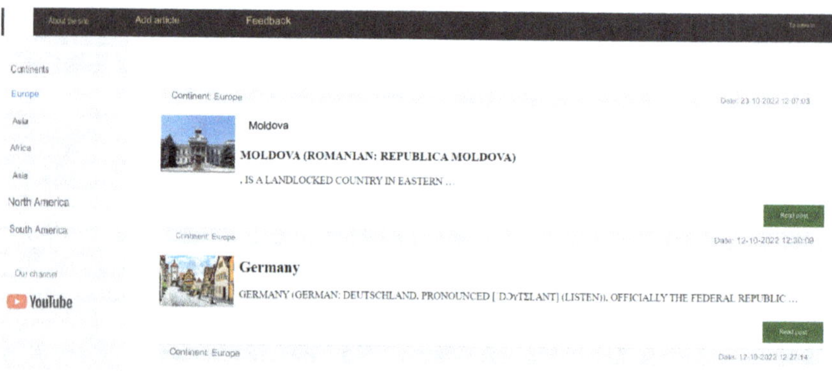

If you click on the '**Europe**' tab, you'll see posts about European countries. Clicking on the '**South America**' tab will display posts about countries in South America. Clicking on a tab where there are no posts yet will result in a **404 error**.

Hence, the category selection is functioning correctly.

Let's further enhance our admin panel. We'll make the **'publication'** field editable.

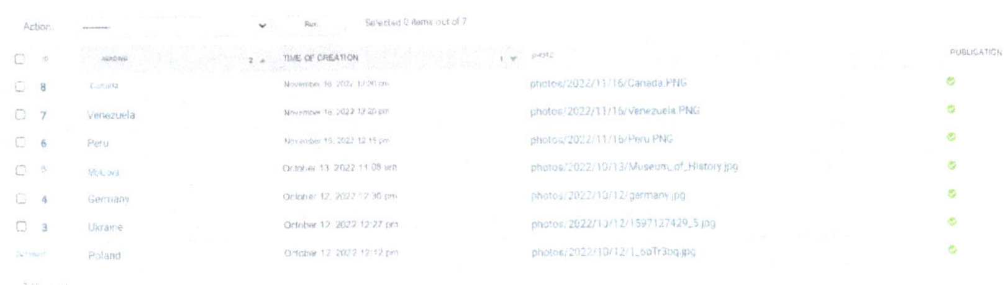

To do this, let's navigate to the **admin.py** file and within the **Dir_travelAdmin** class, add another attribute

```python
class Dir_travelAdmin(admin.ModelAdmin):
    list_display = ('id', 'title', 'time_create', 'photo', 'is_puplished')
    list_display_links = ('id', 'title')
    search_fields = ('title', 'content')
    list_editable = ('is_published',)
```

I made a mistake earlier.

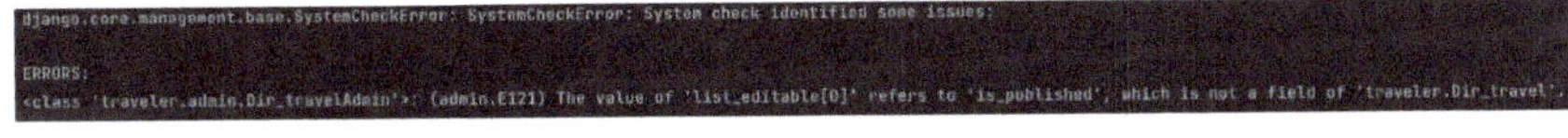

Let's fix that! Instead of **'is_puplished'**, we'll write **'is_published'**. Also, we'll need to rerun the migration commands for the database

```
python manage.py makemigrations
python manage.py migrate
```

Should be

class Dir_travelAdmin(admin.ModelAdmin):

   list_display = ('id', 'title', 'time_create', 'photo', 'is_published')

   list_display_links = ('id', 'title')

   search_fields = ('title', 'content')

   list_editable = ('is_published',)

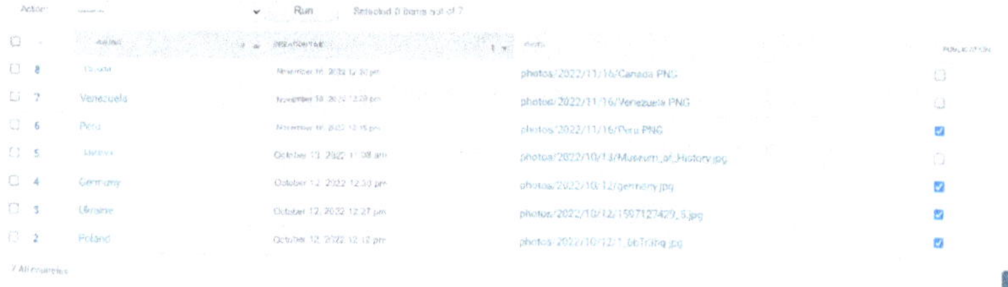

Let's check. Refresh the admin panel. Don't forget to start the server.

Now we have that field editable.

Let's add more fields that we can use to filter our list of articles. We'll do this by adding another line to the same class.

class Dir_travelAdmin(admin.ModelAdmin):

   list_display = ('id', 'title', 'time_create', 'photo', 'is_published')

   list_display_links = ('id', 'title')

   search_fields = ('title', 'content')

   list_editable = ('is_published',)

   list_filter = ('is_published', 'time_create')

```python
class Dir_travelAdmin(admin.ModelAdmin):
    list_display = ('id', 'title', 'time_create', 'photo', 'is_published')
    list_display_links = ('id', 'title')
    search_fields = ('title', 'content')
    list_editable = ('is_published',)
    list_filter = ('is_published', 'time_create')
```

'is_published', **'time_create'** – fields by which we'll filter our list. Let's refresh the page.

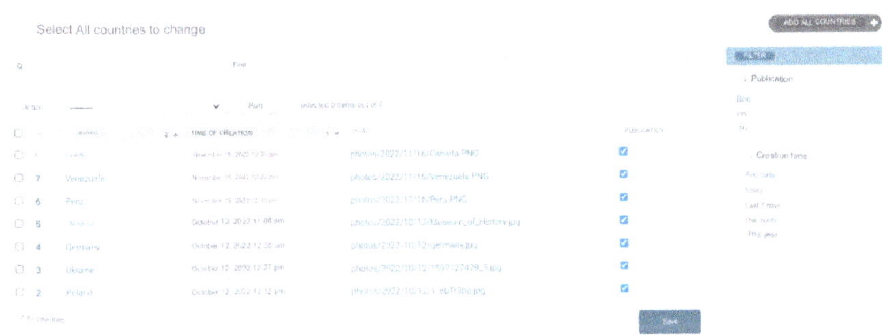

We see the sidebar with filters in the top right corner.

User-defined template tags.

Earlier, we created two functions: index and **show_category**. They are quite similar and violate the principle of "**Don't Repeat Yourself" (DRY).** For instance, the line **cats = Category.objects.all()** exists in both functions. Let's eliminate this duplication by using custom template tags as an example.

In Django, you can create two types of tags

Simple tags – simple tags

Inclusion tags – inclusion tags.

For more details on the topic, you can read by following the link below

https://django.fun/ru/docs/django/4.1/howto/custom-template-tags/

Let's see how to use this feature with a specific example.

Simple tags

Let's move to the project.

Open the views.py file.

Initially, we'll create a simple tag that fetches categories from the database and can be used directly in the template.

According to the **Django** documentation, all tags should be placed in a specific subdirectory within our app, and we'll name it templatetags.

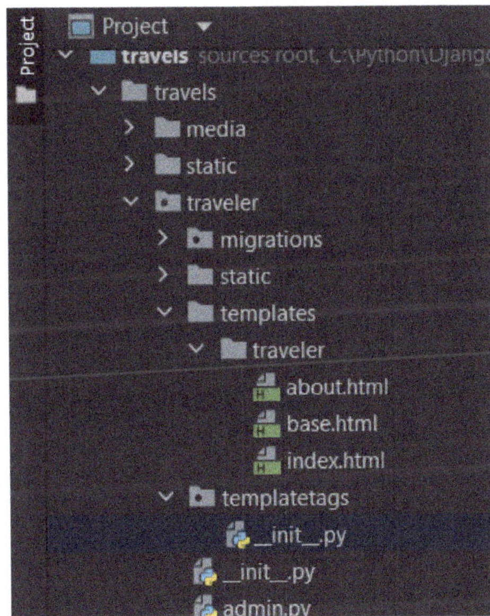

The directory should indeed be a package, which means it needs to contain a special file named **__init__.py**, and this file will remain empty. This file simply informs **Django** that the directory is a package.

We'll define the logic for the new tag in a file named **traveler_tags.py**.

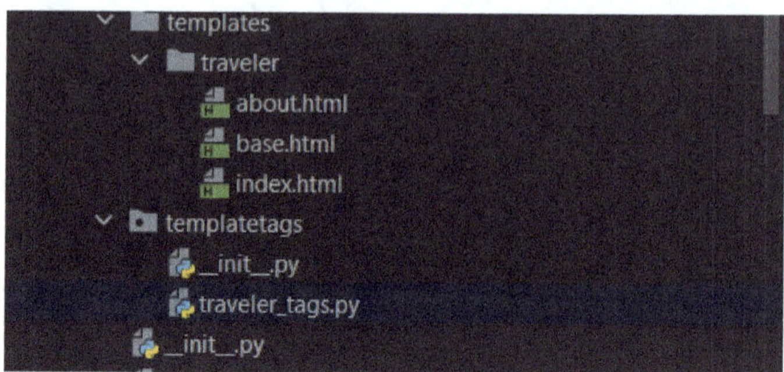

And let's import the '**templates**' module at the beginning to work with templates and our models.

from django import template

*from traveler.models import **

Let's register the tag templates by creating a **Library** class

Register = template.Library()

Next, we'll define a function to work with a simple tag. Since our tag will return categories, let's name it accordingly

def get_categories():

  return Category.objects.all()

In this function, we'll access the database and select all entries from the categories table, which will be returned by this function.

```python
from django import template
from traveler.models import *


Register = template.Library()


def get_categories():
    return Category.objects.all()
```

Next, we need to turn this function into a tag. To do this, we'll use a special decorator.

from django import template

*from traveler.models import ***

Register = template.Library()

@register.simple_tag()

def get_categories():

  return Category.objects.all()

```python
from django import template
from traveler.models import *


Register = template.Library()


@register.simple_tag()
def get_categories():
    return Category.objects.all()
```

This simple process turns our function into a tag that can be used in the templates of our application. Next, let's open the base template, **base.html**, and load our tag at the very beginning of the file.

{% load static %}

{% load traveler_tags %}

```
1   {% load static %}
2   {% load traveler_tags %}
3   <!DOCTYPE html>
```

In this case, it currently contains just one simple tag that we can use in this template.

Let's save it

<!--Sidebar To the left -->

  <td valign="top" class="left-chapters">

    {% get_categories %}

<ul id="leftchapters">

And let's see how this simple tag works. Let's navigate to the terminal and start our test server.

We have an error

```
File "C:\Python\Django\travels\venv\lib\site-packages\django\template\backends\django.py", line 117, in get_installed_libraries
File "C:\Python\Django\travels\travels\traveler\templatetags\traveler_tags.py", Line 6, in <module>
  return {
File "C:\Python\Django\travels\venv\lib\site-packages\django\template\backends\django.py", line 117, in <dictcomp>
  @register.simple_tag()
NameError: name 'register' is not defined. Did you mean: 'Register'?
```

Let's correct **'Register'** to **'register'**

```python
1    from django import template
2    from traveler.models import *
3
4    register = template.Library()
5
6    @register.simple_tag()
7    def get_categories():
8        return Category.objects.all()
9
```

Let's restart our server. The command is...

Python manage.py runserver

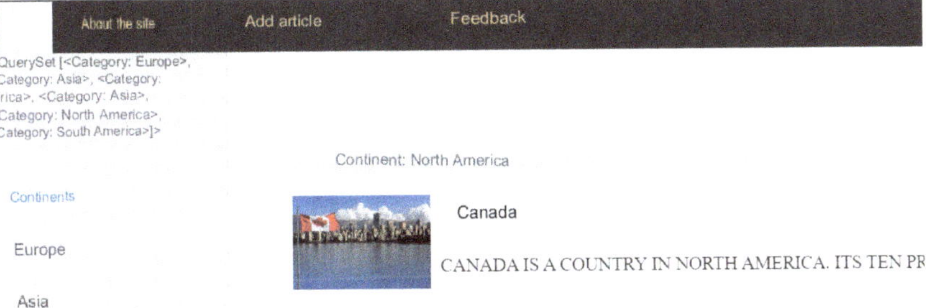

We see on the top left our list, which appeared thanks to the tag that simply returns a list of categories from the database. Let's iterate through our tag.

Since this is a tag, we won't be able to use it directly in a loop. Therefore, we need to first create a reference to this tag using a variable.

<!--Sidebar On the left -->

<td valign="top" class="left-chapters">

{% get_categories as categories %}

Now we can work in a loop using this variable.

*{% for c in **categories** %}*

```
{% if c.pk == cat_selected %}

    <li class="selected">{{c.name}}</li>

{% else %}

    <li><a href="{{ c.get_absolute_url }}">{{c.name}}</a></li>

{% endif %}

{% endfor %}
```

```
44    {% for c in categories %}
45        {% if c.pk == cat_selected %}
46            <li class="selected">{{c.name}}</li>
47        {% else %}
48            <li><a href="{{ c.get_absolute_url }}">{{c.name}}</a></li>
49        {% endif %}
50    {% endfor %}
```

Next, let's go to the main page, refresh, and observe that everything works without changes. Then, we'll rewrite the functions **show_category** and index in the **views.py** file

```python
def index(request):
    posts = Dir_travel.objects.all()
    context = {
        'posts': posts,
        'menu': menu,
        'title': 'The main page',
        'cat_selected': 0,
    }
    return render(request, 'traveler/index.html', context=context)


def show_category(request, cat_id):
    posts = Dir_travel.objects.filter(cat_id=cat_id)

    if len(posts) == 0:
        raise Http404()
```

```python
context = {
    'posts': posts,
    'menu': menu,
    'title': ' Display by categories ',
    'cat_selected': cat_id,
}
return render(request, 'traveler/index.html', context=context)
```

Let's refresh the page again. Everything is working fine. Additionally, if needed, we can change the tag name. Let's write it like this:

```python
@register.simple_tag(name='getcats')
def get_categories():
    return Category.objects.all()
```

```python
from django import template
from traveler.models import *


register = template.Library()


@register.simple_tag(name='getcats')
def get_categories():
    return Category.objects.all()

```

And now in the template, we can use this name

```html
<!--Sidebar On the left -->
<td valign="top" class="left-chapters">
    {% getcats as categories %}
```

<ul id="leftchapters">

```
34    <!--Sidebar слева -->
35        <td valign="top" class="left-chapters">
36            {% getcats as categories %}
37        <ul id="leftchapters">
38    {% if cat_selected == 0 %}
39            <li class="selected">Continents </li>
```

Let's refresh the page. Everything is working again. Let's now consider the second type of custom template tags.

Inclusion tag

Inclusion tags allow the creation of a custom template based on certain data and return an **HTML** snippet. Previously, we returned not an entire **HTML** page but a collection of data that was then used in the template. That is, in the **base.html** file, we can take an entire fragment of code, place it in a separate template file, and put a small tag in the base file. Let's start. First, in the **traveler_tags.py** file we previously created, let's define the second inclusion tag.

@register.inclusion_tag('traveler/list_categories.html')

def show_categories():

  cats = Category.objects.all()

  return {"cats": cats}

```python
1   from django import template
2   from traveler.models import *
3
4   register = template.Library()
5
6   @register.simple_tag(name='getcats')
7   def get_categories():
8       return Category.objects.all()
9
10  @register.inclusion_tag('traveler/list_categories.html')
11  def show_categories():
12      cats = Category.objects.all()
13      return {"cats": cats}
14
```

The name of this tag is **show_categories** because it will return a complete page.

cats = Category.objects.all() – This function will retrieve all categories.

{"cats": cats} – It returns a dictionary.

The parameter cats will be automatically passed to the template **'traveler/list_categories.html'**, which we will define below.

This template, **list_categories.html**, will generate an **HTML** page fragment.

Let's place this template in the same folder where all the **HTML** files are located..

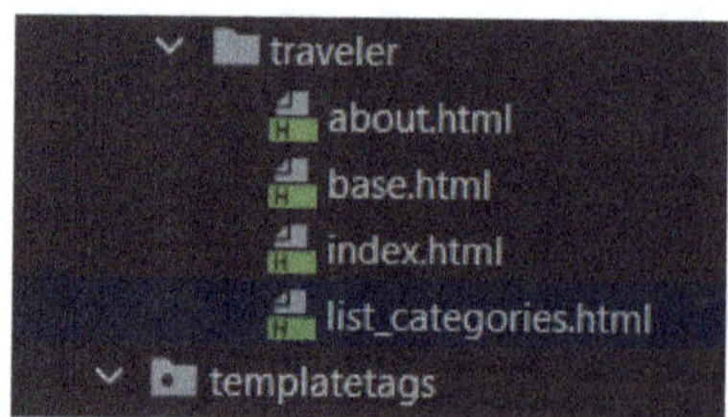

Let's copy the code fragment from **base.html** and place it in the file **list_categories.html**

```
{% for c in categories %}
    {% if c.pk == cat_selected %}
       <li class="selected">{{c.name}}</li>
    {% else %}
       <li><a href="{{ c.get_absolute_url }}">{{c.name}}</a></li>
    {% endif %}
{% endfor %}
```

We need to change the line **{% for c in categories %} to {% for c in cats %},** which we obtain from return **{"cats": cats}**

```
1    {% for c in cats %}
2        {% if c.pk == cat_selected %}
3            <li class="selected">{{c.name}}</li>
4        {% else %}
8            <li><a href="{{ c.get_absolute_url }}">{{c.name}}</a></li>
6        {% endif %}
7    {% endfor %}
```

Let's go back to the base.html file and instead of...

```
{% for c in categories %}
    {% if c.pk == cat_selected %}
       <li class="selected">{{c.name}}</li>
    {% else %}
       <li><a href="{{ c.get_absolute_url }}">{{c.name}}</a></li>
    {% endif %}
{% endfor %}
```

Let's write...

```
{% show_categories %}
```

```
41                    <li><a href="{% url 'home' %}">Continents </a></li>
42       {% endif %}
43
44       {% show_categories %}
45
46            <li class="share">
47            <p>Our channel </p>
```

And remove the line...

```
{% getcats as categories %}
```

```
35            <td valign="top" class="left-chapters">
36               {% getcats as categories %}
37            <ul id="leftchapters">
38       {% if cat_selected == 0 %}
```

Let's check how everything works after the changes. Start our server and refresh the page. As we can see, everything is working.

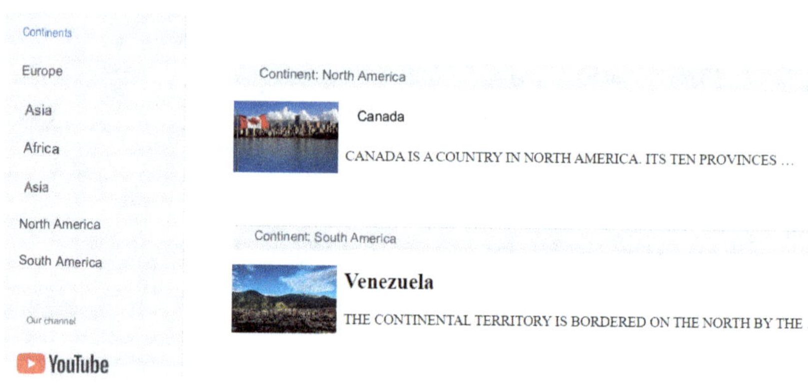

Let's remove the **{% show_categories %}** tag and see how it affects the functionality of our page

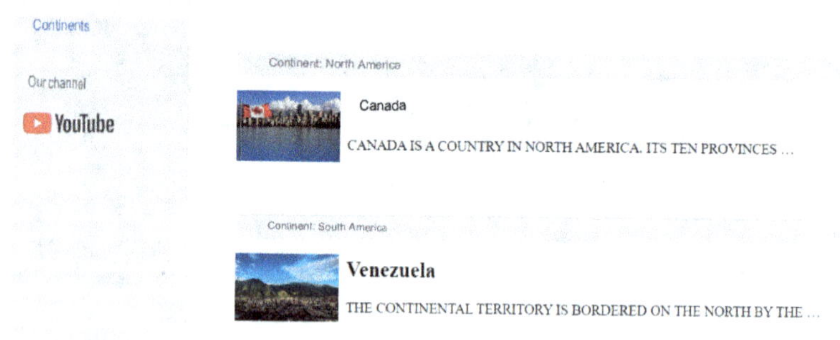

The sidebar menu is missing. Everything is working, but with some adjustments.

The sidebar menu currently doesn't work fully.

When selecting a menu item under the **'Continents'** button, such as **'Europe,'** it doesn't get highlighted in any way to emphasize the selection of that category.

We'll fix this now by passing parameters to the tags. Let's open the **'traveler_tags.py'** file and see how we can pass parameters to our simple tag.

For this tag function, we can define a named parameter, for example, **'filter=None,'** which filters data based on the categories table.

@register.simple_tag(name='getcats')

```python
def get_categories(filter=None):

  if not filter:

    return Category.objects.all()

  else:

    return Category.objects.filter(pk=filter)
```

If our filter has a value of None, i.e., **filter=None**,

then we simply select everything that exists in these categories,

return Category.objects.all()

If it takes any other value, then we use the respective method

return Category.objects.filter(pk=filter)

and select the 'pk' that corresponds to the specified filter. Let's see how the **'filter'** parameter can be passed to the simple tag **'get_categories**,' which is named **'getcats'** in the **base.html** template.

Open the base.html template and insert the line...

```html
<!--Sidebar Left -->

  <td valign="top" class="left-chapters">

    {% getcats %}

  <ul id="leftchapters">
```

```
34        <!--Sidebar слева -->
35            <td valign="top" class="left-chapters">
36                {% getcats %}
37          💡 <ul id="leftchapters">
```

To simply see how it works and view the entire full list.

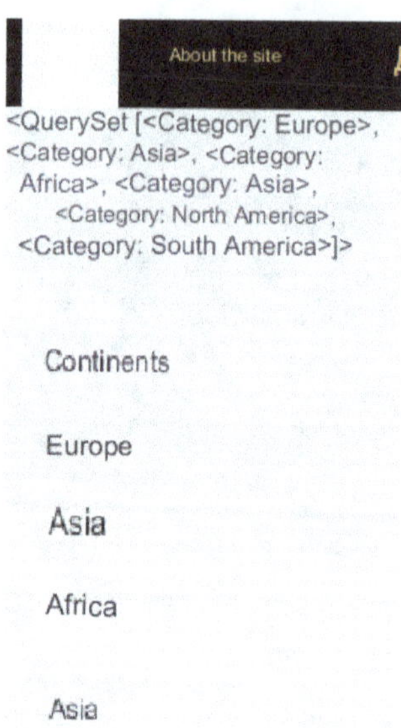

Next, we'll pass the parameter '**filter**' and assign it some value

{% getcats filter=1 %}

So, only one entry with **id=1** should be selected. We navigate to the page, refresh, and indeed, we see only one entry.

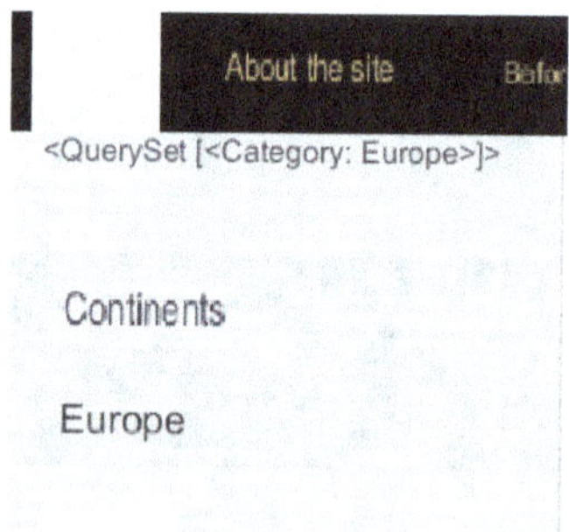

Now let's perform a similar operation for the inclusive tag and pass two parameters instead.

@register.inclusion_tag('traveler/list_categories.html')

```python
def show_categories(sort=None, cat_selected=0):
    if not sort:
        cats = Category.objects.all()
    else:
        cats = Category.objects.order_by(sort)
    return {"cats": cats, "cat_selected": cat_selected}
```

The first parameter, **sort=None**, defines the sorting of these categories.

The second one, **cat_selected=0**, determines which category is selected.

Next, we perform the sorting. If it's not defined, then..

```python
cats = Category.objects.all()
```

and if it's defined, we sort by the specified field

```python
cats = Category.objects.order_by(sort)
```

The second parameter

'cat_selected': cat_selected

is passed directly to the

list_categories.html

template so that we can check which category is selected and display it as regular text.

Now, in the base.html template, we'll remove the **{% getcats filter=1 %}** tag we used for the example and correct it in the line below to

{% show_categories '-name' cat_selected %}.

Here, the filtering will occur based on the name **'-name'**, and **cat_selected** will be passed, which is available in this template as

{% if cat_selected == 0 %}...

```html
<ul id="leftchapters">
{% if cat_selected == 0 %}
    <li class="selected"> Continents </li>
{% else %}
    <li><a href="{% url 'home' %}"> Continents </a></li>
```

{% endif %}

{% show_categories '-name' cat_selected %}

```
37      <ul id="leftchapters">
38      {% if cat_selected == 0 %}
39              <li class="selected">Continents </li>
40      {% else %}
41              <li><a href="{% url 'home' %}">Continents </a></li>
42      {% endif %}
43
44      {% show_categories '-name' cat_selected %}
```

Let's see how this will work. Let's refresh the page. We see that upon entering the category, the link disappears and is displayed as text, and the order changes. Everything is working.

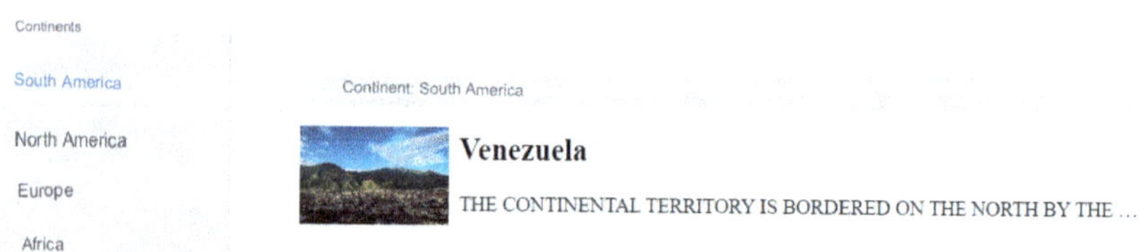

Alternatively, if sorting isn't necessary, we can pass just one parameter:

{% show_categories cat_selected=cat_selected %}.

Let's refresh the page, and we see that nothing has changed.

The use of slugs in URL addresses

Let's display web pages based on their slug.

A slug is a unique part of a **URL** that's associated with a specific record and consists of letters, underscores, and numbers. It's a unique set of characters used to retrieve an article from the database.

For instance, in the

URL https://center-doors.com.ua/mezhkomnatnye-dveri,

'mezhkomnatnye-dveri' is the slug in this practice.

Using slugs is a great practice because such pages are better ranked by search engines and are more understandable to end-users.

In contrast, there's another approach that's less readable and poorly ranked by search engines, like in the **URL**:

https://holz.ua/ua/dveri/vhodnye/?gclid=Cj0KCQiA-JacBhC0ARIsAIxybyP9dhetBuWeBpP9QlZ2wq7eGP7NmqPtdns3sUnJ2q5RRsd6woUNAZs aAhXZEALw_wcB

Firstly, let's display articles by their identifier, and then replace the address with the slug.

Open the **views.py** file where we have a placeholder function called **show_post** - to display the article. Let's modify it slightly to display the article based on its identifier

```python
def show_post(request, post_the):
  post = get_object_or_404(Dir_travel, pk=post_the)


  context = {
    'post': post,
    'menu': menu,
    'title': post.title,
    'cat_selected': 1,
  }
  return render(request, 'traveler/post.html', context=context)
```

```python
35   def show_post(request, post_the):
36       post = get_object_or_404(Dir_travel, pk=post_the)
37
38       context = {
39           'post': post,
40           'menu': menu,
41           'title': post.title,
42           'cat_selected': 1,
43       }
44       return render(request, 'traveler/post.html', context=context)
45
46
47   def show_category(request, cat_id):
48       posts = Dir_travel.objects.filter(cat_id=cat_id)
```

We start by taking a record from the **Dir_travel** model, where the primary key **'pk'** corresponds to the **'post_the'** identifier we pass in the request.

We use the **'get_object_or_404'** function.

It selects a post from the **Dir_travel** model with the primary key **'pk=post_the'** if it exists.

Otherwise, it raises a **404** exception. To use this function, it needs to be imported..

from django.shortcuts import render, redirect, get_object_or_404

```python
1   from django.http import HttpResponse
2   from django.shortcuts import render, redirect, get_object_or_404
```

Next, we form parameters

context = {

    'post': post,

    'menu': menu,

    'title': post.title,

    'cat_selected': post.cat_id,

    }

We'll pass these to the **post.html** template, which, by the way, we don't have yet.

The line **'cat_selected': 1**, will be changed to **'cat_selected': post.cat_id**,

That means we're passing the property **cat_id**, which exists in the **Dir_travel** object.

In other words, it's a reference to an object of **class Dir_travel(models.Model):**

And when an instance of this class is created, cat_id is automatically generated, containing the identifier of the current category related to the articles.

Then, we pass all these parameters to the template

*return render(request, 'traveler/**post.html**', context=context)*

All our templates are located in the folder **traveler**

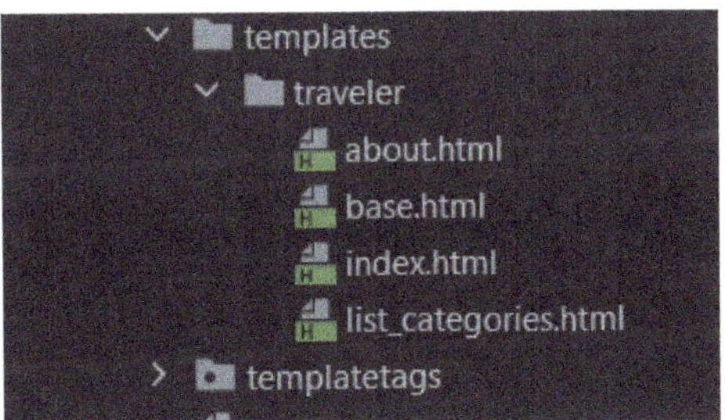

Let's create this file.

```
travels
    media
    static
    traveler
        migrations
        static
        templates
            traveler
                about.html
                base.html
                index.html
                list_categories.html
                post.html
    templatetags
```

```html
1  <!DOCTYPE html>
2  <html lang="en">
3  <head>
4      <meta charset="UTF-8">
5      <title>Title</title>
6  </head>
7  <body>
8
9  </body>
10 </html>
```

Instead of the automatically generated template, we add our base template.

```
{% extend 'traveler/base.html' %}

{% block content %}

<h1>{{post.title}}</h1>

{% if post.photo %}

<p><img class="img-article-left" src="{{post.photo.url}}"></p>

{% endif %}

{{post.content|linebreaks}}

{% endblock %}
```

```
1   {% extend 'traveler/base.html' %}
2
3   {% block content %}
4   <h1>{{post.title}}</h1>
5
6   {% if post.photo %}
7   <p><img class="img-article-left" src="{{post.photo.url}}"></p>
8   {% endif %}
9
10  {{post.content|linebreaks}}
11  {% endblock %}
```

In it, we extend the base template

{% extend 'traveler/base.html' %}

In the content block, we display a first-level heading

<h1>{{post.title}}</h1>

If there's a photo

{% if post.photo %}

then we show the photo

<p><img class="img-article-left" src="{{post.photo.url}}"></p>

That is, we pass **post.photo.url** of the image associated with the post

and then display the content

{{post.content|linebreaks}}

with the

|linebreaks filter, which adds paragraph tags to our article.

Additionally, we have the route specified.

path('post/int:post_the/', show_post, name='post'),

Let's see how this will work.

We'll start the web server.

Continent: North America

We click on the **'Read Post'** button and navigate to the page

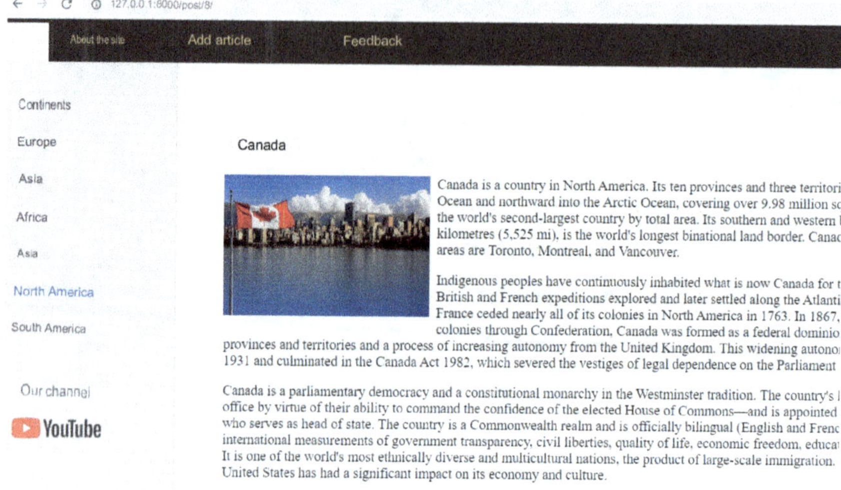

Page with the full article will open.

Additionally, the category **'North America'** is selected, while the other categories are highlighted as links, and we can navigate to them as well.

All this is made possible thanks to the line **'cat_selected': post.cat_id**.

If an invalid identifier is set in the search bar, for example

http://127.0.0.1:8000/category/141/

, then we will encounter a **404** error.

Let's display articles by slug.

For this, in **models.py**, we'll add one more field.

```python
class Dir_travel(models.Model):

    title = models.CharField(max_length=255, verbose_name = "Header")

    slug = models.SlugField(max_length=255, unique=True, db_index=True,
verbose_name="URL")

    content = models.TextField(blank=True, verbose_name = " Article text ")

    photo = models.ImageField(upload_to="photos/%Y/%m/%d/", verbose_name = "Photo")

    time_create = models.DateTimeField(auto_now_add=True, verbose_name = " Time of creation ")

    time_update = models.DateTimeField(auto_now=True, verbose_name = " Time of modification ")

    is_published = models.BooleanField(default=True, verbose_name = " Publication ")

    cat = models.ForeignKey('Category', on_delete=models.PROTECT, null=True, verbose_name = " Category ")
```

```python
from django.urls import reverse


class Dir_travel(models.Model):
    title = models.CharField(max_length=255, verbose_name = "Header ")
    slug = models.SlugField(max_length=255, unique=True, db_index=True, verbose_name="URL")
    content = models.TextField(blank=True, verbose_name = "Article text ")
    photo = models.ImageField(upload_to="photos/%Y/%m/%d/", verbose_name = "Photo ")
    time_create = models.DateTimeField(auto_now_add=True, verbose_name = "Time of creation ")
    time_update = models.DateTimeField(auto_now=True, verbose_name = "Change time ")
    is_published = models.BooleanField(default=True, verbose_name = "Publication ")
    cat = models.ForeignKey('Category', on_delete=models.PROTECT, null=True, verbose_name = "Category ")


    def __str__(self):
        return self.title


    def get_absolute_url(self):
        return reverse('post', kwargs={'post_the': self.pk})
```

For this purpose, there is a special class called SlugField.

max_length=255 – maximum length for this slug.

unique=True – this field will be unique, as each article's slug must be unique.

db_index=True – the field will be indexed for faster searching by this slug.

verbose_name="URL" – in the admin panel, we'll see the URL field.

Since we added a new attribute, accordingly, we need to change the database table as well.

For this, in the terminal, we'll execute the familiar command

Python manage.py makemigrations

Resulting in the following message:

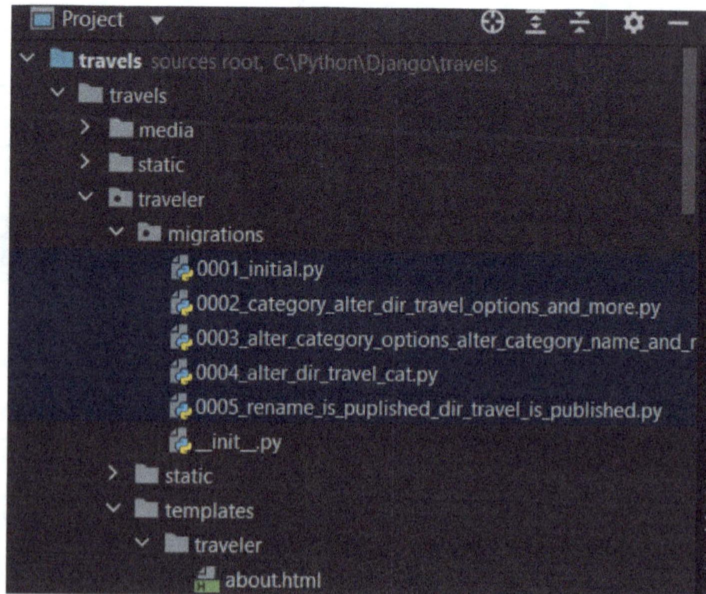

Which informs us that the field cannot be empty because our table already contains records, and when we add a new field, it cannot be empty by requirement. Additionally, this field should also be unique.

Let's make some adjustments.

The first thing we'll do is remove the highlighted parameter in the line

cat = models.ForeignKey('Category', on_delete=models.PROTECT, null=True, verbose_name="Category")

and rebuild our database structure.

We'll delete all migrations.

We'll remove the checkmarks to physically delete from the hard drive

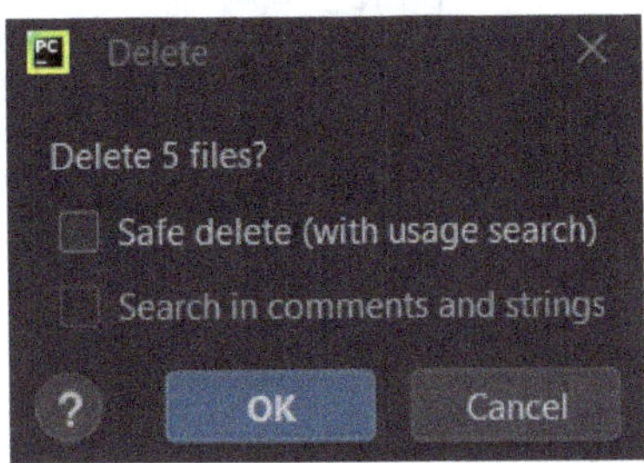

And click '**OK**'.

Next, press '**2**' to exit

```
Please select a fix:
1) Provide a one-off default now (will be set on all existing rows with a null value for this column)
2) Quit and manually define a default value in models.py.
Select an option: 2
```

Let's immediately add a slug to the **Category** class as well to avoid unnecessary migrations.

```
class Category(models.Model):

  name = models.CharField(max_length=100, db_index=True, verbose_name = " Continent ")

  slug = models.SlugField(max_length=255, unique=True, db_index=True,
verbose_name="URL")


  def __str__(self):

    return self.name

......
```

```python
class Category(models.Model):
    name = models.CharField(max_length=100, db_index=True, verbose_name = "Continent")
    slug = models.SlugField(max_length=255, unique=True, db_index=True, verbose_name="URL")

    def __str__(self):
        return self.name

    def get_absolute_url(self):
        return reverse('category', kwargs={'cat_id': self.pk})
```

Let's enter the command in the terminal once again

Python manage.py makemigrations

```
(venv) PS C:\Python\Django\travels\travels> Python manage.py makemigrations
Migrations for 'traveler':
  traveler\migrations\0001_initial.py
    - Create model Category
    - Create model Dir_travel
(venv) PS C:\Python\Django\travels\travels>
```

And we see that it has been applied.

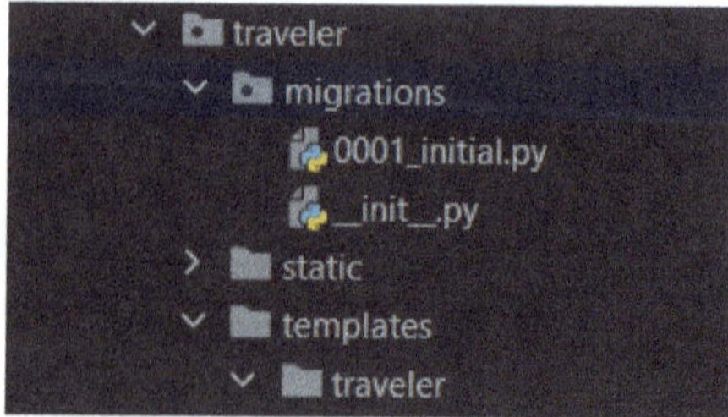

Next, we apply the migration using the command

'Python manage.py migrate.'

We see that it doesn't get created because the database already contains such tables, and it simply cannot be rebuilt.

```
(venv) PS C:\Python\Django\travels\travels> Python manage.py migrate
Operations to perform:
  Apply all migrations: admin, auth, contenttypes, sessions, traveler
Running migrations:
  No migrations to apply.
(venv) PS C:\Python\Django\travels\travels>
```

To do this, let's delete the previous database and repeat the migration command.

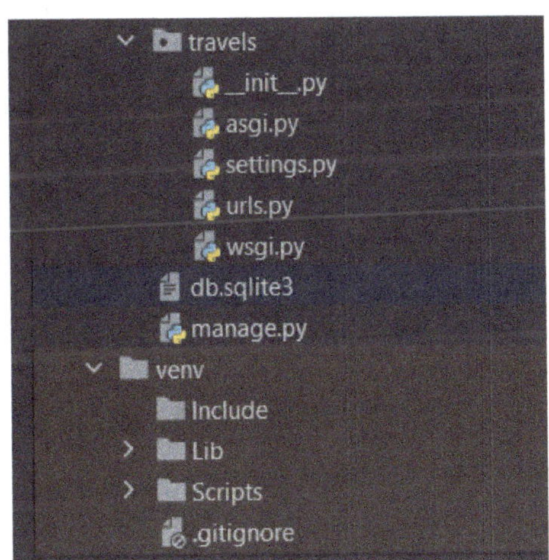

```
(venv) PS C:\Python\Django\travels\travels> Python manage.py migrate
Operations to perform:
  Apply all migrations: admin, auth, contenttypes, sessions, traveler
Running migrations:
  Applying contenttypes.0001_initial... OK
  Applying auth.0001_initial... OK
  Applying admin.0001_initial... OK
  Applying admin.0002_logentry_remove_auto_add... OK
  Applying admin.0003_logentry_add_action_flag_choices... OK
  Applying contenttypes.0002_remove_content_type_name... OK
  Applying auth.0002_alter_permission_name_max_length... OK
  Applying auth.0003_alter_user_email_max_length... OK
  Applying auth.0004_alter_user_username_opts... OK
  Applying auth.0005_alter_user_last_login_null... OK
  Applying auth.0006_require_contenttypes_0002... OK
  Applying auth.0007_alter_validators_add_error_messages... OK
  Applying auth.0008_alter_user_username_max_length... OK
  Applying auth.0009_alter_user_last_name_max_length... OK
  Applying auth.0010_alter_group_name_max_length... OK
  Applying auth.0011_update_proxy_permissions... OK
  Applying auth.0012_alter_user_first_name_max_length... OK
  Applying sessions.0001_initial... OK
  Applying traveler.0001_initial... OK
(venv) PS C:\Python\Django\travels\travels>
```

Everything was created as we see. The database table completely rebuilt, including the admin panel. The superuser created earlier has disappeared. Therefore, let's create the superuser again to access the admin panel. To do this, execute the following command:

Python manage.py createsuperuser

```
(venv) PS C:\Python\Django\travels\travels> Python manage.py createsuperuser
Username (leave blank to use 'user'): root
Email address: root@gmail.com
Password:
Password (again):
The entered password is too short. It must contain at least 8 characters.
The entered password is too wide.
The entered password consists of numbers only.
Bypass password validation and create user anyway? [y/N]: y
Superuser created successfully.
(venv) PS C:\Python\Django\travels\travels>
```

We'll start the test web server and check. Enter the command

'Python manage.py runserver'.

Then input your login and password

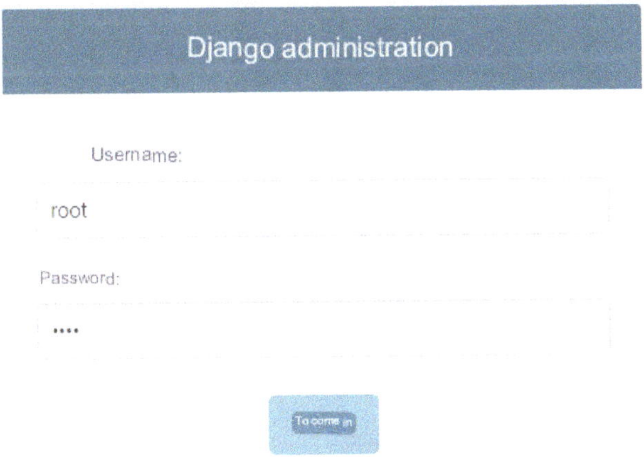

Django administration

Username:

root

Password:

••••

To come in

Everything is working as before. However, if we enter '**Continents**,' it will be empty because we deleted the database.

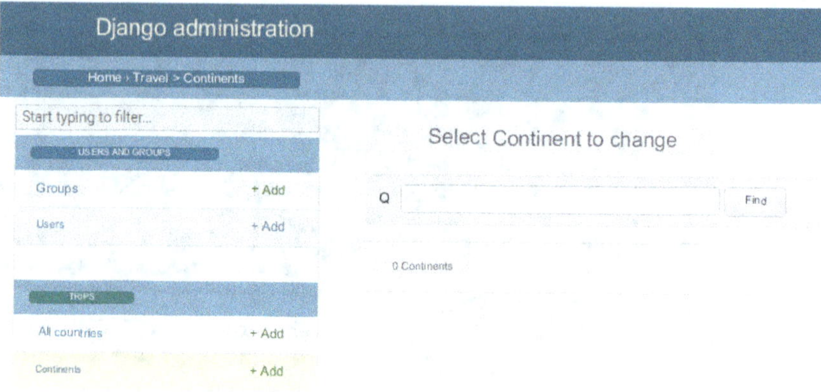

If you click on the **'Add'** button next to **'Continents'** to refill it with content, in the **'Continent'** field, enter, for instance, **'Europe,'** and a little below, you'll need to enter a **URL** address, such as **'europa'**.

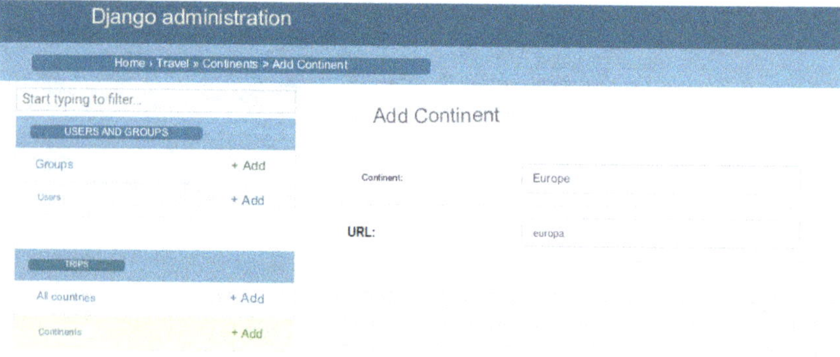

This is the slug fragment. We can input it manually, but since the slug replicates the title, it would be good for the slug to automatically populate in this field when the title is filled.

This can be achieved as follows:

Open **admin.py** where the **CategoryAdmin** class is located. We can add a line to this class

class CategoryAdmin(admin.ModelAdmin):

  list_display = ('id', 'name')

  list_display_links = ('id', 'name')

  search_fields = ('name',)

  prepopulated_fields = {"slug": ("name",)}

```
14      class CategoryAdmin(admin.ModelAdmin):
15          list_display = ('id', 'name')
16          list_display_links = ('id', 'name')
17          search_fields = ('name',)
18          prepopulated_fields = {"slug": ("name",)}
```

Thanks to this entry, we can fill in the '**name**' field, based on which the '**slug**' field will automatically be filled in transliteration.

Let's check it.

Add Continent

Continent: Europe

URL: europa

Everything is working as intended. If, for any reason, the slug isn't unique, we can always make adjustments to it.

Add Continent

Continent: Europe

URL: evropa-2

Since all previous records in the database were deleted, let's recreate all those records of continents that were there before, following the same process.

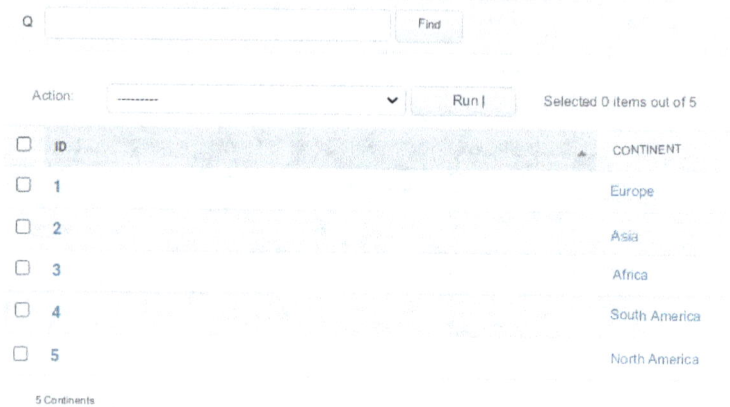

Next, let's add **all countries**

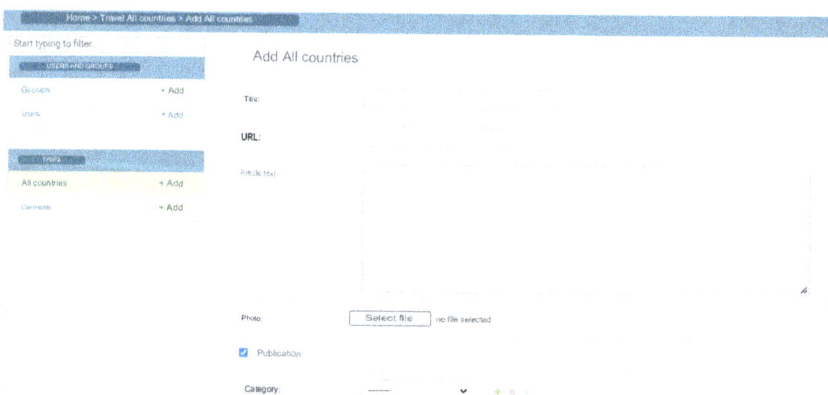

Here, we also want the **URL** field to be automatically filled in. We'll do everything similarly to the previous example

```
class Dir_travelAdmin(admin.ModelAdmin):
    list_display = ('id', 'title', 'time_create', 'photo', 'is_published')
```

list_display_links = ('id', 'title')

search_fields = ('title', 'content')

list_editable = ('is_published',)

list_filter = ('is_published', 'time_create')

prepopulated_fields = {"slug": ("title",)}

```python
class Dir_travelAdmin(admin.ModelAdmin):
    list_display = ('id', 'title', 'time_create', 'photo', 'is_published')
    list_display_links = ('id', 'title')
    search_fields = ('title', 'content')
    list_editable = ('is_published',)
    list_filter = ('is_published', 'time_create')
    prepopulated_fields = {"slug": ("title",)}
```

Instead of **'name,'** we write **'title.'**

Let's fill the database together with uploading photos for different countries.

Add All countries

Title: Ukraine

URL: ukraine

Article text:
beginning of the ongoing Russo-Ukrainian War, and in a major escalation of the conflict in February 2022, Russia launched a full-scale invasion of Ukraine. Since the outbreak of war with Russia in 2014, Ukraine has continued to seek closer economic, political, and military ties with the Western world, including with the United States, European Union, and NATO.[16]

Ukraine is a unitary republic under a semi-presidential system and a developing country, ranking 77th on the Human Development Index. Ukraine is the poorest country in Europe by nominal GDP per capita, [17] and has high levels of corruption.[18][19] However, due to its extensive fertile land, pre-war Ukraine was one of the largest grain exporters in the world.[20][21] It is a founding member of the United Nations, as well as a member of the Council of Europe, the World Trade Organization, and the OSCE, and is in the process of joining the European Union and becoming a NATO member.[22]

Photo: [Choose File] ukraine.jpg

☑ Publication

Category: Europe

After filling in, here is the resulting list of countries

Select All countries to change

Q [   ] [Find]

Action [———— ▾] [Run] Selected 0 items out of 13

	ID	HEADING		TIME OF CREATION		PHOTO	PUBLICATION
☐	13	Tanzania		December 2, 2022 12:00 pm		photos/2022/12/02/tanzania.jpg	✔
☐	12	Zimbabwe		December 2, 2022 11:58 am		photos/2022/12/02/zimbabwe.jpg	✔
☐	11	Cambodia		December 2, 2022 11:57 am		photos/2022/12/02/cambodia.jpg	✔
☐	10	China		December 2, 2022 11:56 am		photos/2022/12/02/china.jpg	✔
☐	9	Canada		December 2, 2022 11:54 am		photos/2022/12/02/Canada.jpg	✔
☐	8	United States		December 2, 2022 11:52 am		photos/2022/12/02/usa.jpg	✔
☐	7	Mexico		December 2, 2022 11:44 am		photos/2022/12/02/mexico.jpg	✔
☐	6	Peru		December 2, 2022 11:41 am		photos/2022/12/02/Peru.jpg	✔
☐	5	Brazil		December 2, 2022 11:39 am		photos/2022/12/02/brazil.jpg	✔
☐	4	Italy		December 2, 2022 11:36 am		photos/2022/12/02/italy.jpeg	✔
☐	3	Germany		December 2, 2022 11:35 am		photos/2022/12/02/germany.jpg	✔
☐	2	Poland		December 2, 2022 11:31 am		photos/2022/12/02/poland.jpg	✔
☐	1	Ukraine		December 2, 2022 11:28 am		photos/2022/12/02/ukraine.jpg	✔

13 All countries

[Save]

Let's go to the website

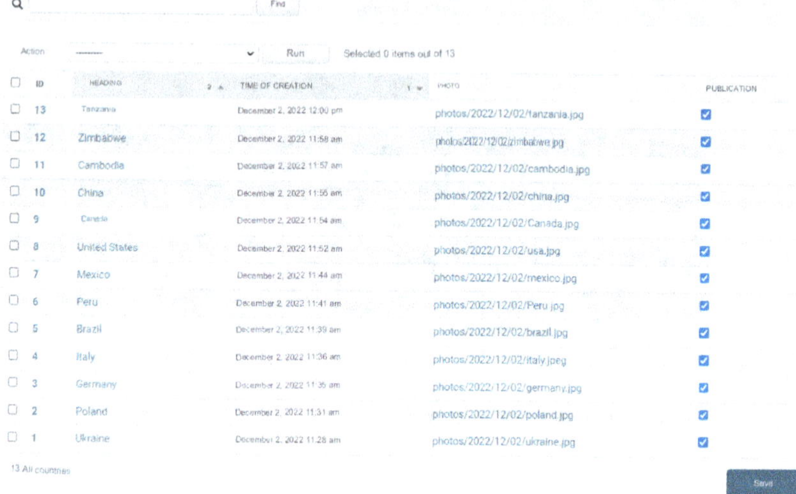

If you click on the 'Read' button, you'll be directed to a page with a detailed description

Tanzania

Tanzania /ˌtænzəˈniːə/[8][9][b] Swahili: [tanzaniˈa]), officially the United Republic of Tanzania (Swahili: Jamhuri ya Muungano wa Tanzania), is a country in East Africa within the African Lakes region. It borders Uganda to the north; Kenya to the northeast; Comoro Islands and the Indian Ocean to the east; Mozambique and Malawi to the south; Zambia to the southwest; and Burundi, and the Democratic Republic of the Congo to the west. Mount Kilimanjaro, Africa's highest mountain, is in northeastern Tanzania. According to the United Nations, Tanzania has a population of 63.59 million, making it the most populous country located entirely south of the equator.

Many important hominid fossils have been found in Tanzania, such as 6-million-year-old Pliocene hominid fossils. The genus Australopithecus ranged across Africa between 4 and 2 million years ago, and the oldest remains of the genus Homo are found near Lake Olduvai. Following the rise of Homo erectus 1.8 million years ago, humanity spread all over the Old World, and later in the New World and Australia under the species Homo sapiens. H. sapiens also overtook Africa and absorbed the older species of humanity.

Later in the Stone and Bronze Age, prehistoric migrations into Tanzania included Southern Cushitic speakers who moved south from present-day Ethiopia.[10] Eastern Cushitic people who moved into Tanzania from north of Lake Turkana about 2,000 and 4,000 years ago;[10] and the Southern Nilotes, including the Datoog, who originated from the present-day South Sudan–Ethiopia border region, between 2,900 and 2,400 years ago. These movements took place at about the same time as the settlement of the Mashariki Bantu from West Africa in the Lake Victoria and Lake Tanganyika areas. They subsequently migrated across the rest of Tanzania between 2,300 and 1,700 years ago.[10][11]

German rule began in mainland Tanzania during the late 19th century when Germany formed German East Africa. This was followed by British rule after World War I. The mainland was governed as Tanganyika, with the Zanzibar Archipelago remaining a separate colonial jurisdiction. Following their respective independence in 1961 and 1963, the two entities merged in 1964 to form the United Republic of Tanzania.[12] Tanganyika joined the British Commonwealth in 1961 and Tanzania remains a member of the Commonwealth as a unified republic.[13]

Tanzania's population is composed of about 120 ethnic,[14] linguistic, and religious groups. The sovereign state of Tanzania is a presidential constitutional republic and since 1996 its official capital city has been Dodoma where the president's office, the National Assembly, and all government ministries are located.[15] Dar es Salaam, the former capital, retains most government offices and is the country's largest city, principal port, and leading commercial centre.[16][17] Tanzania is a de facto one-party state with the democratic socialist Chama Cha Mapinduzi party in power.

Tanzania is mountainous and densely forested in the north-east, where Mount Kilimanjaro is located. Three of Africa's Great Lakes are partly within Tanzania. To the north and west lie Lake Victoria, Africa's largest lake, and Lake Tanganyika, the continent's deepest lake, known for its unique species of fish. To the south lies Lake Malawi. The eastern shore is hot and humid, with the Zanzibar Archipelago just offshore. The Menai Bay Conservation Area is Zanzibar's largest marine protected area. The Kalambo Falls, located on the Kalambo River at the Zambian border, is the second-highest uninterrupted waterfall in Africa.[18]

Christianity is the largest religion in Tanzania, but there are also substantial Muslim and animist minorities.[19] Over 100 different languages are spoken in Tanzania, making it the most linguistically diverse country in East Africa. The country does not have a de jure official language[21][22] although the national language is Swahili.[23] Swahili is used in parliamentary debate, in the lower courts, and as a medium of instruction in primary school. English is used in foreign trade, in diplomacy, in higher courts, and as a medium of instruction in secondary and higher education,[20] although the Tanzanian government is planning to discontinue English as the primary language of instruction and make it available as an optional course.[24] Approximately 10% of Tanzanians speak Swahili as a first language, and up to 90% speak it as a second language.[20]

Currently, articles are being displayed by identifier. However, we need to display them by slug.

Let's open urls.py and in the route

path('post/int:post_slug/', show_the, name='post'),

make some modifications

```python
urlpatterns = [
    path('', index, name='home'),
    path('about/', about, name='about'),
    path('addpage/', addpage, name='add_page'),
    path('contact/', addpage, name='contact'),
    path('login/', login, name='login'),
    path('post/<slug:post_slug>/', show_post, name='post'),
    path('category/<int:cat_id>/', show_category, name='category'),
```

```python
urlpatterns = [
    path('', index, name='home'),
    path('about/', about, name='about'),
    path('addpage/', addpage, name='add_page'),
    path('contact/', addpage, name='contact'),
    path('login/', login, name='login'),
    path('post/<slug:post_slug>/', show_post, name='post'),
    path('category/<int:cat_id>/', show_category, name='category'),
]
```

Next, in the **views.py** file, we'll also make changes to the view function

*def show_post(request, **post_slug**):*

  *post = get_object_or_404(Dir_travel, **slug=post_slug**)*

  context = {

    'post': post,

    'menu': menu,

    'title': post.title,

    'cat_selected': post.cat_id,

  }

  return render(request, 'traveler/post.html', context=context)

```python
def show_post(request, post_the):
    post = get_object_or_404(Dir_travel, pk=post_the)

    context = {
        'post': post,
        'menu': menu,
        'title': post.title,
        'cat_selected': post.cat_id,
    }
    return render(request, 'traveler/post.html', context=context)
```

Next, in the **models.py** file, within the **get_absolute_url** function, we'll correctly form the route to the article.

def get_absolute_url(self):

   *return reverse('post', kwargs={'**post_slug**': **self.slug**})*

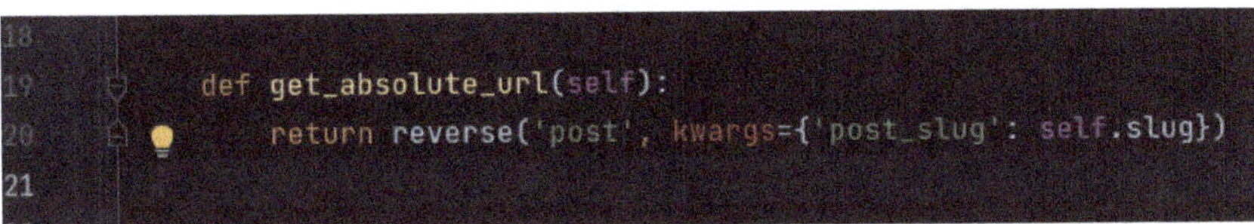

```
18
19    def get_absolute_url(self):
20        return reverse('post', kwargs={'post_slug': self.slug})
21
```

Consequently, the **'post_slug'** parameter will be passed into **urls.py**, in the **path('post/slug:post_slug/', show_post, name='post')** route, forming a complete path to our page.

So, let's go to the website, open the main page, and click on the **'Read Post'** button.

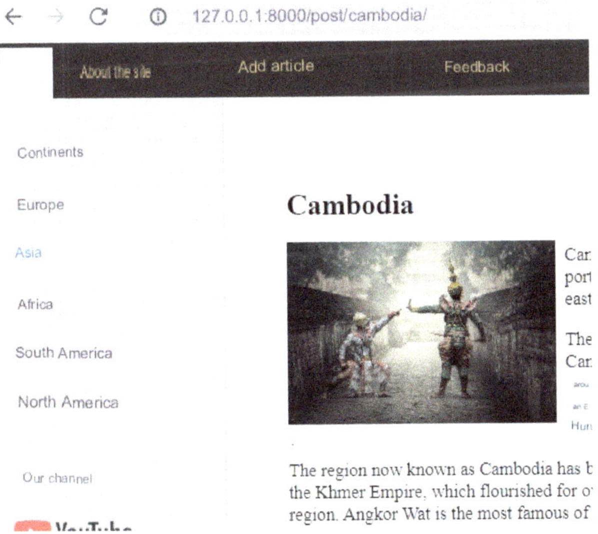

So, this article was retrieved from the database using the **'cambodia'** slug. Moreover, we made absolutely no changes in the templates thanks to the use of the **get_absolute_url** method.

Furthermore, **Django** protects such addresses from so-called **SQL** injections that malicious users might attempt by manipulating the browser's address bar to execute **SQL** queries.

Forms not related to models.

Forms are one of the most crucial elements in website development. For instance, when we perform authentication or registration on a website, a corresponding page appears with input fields, lists, checkboxes, and so forth.

HTML forms are defined using the <form>...</form> tag and are used to transmit user information to the server. For instance, login and password for accessing a website.

You can find detailed information on the website **https://django.fun/ru/docs/django/4.1/topics/forms/.**

In **Django**, forms can be created either in conjunction with database tables or independently. There exists a functional difference between these two types of forms.

For instance, when we authenticate or register a user on a website, it involves databases. In such cases, it's advisable to use the form in conjunction with a database model.

On the other hand, if the task involves site search or sending an email to the user, it's evident that creating a connection to the database is unnecessary.

Let's first consider a form not associated with a model. We'll do this using the example of adding articles to the database. Later on, we'll modify it and link it to a model.

Firstly, let's start the test web server using the familiar command.

Python manage.py runserver

We open the main page and click on **'Add article**

Here is where we'll create our form

Adding an article

Let's open the **views.py** file and find the function responsible for this page. It's the function...

def addpage(request):

return HttpResponse("Adding an article ")

```
26    def addpage(request):
27        return HttpResponse("Adding an article ")
```

Let's modify it.

def addpage(request):

return render(request, 'traveler/addpage.html', {'menu': menu, 'title': ' Adding an article '})

Where we'll be passing the main menu and the title

{'menu': menu, 'title': 'Adding an article'}.

Next, we need to specify the **addpage.html** template. Let's create it first

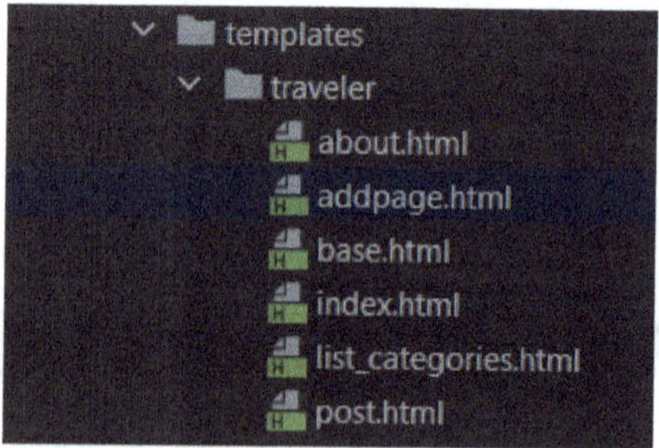

Let's display the content as follows for now

```
{% extends 'traveler/base.html' %}


{% block content %}
<h1>{{title}}</h1>
<p> Page content </p>
{% endblock %}
```

```
1    {% extends 'traveler/base.html'  %}
2
3    {% block content %}
4    <h1>{{title}}</h1>
5    <p> The content of the article </p>
6    {% endblock %}
```

Extending the base template

{% extends 'traveler/base.html' %}

In the content block, simply display the header and paragraph.

Then, in the browser, refresh, and we'll see the next page already appearing

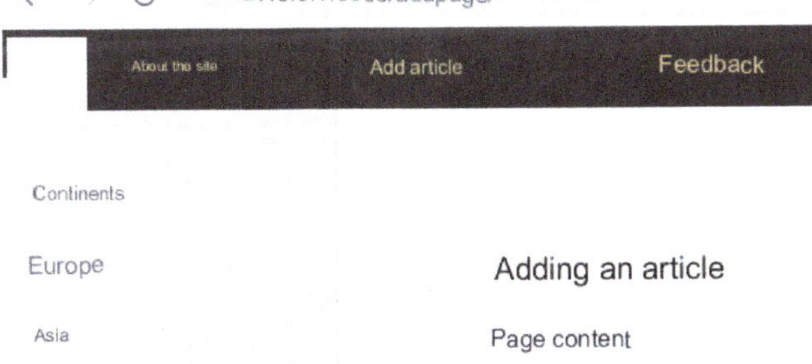

Everything is ready for us to place the form.

In Django, there's a special class

<form>...</form>

on which child classes are built, like class

AddPostForm(forms.Form).

Let's place this class and other logic in the forms.py file, which we'll create in the application folder.

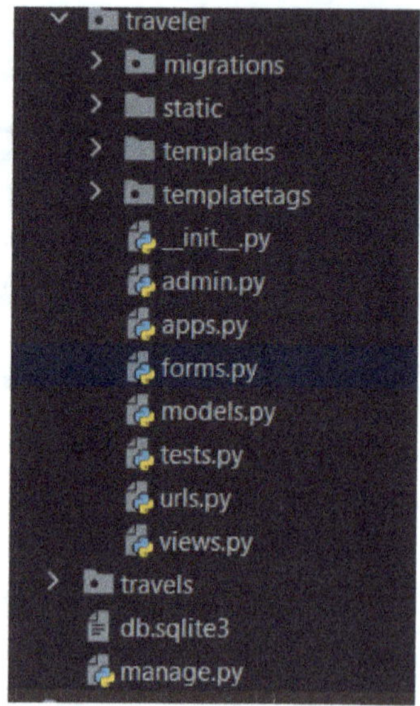

Let's write in this file

from django import forms

*from .models import ***

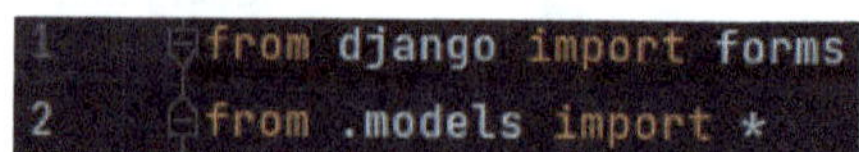

Let's import the forms module where all the information for creating our classes is located.

Also, let's import models that we'll need later.

Next, we'll define the form class that describes the post addition form.

```python
class AddPostForm(forms.Form):

    title = forms.CharField(max_length=255)

    slug = forms.SlugField(max_length=255)

    content = forms.CharField(widget=forms.Textarea(attrs={'cols': 60, 'rows': 10}))

    is_published = forms.BooleanField()

    cat = forms.ModelChoiceField(queryset=Category.objects.all())
```

```python
from django import forms
from .models import *


class AddPostForm(forms.Form):
    title = forms.CharField(max_length=255)
    slug = forms.SlugField(max_length=255)
    content = forms.CharField(widget=forms.Textarea(attrs={'cols': 60, 'rows': 10}))
    is_published = forms.BooleanField()
    cat = forms.ModelChoiceField(queryset=Category.objects.all())
```

All these attributes represent the fields that will be displayed on our form, on the page.

Please note that some attributes, such as **time_create** and **time_update**, are not specified here because they will be automatically populated. We need to allow users to fill in only some important fields.

It's also worth noting that **the is_published** field is defined as a BooleanField, which results in a checkbox on the page, allowing us to indicate whether the entry is published or not.

The field for selecting the category cat is created using the **ModelChoiceField** class, displaying a dropdown list where we can choose the relevant categories. This list will be retrieved using **Category.objects.all()** and will be contained within a queryset.

For more detailed information about built-in fields, you can read at the following link

https://django.fun/ru/docs/django/4.1/ref/forms/fields/

Thus, the form is defined and it can be used in the presentation function def addpage in the **views.py** file.

def addpage(request):

  form = AddPostForm()

  *return render(request, 'traveler/addpage.html', {**'form': form**, 'menu': menu, 'title': 'Добавление статьи'})*

```python
def addpage(request):
    form = AddPostForm()
    return render(request, 'traveler/addpage.html', {'form': form, 'menu': menu, 'title': 'Adding an article'})
```

We create an instance of the **class: form = AddPostForm(),** then pass this parameter to the **addpage.html** template, for instance, **'form': form**, and, of course, import it

from .forms import AddPostForm

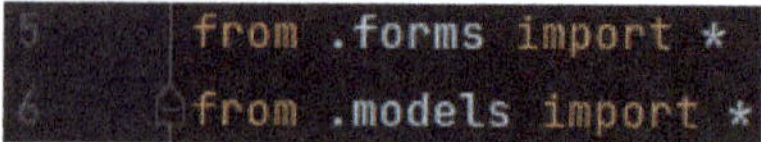
```python
from .forms import AddPostForm
from .models import *
```

It's better to write it like this:

from .forms import *,

so you can import any forms from this file.

```python
from .forms import *
from .models import *
```

Next, open the file **addpage.html** and instead of the paragraph, insert the following code.

{% extends 'traveler/base.html' %}

{% block content %}

<h1>{{title}}</h1>

```
<form action="{% url 'add_page' %}" method="post">

  {% csrf_token %}

  {{ form.as_p }}

  <button type="submit"> Add </button>

</form>

{% endblock %}
```

```
 1    {% extends 'traveler/base.html'   %}
 2
 3    {% block content %}
 4    <h1>{{title}}</h1>
 5
 6    <form action="{% url 'add_page' %}" method="post">
 7        {% csrf_token %}
 8        {{ form.as_p }}
 9        <button type="submit"> Add </button>
10    </form>
11
12    {% endblock %}
```

action="{% url 'add_page' %}"

indicates the **URL** to which we should submit this form, specifying where to send the data to the server. In this case, we're redirecting to the same **URL** where our form is displayed, essentially refreshing the page.

"method="post"" is the data transfer method. Usually, when using forms, the post method is specified. For instance, when we're sending login and password, we don't want the transfer of this data to be visible externally for security reasons.

"{% csrf_token %}" serves to protect the form from Cross-Site Request Forgery **(CSRF)** attacks. These attacks occur when a form that looks like yours is created on a phishing site. Users might unwittingly input genuine login and password details, which the attackers can intercept. **Django** processes only those forms where this token is specified, generating a hidden field with a token that refreshes upon each page reload. If the token matches, the form is processed accordingly.

"{{ form.as_p }}"

displays all form fields using **HTML** paragraph elements (**'p'**).

In reality, **as_p()** is a function. However, when we want this function to be called at this point, we write it without parentheses. We're not directly calling it as a function; rather, we're passing a reference to it, and the template engine will execute it.

"<button type="submit">Add</button>" - this button allows sending data to the server.

Let's check how all of this will work. Let's go to the site and refresh the page.

Adding an article

Title: [   ]

Slug: [   ]

Content: [   ]

Is published: ☐

Cat: [--------- ▾]

[Add]

Let's further examine this form.

When this form is initially displayed on the page, its fields are empty.

After the user enters some data and clicks **'Submit'**, this data is sent to the server, where it undergoes validation.

If everything is okay, the user might be redirected to another page. If errors occur, the form is displayed again to the user.

At this point, the form should not be empty; it should display the data previously entered by the user.

How do we achieve this in our program?

Let's demonstrate first on a diagram.

```
def addpage(request):
    if request.method == 'POST':
        form = AddPostForm(request.POST)
        if form.is_valid():
            print(form.cleaned_data)
    else:
        form = AddPostForm()
    return ...
```

Let's break it down now.

When the form is first sent to this page, the request object's method property is set to **NONE** because we haven't sent any data yet.

Therefore, the condition

if request.method == 'POST':

won't trigger, and we'll move to the else: line, where we generate a standard empty form:

form = AddPostForm().

However, when the user enters all the data and clicks the '**Add**' button, the check if **request.method == 'POST':**

triggers, and the form

 form = AddPostForm(request.POST)

is created, containing the data filled in by the user. If the data validation fails, the form will be displayed a second time with the fields pre-filled.

If the validation passes, print(**form.cleaned_data**) will display the sanitized data in the console.

Let's implement this functionality in our program.

```python
def addpage(request):
    if request.method == 'POST':
        form = AddPostForm(request.POST)
        if form.is_valid():
            print(form.cleaned_data)
    else:
        form = AddPostForm()
    return render(request, 'traveler/addpage.html', {'form': form, 'menu': menu, 'title': 'Adding an article'})
```

Let's check how this will work.

Adding an article

Title: Egypt

Slug: Egypt

Content: Egypt

Is published: ☑

Cat: Africa

Add

After clicking '**Add**,' the form was saved a second time.

In the terminal...

```
{'title': 'Египет', 'slug': 'Egypt', 'content': 'Egypt', 'is_published': True, 'cat': <Category: Africa >}
[13/Dec/2022 11:15:23] "POST /addpage/ HTTP/1.1" 200 3564
```

As you can see, everything was processed correctly as well.

Now, let's make it so that when filling out the form, we encounter some errors.

For instance, in the **'slug'** field, let's input prohibited characters, in simpler terms, using Cyrillic.

Adding an article

Title: [Tunis]

• The value must contain only Latin letters, numbers, underscores or hyphens.

Slug: [jhjhjjjjpopn]

We see that the framework automatically generated this message.

Nothing was displayed in the console because the form submission didn't pass the validation.

Let's enhance the appearance of the form a bit.

Firstly, let's change the field names to Russian.

Go to the **forms.py** file and add something to the necessary fields in the AddPostForm class.

```python
class AddPostForm(forms.Form):
    title = forms.CharField(max_length=255, label=" Title ")
    slug = forms.SlugField(max_length=255, label="URL")
    content = forms.CharField(widget=forms.Textarea(attrs={'cols': 60, 'rows': 10}), label=" Content ")
    is_published = forms.BooleanField(label=" Publication ")
    cat = forms.ModelChoiceField(queryset=Category.objects.all(), label=" Categories ")
```

```python
from django import forms
from .models import *


class AddPostForm(forms.Form):
    title = forms.CharField(max_length=255, label="header ")
    slug = forms.SlugField(max_length=255, label="URL")
    content = forms.CharField(widget=forms.Textarea(attrs={'cols': 60, 'rows': 10}), label="Content ")
    is_published = forms.BooleanField(label="Publication ")
    cat = forms.ModelChoiceField(queryset=Category.objects.all(), label="Categories ")
```

After refreshing the page, we'll see the field names in Russian.

Let's continue modernizing further.

```python
is_published = forms.BooleanField(label=" Publication ", required=False , initial=True)
```

Thus, **required=False** makes this field optional, while **initial=True** will pre-select the checkbox by default

cat = forms.ModelChoiceField(queryset=Category.objects.all(), label=" Categories ",
empty_label=" Category not selected ")

This parameter allows writing this message instead of dashes in the field.

```python
class AddPostForm(forms.Form):
    title = forms.CharField(max_length=255, label="header")
    slug = forms.SlugField(max_length=255, label="URL")
    content = forms.CharField(widget=forms.Textarea(attrs={'cols': 60, 'rows': 10}), label="Content")
    is_published = forms.BooleanField(label="Publication", required=False, initial=True)
    cat = forms.ModelChoiceField(queryset=Category.objects.all(), label="Categories", empty_label="Category not selected")
```

Again, to know all the parameters, please refer to the documentation, the link to which is provided above.

Let's spruce up our form a bit.

To do this, go to the **addpage.html** template and change it to

```
<p>
    <label class="form-label" for="{{ form.title.id_for_label }}">{{ form.title.label }}: </label>
    {{ form.title }}
</p>
<div class="form-error">{{ form.title.errors }}</div>


<p>
    <label class="form-label" for="{{ form.slug.id_for_label }}">{{ form.slug.label }}: </label>
    {{ form.slug }}
</p>
<div class="form-error">{{ form.slug.errors }}</div>


<p>
    <label class="form-label" for="{{ form.content.id_for_label }}">{{ form.content.label }}: </label>
    {{ form.content }}
```

```html
    </p>
    <div class="form-error">{{ form.content.errors }}</div>


    <p>
        <label class="form-label" for="{{ form.is_published.id_for_label }}">{{ form.is_published.label }}: </label>
        {{ form.is_published }}
    </p>
    <div class="form-error">{{ form.is_published.errors }}</div>


    <p>
        <label class="form-label" for="{{ form.cat.id_for_label }}">{{ form.cat.label }}: </label>
        {{ form.cat }}
    </p>
    <div class="form-error">{{ form.cat.errors }}</div>
```

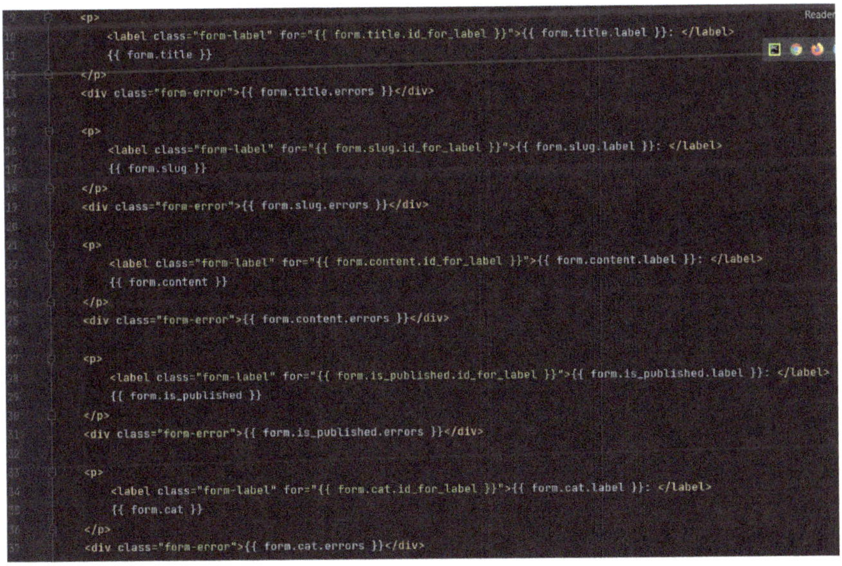

```html
    <p>
        <label class="form-label" for="{{ form.title.id_for_label }}">{{ form.title.label }}: </label>
        {{ form.title }}
    </p>
    <div class="form-error">{{ form.title.errors }}</div>

    <p>
        <label class="form-label" for="{{ form.slug.id_for_label }}">{{ form.slug.label }}: </label>
        {{ form.slug }}
    </p>
    <div class="form-error">{{ form.slug.errors }}</div>

    <p>
        <label class="form-label" for="{{ form.content.id_for_label }}">{{ form.content.label }}: </label>
        {{ form.content }}
    </p>
    <div class="form-error">{{ form.content.errors }}</div>

    <p>
        <label class="form-label" for="{{ form.is_published.id_for_label }}">{{ form.is_published.label }}: </label>
        {{ form.is_published }}
    </p>
    <div class="form-error">{{ form.is_published.errors }}</div>

    <p>
        <label class="form-label" for="{{ form.cat.id_for_label }}">{{ form.cat.label }}: </label>
        {{ form.cat }}
    </p>
    <div class="form-error">{{ form.cat.errors }}</div>
```

Using the tag **for="{{ form.title.id_for_label }}"** we set a unique identifier using the **id_for_label** property.

{{ form.title.label }}: allows displaying the actual label.

{{ form.title }}: will insert the corresponding input tag for the title.

<div class="form-error">{{ form.title.errors }}</div>: shows potential errors when entering the title. This utilizes the errors collection.

class="form-label": styling classes that I've predefined and placed in the style sheet.

Let's navigate to the page and refresh.

Adding an article

Title:

URL:

Content:

Publication:

Categories: Category not selected

Add

Everything seems to be working fine.

However, it's noticeable that the amount of code has significantly increased. This can be substantially reduced by addressing repetitive lines and utilizing a for loop.

```
{% csrf_token %}


{% for f in form %}


<p> <label class="form-label" for="{{ f.id_for_label }}">{{f.label}}: </label>{{ f }}</p>
<div class="form_error">{{ f.errors }}</div>
```

{% endfor %}

```
{% for f in form %}

    <p> <label class="form-label" for="{{ f.id_for_label }}">{{f.label}}: </label>{{ f }}</p>
    <div class="form_error">{{ f.errors }}</div>

{% endfor %}
```

We go to the page, refresh, and see that nothing has changed. Everything is working.

Adding an article

Title:

URL:

Content:

Publication: ☑

Categories: Category not selected ▾

Add

All fields now have the same formatting styles under **class="form-label"** and **class="form_error,"** but they can be customized if desired. Each field can have its own style assigned to it. Let's navigate to the **forms.py** file and within the **AddPostForm** class, specify a special parameter called widget

class AddPostForm(forms.Form):

title = forms.CharField(max_length=255, label=" Title ",
widget=forms.TextInput(attrs={'class': 'form-input'}))

slug = forms.SlugField(max_length=255, label="URL")

```python
content = forms.CharField(widget=forms.Textarea(attrs={'cols': 60, 'rows': 10}),
label="Контент")

is_published = forms.BooleanField(label=" Publication ", required=False, initial=True)

cat = forms.ModelChoiceField(queryset=Category.objects.all(), label=" Categories ",
empty_label=" Not selected category ")
```

This parameter is assigned corresponding attributes

TextInput(attrs={'class': 'form-input'}))

In this case, the line **attrs={'class': 'form-input'}))** will mean that for the title...

Title: [____________________________]

we will be specifying our own styling class

```html
<input type="text" name="title" class="form-input" maxlength="255" required
id="id_title"> == $0
```

As we can see, **class='form-input'** has been added. To view the code, use the code inspector in your browser.

This way, fine-tuning each field is possible when needed.

Here's what has been achieved.

Adding an article

Title:

URL:

Content:

Publication: ☑

Categories: Category not selected ▾

Add

Next, let's proceed with adding the data from the form into the database.

Open **views.py** and add a few lines of code to the **addpage** module

```python
def addpage(request):
    if request.method == 'POST':
        form = AddPostForm(request.POST)
        if form.is_valid():
            #print(form.cleaned_data)
            try:
                Dir_travel.objects.create(**form.cleaned_data)
                return redirect('home')
            except:
                form.add_error(None, 'Post addition error')
    else:
        form = AddPostForm()
    return render(request, 'traveler/addpage.html', {'form': form, 'menu': menu, 'title': 'Adding an article'})
```

```python
def addpage(request):
    if request.method == 'POST':
        form = AddPostForm(request.POST)
        if form.is_valid():
            #print(form.cleaned_data)
            try:
                Dir_travel.objects.create(**form.cleaned_data)
                return redirect('home')
            except:
                form.add_error(None, 'Error adding post')
    else:
        form = AddPostForm()
    return render(request, 'traveler/addpage.html', {'form': form, 'menu': menu, 'title': 'Adding an article'})
```

In the **'try'** block, we add a new entry using **Dir_travel.objects.create(**form.cleaned_data).** If the addition is successful, we redirect to the home page using return redirect(**'home'**). If any issues arise, we move to **'except'** and add an error to display on the form page using **form.add_error(None, Post addition error).**

#print(form.cleaned_data) – we will comment this out.

To display this error on the page, we'll add a line to the template

{% csrf_token %}

  <div class="form-error">{{ form.non_field_errors }}</div>

  {% for f in form %}

```html
    {% csrf_token %}
    <div class="form-error">{{ form.non_field_errors }}</div>
    {% for f in form %}
```

And we'll display errors not related to the fields. Now, let's go to the form, refresh it, and fill it in with some data.

Adding an article

Error adding post

Title: Italy

URL: italy

Content:
```
Italy (Italian: Italia [i'taːlja] (listen)), officially the
Italian Republic[11][12] (Italian: Repubblica Italiana [re
'pubblika itaˈljaːna]),[13][14] is a country located in the
middle of the Mediterranean Sea, in Southern Europe;[15][16]
[17] its territory largely coincides with the homonymous
geographical region.[18] Italy is also considered part of
Western Europe.[19][note 1] A unitary parliamentary republic
with Rome as its capital and largest city, the country covers
a total area of 301,230 km2 (116,310 sq mi) and shares land
borders with France, Switzerland, Austria, Slovenia and the
```

Publication: ☑

Categories: Europe ⌄

Add

We received an error because we already have a slug like that in our database. This record exists in the database, and as we recall, the slug must be unique. Let's change the slug, for example, **to Italy_1**

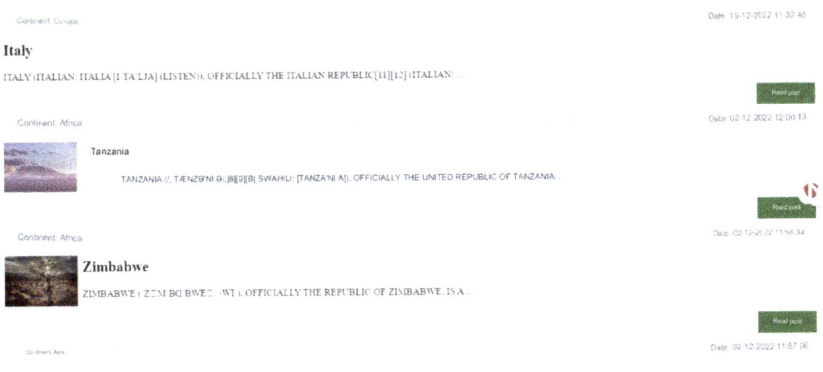

Great, it all worked out! Although without a photo for now, that's not crucial at the moment. Next, let's try using forms in conjunction with a model.

Forms related to models. Custom validators.

The previous example was somewhat artificial since adding a new post is inevitably linked to accessing the database in one way or another. Consequently, we've encountered code duplication in both the **forms.py** and **models.py** files, which isn't exemplary. Let's do the following: navigate to the **forms.py** file and make the **AddPostForm** class inherit from another class. Inside this class, we'll remove all the fields and specify them within a nested Meta class.

```
class AddPostForm(forms.ModelForm):

    class Meta:

        model = Dir_travel

        fields = '__all__'
```

model = Dir_travel associates this class with our model, while **"fields = 'all'"** indicates which fields should be displayed in the form. It means to show all fields except those that are filled in automatically.

Let's test how this works. Start the server, go to the main page, and click on **'Add Article'**. You'll see a form linked to the model, with fields automatically generated in conjunction with our model, including the **'Photo'** field.

Adding an article

Title:

URL:

Article text:

Photo: Choose File | File not selected

Publication: ☑

Category: ---------- ▾

Add

However, in practice, it's recommended to explicitly specify the list of fields. Let's specify the fields excluding photographs.

```
class AddPostForm(forms.ModelForm):

    class Meta:

        model = Dir_travel

        fields = ['title', 'slug', 'content', 'is_published', 'cat']
```

Adding an article

Title:

URL:

Article text:

Publication: ☑

Category: ---------

Add

Let's set up styling for the first three fields.

```
class AddPostForm(forms.ModelForm):

    class Meta:

        model = Dir_travel

        fields = ['title', 'slug', 'content', 'is_published', 'cat']

        widgets = {

            'title': forms.TextInput(attrs={'class': 'form-input'}),

            'content': forms.Textarea(attrs={'cols': 60, 'rows': 10}),

        }
```

```python
class AddPostForm(forms.ModelForm):
    class Meta:
        model = Dir_travel
        fields = ['title', 'slug', 'content', 'is_published', 'cat']
        widgets = {
            'title': forms.TextInput(attrs={'class': 'form-input'}),
            'content': forms.Textarea(attrs={'cols': 60, 'rows': 10}),
        }
```

Title:

URL:

Article text:

The sizes have changed slightly.

Next, for the '**Category**' field, instead of dashes, it should display '**Category not selected**'. Let's define a constructor in the **AddPostForm** class.

```python
class AddPostForm(forms.ModelForm):
    def __init__(self, *args, **kwargs):
        super().__init__(*args, **kwargs)
        self.fields['cat'].empty_label = 'Category not selected'

    class Meta:
        model = Dir_travel
        fields = ['title', 'slug', 'content', 'is_published', 'cat']
        widgets = {
            'title': forms.TextInput(attrs={'class': 'form-input'}),
            'content': forms.Textarea(attrs={'cols': 60, 'rows': 10}),
```

```python
        }


 4  class AddPostForm(forms.ModelForm):
 5      def __init__(self, *args, **kwargs):
 6          super().__init__(*args, **kwargs)
 7          self.fields['cat'].empty_label = 'Category not selected'
 8
 9      class Meta:
10          model = Dir_travel
11          fields = ['title', 'slug', 'content', 'is_published', 'cat']
12          widgets = {
13              'title': forms.TextInput(attrs={'class': 'form-input'}),
14              'content': forms.Textarea(attrs={'cols': 60, 'rows': 10}),
15          }
```

When an instance of the form class **AddPostForm** is created, the constructor is invoked: **def init(self, *args, **kwargs):,** which in turn should call the constructor of the base **class super().init(*args, **kwargs)** to execute automatic actions, specifically to access the fields property with the key **'cat'**, and only after that, we modify the empty_label property for the **'cat'** field.

Category: | Category not selected ⌄

Inside this form, a method called save has appeared, allowing the form data to be directly saved into the database.

Moving to the **views.py** file, instead of the line **Dir_travel.objects.create(**form.cleaned_data)** within the addpage module,

let's simply use **form.save().**

As a result, all data submitted in the form will be automatically added to the database. Moreover, this method no longer needs to be placed within a try/except block, as it inherently performs all necessary checks.

Therefore, this block can be removed, simplifying the code even further. In the end, it will look like this:

def addpage(request):

  if request.method == 'POST':

form = AddPostForm(request.POST)

if form.is_valid():

   form.save()

   return redirect('home')

  else:

  form = AddPostForm()

 return render(request, 'traveler/addpage.html', {'form': form, 'menu': menu, 'title': 'Adding an article'})

```python
def addpage(request):
    if request.method == 'POST':
        form = AddPostForm(request.POST)
        if form.is_valid():
            #print(form.cleaned_data)
            form.save()
            return redirect('home')

    else:
        form = AddPostForm()
    return render(request, 'traveler/addpage.html', {'form': form, 'menu': menu, 'title': 'Adding an article'})
```

Let's go to the browser, click on **'Add Article**,' and fill out the form. Specifically input a non-unique slug in the **URL** field, one that already exists, to check the message **Django** will provide us.

Adding an article

Title: Italy

URL: italy_1

• All countries with this URL already exist.

Article text: hgghghghg

Publication: ☑

Category: Europe

Add

Indeed, we received a specific message indicating that such a **URL** already exists.

It means the save method automatically generated a message related to that specific issue, which is quite practical.

Let's still add a new post. The article text isn't important for now.

Continent: Europe

Spain

GHGCDHVSDH SHCDJ SDCJBSJHDBC

That's great! You've got a new post.

If you click on the **'Read Post'** link, you'll navigate to the page displaying that post. In the browser's address bar, you'll also see the unique slug associated with it.

127.0.0.1:8000/post/spain/

Add article   Feedback

Spain

ghgcdhvsdh shcdj sdcjbsjhdbc

From this point, let's focus on the **'Photo'** field, which was previously ignored to avoid overwhelming attention. We'll work with forms associated with models.

In the forms.py file, within the **AddPostForm** class, within the Meta subclass, let's add this field

class AddPostForm(forms.ModelForm):

```python
def __init__(self, *args, **kwargs):
    super().__init__(*args, **kwargs)
    self.fields['cat'].empty_label = 'Category not selected'


class Meta:
    model = Dir_travel
    fields = ['title', 'slug', 'content', 'photo', 'is_published', 'cat']
    widgets = {
        'title': forms.TextInput(attrs={'class': 'form-input'}),
        'content': forms.Textarea(attrs={'cols': 60, 'rows': 10}),
    }
```

```python
class AddPostForm(forms.ModelForm):
    def __init__(self, *args, **kwargs):
        super().__init__(*args, **kwargs)
        self.fields['cat'].empty_label = 'Category not selected'

    class Meta:
        model = Dir_travel
        fields = ['title', 'slug', 'content', 'photo', 'is_published', 'cat']
        widgets = {
            'title': forms.TextInput(attrs={'class': 'form-input'}),
            'content': forms.Textarea(attrs={'cols': 60, 'rows': 10}),
        }
```

Next, open the **views.py** file, and within the addpage function, add the line

form = AddPostForm(request.POST, request.FILES),

where, when creating an instance of the **AddPostForm** form, we pass a list of files sent from the form to the server via **request.FILES** as the second argument. This means accessing the request object and retrieving its FILES collection.

```python
def addpage(request):
    if request.method == 'POST':
        form = AddPostForm(request.POST, request.FILES)
        if form.is_valid():
```

#print(form.cleaned_data)

form.save()

return redirect('home')

else:

form = AddPostForm()

return render(request, 'traveler/addpage.html', {'form': form, 'menu': menu, 'title': 'Adding an article'})

```python
def addpage(request):
    if request.method == 'POST':
        form = AddPostForm(request.POST, request.FILES)
        if form.is_valid():
            #print(form.cleaned_data)
            form.save()
            return redirect('home')

    else:
        form = AddPostForm()
    return render(request, 'traveler/addpage.html', {'form': form, 'menu': menu, 'title': 'Adding an article'})
```

Finally, in the **addpage.html** file, let's add the line

*<form action="{% url 'add_page' %}" method="post" **enctype="multipart/form-data"**>*

```html
6   <form action="{% url 'add_page' %}" method="post" enctype="multipart/form-data">
7       {% csrf_token %}
8       <div class="form-error">{{ form.non_field_errors }}</div>
9       {% for f in form %}
```

If we're submitting any files along with the form data, it's essential to specify the attribute **enctype='multipart/form-data'**.

Let's navigate to the browser, refresh the page, and post something, but this time with an uploaded photo.

Adding an article

Title: Netherlands

URL: netherlands

Article text:

With a population of 17.7 million people, all living within a total area of 41,850 km2 (16,160 sq mi)—of which the land area is 33,500 km2 (12,900 sq mi)—the Netherlands is the 16th most densely populated country in the world and the second-most densely populated country in the European Union, with a density of 529 people per square kilometre (1,370 people/sq mi). Nevertheless, it is the world's second-largest exporter of food and agricultural products by value, owing to its fertile soil, mild climate, intensive agriculture, and inventiveness.[29][30][31][32]

Photo: Choose File Nederland.jpg

Publication: ☑

Category: Europe

Add

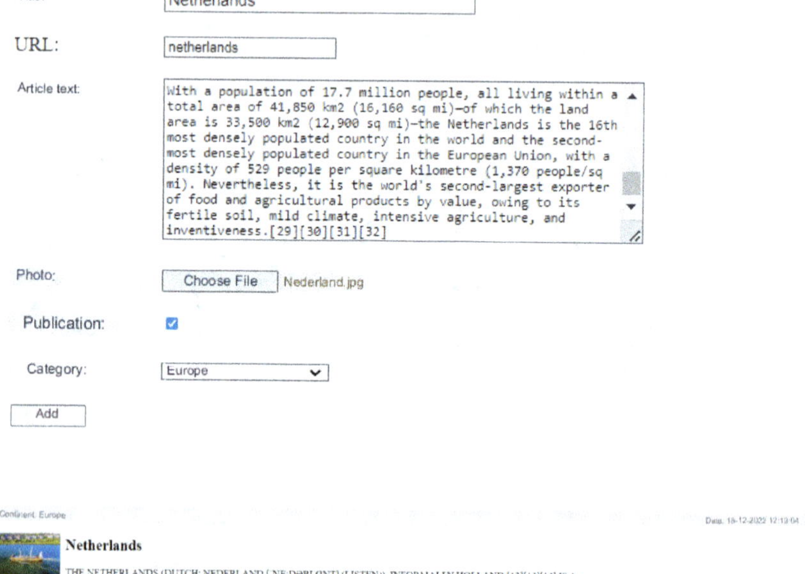

Yes, everything worked out.

Let's click on **'Read Post**,' and here too, everything worked

Netherlands

The Netherlands (Dutch: Nederland [ˈneːdər
Caribbean. It is the largest of four constituen
Germany to the east, and Belgium to the sou
Belgium in the North Sea.[18] The country's
Saxon and Limburgish are recognised region
English and Papiamento are official in the C;

The four largest cities in the Netherlands are
[20] The Hague holds the seat of the States General, Cabinet and Supreme Court.[2
busiest in Europe. The Netherlands is a founding member of the European Union. E
several intergovernmental organisations and international courts, many of which are

Netherlands literally means "lower countries" in reference to its low elevation and t
level.[24] Most of the areas below sea level, known as polders, are the result of land
unique era of political, economic, and cultural greatness, ranked among the most po
trading companies, the Dutch East India Company and the Dutch West India Comp;

With a population of 17.7 million people, all living within a total area of 41,850 km
country in the world and the second-most densely populated country in the Europea
largest exporter of food and agricultural products by value, owing to its fertile soil.

If we navigate to the project, we'll see that our image has been uploaded where it
should be.

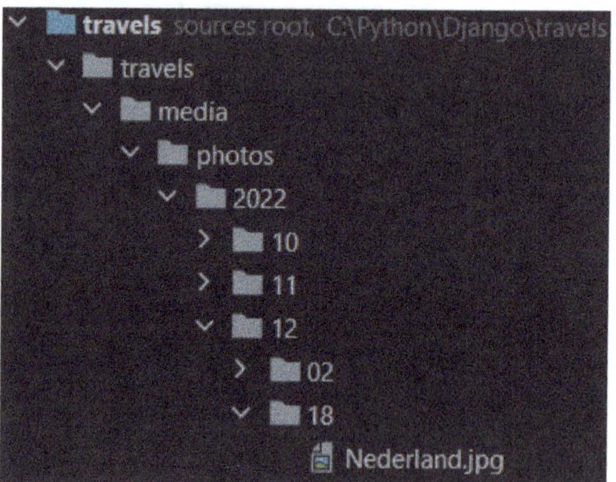

Django took care of all the photo upload operations – placing it on the server, creating a path to it, and storing that path in the database. We didn't have to do all of this manually.

Validation of form fields

Let's consider the validation of form fields. Currently, the correctness check of fields is executed according to the **Dir_travel** model. For example:

max_length=255 - maximum of 255 characters.

unique=True - field must be unique.

blank=True - field is not mandatory.

All these parameters that we specify participate in the validation process. However, there are nuances. For instance, when working with the **SQLite** database, the condition **max_length=255** doesn't trigger. This is a peculiarity of this **DBMS**.

Often, standard checks are insufficient, and there's a need to create a custom validator at the form level. Let's create such a validator for the 'title' field, which every time the length of the field exceeds 200 characters, will display an appropriate message.

The process of verifying the data's correctness occurs according to the following principle. When the user fills in all the form fields and clicks the '**Submit**' button, the data goes to the server, where it's checked using the methods **is_valid()** and **save().** Initially, the standard validators are executed, and only when they succeed, the user-defined validators are activated.

We'll create one such user-defined validator. To do this, open the **forms.py** file and within the **AddPostForm** class, create a method that should start like this:

def clean_ ... then comes the field, in this case, '**title**'. This is the field upon which we'll perform the validation.

Therefore, the complete method will look like this:

def clean_title(self):

So, let's write down.....

```
def clean_title(self):
    title = self.cleaned_data['title']
    if len(title) > 200:
        raise ValidationError('The length exceeds 200 characters')
    return title
```

```python
17      def clean_title(self):
18          title = self.cleaned_data['title']
19          if len(title) > 200:
20              raise ValidationError('Length exceeds 200 characters ')
21          return title
```

title = self.cleaned_data['title'] - retrieves data for the title, where we access the **cleaned_data** collection available in the instance of the **AddPostForm** class. Then, using the key **['title'],** we obtain the title entered by the user. If the length of this title is greater than 200 characters **(if len(title) > 200:),** it raises a ValidationError exception. Otherwise, it returns the title (return title).

In order to use the **ValidationError** class, we need to import it.

from django.core.exceptions import ValidationError

```python
1   from django import forms
2   from .models import *
3   from django.core.exceptions import ValidationError
```

Let's check how this will work. Right now, it doesn't matter what exactly we're adding. The main thing is to input more than 200 characters in the **'Title'** field

Adding an article

Title: dfg fdddddddddddddddddddddg dfgddddddd

• Length exceeds 200 characters

URL: fggg

Article text: dfgdfgdfgdfg

Photo: Choose File File not selected

Publication: ☑

Category: Asia ▾

Add

We see the expected message, indicating that our validator has been triggered. Similarly, of course, we can define a validator for any other field.

View classes.

Let's consider how we can use view classes instead of functions. Previously, we used functions, which is a way to implement simple functionality.

Let's move on to a somewhat different and more advanced way of implementing our functionality—using classes. View classes in English are denoted as **CBV – Class-Based** Views. Object-oriented programming, as known, notably simplifies code writing when applied to classes.

For more detailed information about class-based views, you can read by following this link: **Django Class-Based** Views Documentation

At this moment, we'll replace the '**index**' function, responsible for processing the main page, with a view class.

After reading the documentation page on classes, we understand that the '**ListView**' class would be most suitable for our purposes. This class creates a list of something.

To start, let's import this class.

from django.views.generic import ListView

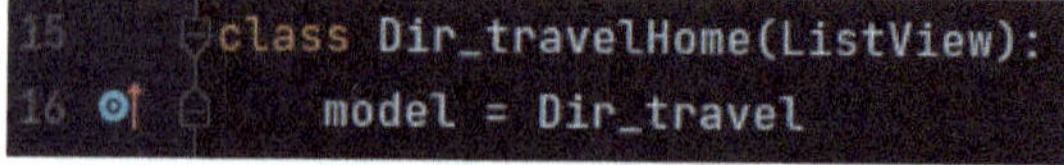

Next, let's create a class that will handle the main page and name it

Dir_travelHome.

class Dir_travelHome(ListView):

  model = Dir_travel

```
15        class Dir_travelHome(ListView):
16            model = Dir_travel
```

Our class will be based on the base class '**ListView**'.

model = Dir_travel - the '**model**' attribute refers to the '**Dir_travel**' model associated with this list of articles. This statement **model = Dir_travel** selects all records from the list and attempts to display them as a list.

By default, the 'ListView' class uses the following template:

<app_name>/<model_name>_list.html

Next, let's connect this in our route, in the **'urls.py'** file. Instead of **'index'** in the line below

Dir_travelHome - path('', Dir_travelHome, name='home'),

To link the route to this class, you need to call a special function **'as_view()'**:

path('', Dir_travelHome.as_view(), name='home'),

We're not just giving a reference to this function; we're specifically calling it.

```
6          path('', Dir_travelHome.as_view(), name='home'),
```

Let's start our server. And we have an error!

```
ImportError: cannot import name 'index' from 'traveler.views' (C:\Python\Django\travels\travels\traveler\views.py)
```

The issue is that we haven't created the template that is searched for by default at this address:

'traveler/Dir_travel_list.html'.

That means we should create a template at this address. However, we won't do that because we already have a template named **index.html**.

Let's specify this in our class.

class Dir_travelHome(ListView):

   model = Dir_travel

_template_name = 'traveler/index.html'_

```
15      class Dir_travelHome(ListView):
16          model = Dir_travel
17          template_name = 'traveler/index.html'
```

And again, there's an error in the console

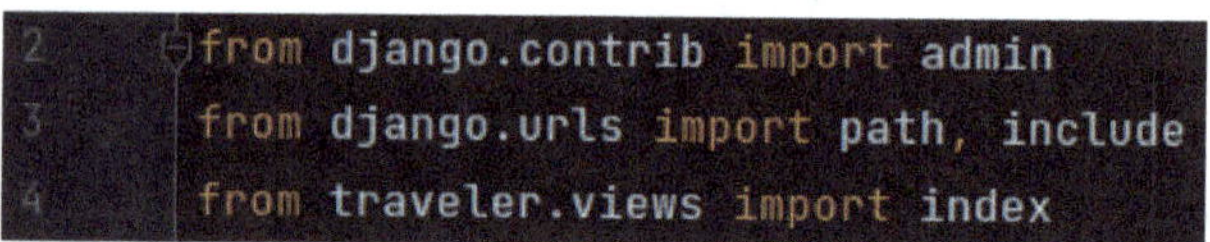

It's referring to the same '**index**' again.

Let's go to the **'urls.py'** file using the path **'travels\urls.py'** and remove the reference to the module that no longer exists

from django.contrib import admin

from django.urls import path, include

from traveler.views import index

Let's start the server again

The page appeared but without posts and the menu. The issue is that in the **'index.html'** file, the line

{% for p in posts %} uses **'posts,'** whereas the **'Dir_travelHome'** class forms another collection named **'object_list.'** Let's change **'posts'** to **'object_list'**

{% for p in object_list %}

```
5              {% for p in object_list %}
6                 <li><div class="article-panel">
```

Now we see all our articles. However, if we want to use the '**posts**' variable in the template, we also need to specify it explicitly in the view class.

class Dir_travelHome(ListView):

model = Dir_travel

template_name = 'traveler/index.html'

context_object_name = 'posts'

```
16    class Dir_travelHome(ListView):
17        model = Dir_travel
18        template_name = 'traveler/index.html'
19        context_object_name = 'posts'
```

Let's go to the browser and refresh the page. Everything should still work as before.

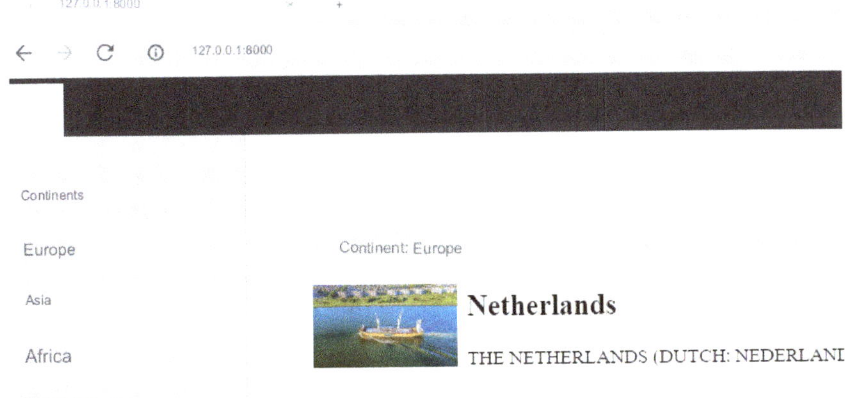

Missing the main header and the top horizontal menu.

Let's add the title **'Home Page'**.

We'll indicate the easiest way. Let's add one more line to our class.

class Dir_travelHome(ListView):

model = Dir_travel

template_name = 'traveler/index.html'

context_object_name = 'posts'

extra_context = {'title': 'Home Page'}

```
16      class Dir_travelHome(ListView):
17  O      model = Dir_travel
18  O      template_name = 'traveler/index.html'
19  O      context_object_name = 'posts'
20  O      extra_context = {'title': 'Main page'}
```

But with this parameter, only static, unchangeable data can be passed. In other words, lists, tuples, collections cannot be passed.

Let's update the home page and check the tab.

Our main horizontal menu is already represented as a dynamic list.

Let's create a function that will generate both static and dynamic contexts to be passed into the template.

Alternatively, we need to pass not only all other contexts but also the list

menu = [{'title': " About the site ", 'url_name': 'about'},

{'title': " Add article ", 'url_name': 'add_page'},

{'title': " Feedback ", 'url_name': 'contact'},

{'title': " Sign in ", 'url_name': 'login'}

We'll define this function in our class

```
class Dir_travelHome(ListView):
    model = Dir_travel
    template_name = 'traveler/index.html'
    context_object_name = 'posts'
    extra_context = {'title': 'Home Page'}


    def get_context_data(self, *, object_list=None, **kwargs):
        context = super().get_context_data(**kwargs)
        context['menu'] = menu
        return context
```

```
16    class Dir_travelHome(ListView):
17        model = Dir_travel
18        template_name = 'traveler/index.html'
19        context_object_name = 'posts'
20        extra_context = {'title': 'Main page '}
21
22        def get_context_data(self, *, object_list=None, **kwargs):
23            context = super().get_context_data(**kwargs)
24            context['menu'] = menu
25            return context
```

First, let's obtain the context that is already formatted for our template.

context = super().get_context_data(kwargs)**

For instance, **'posts'** already exists. We cannot overwrite this collection.

super() - refers to the base ListView class and retrieves the existing context

get_context_data(kwargs)** - retrieves all named parameters.

Next, we pass the named menu into this context using the key

context['menu'] = menu,

assigning the menu list to this key.

Finally, we return this context using return context.

Once again, this function dynamically generates the existing context and adds the menu list to it.

Let's update the home page.

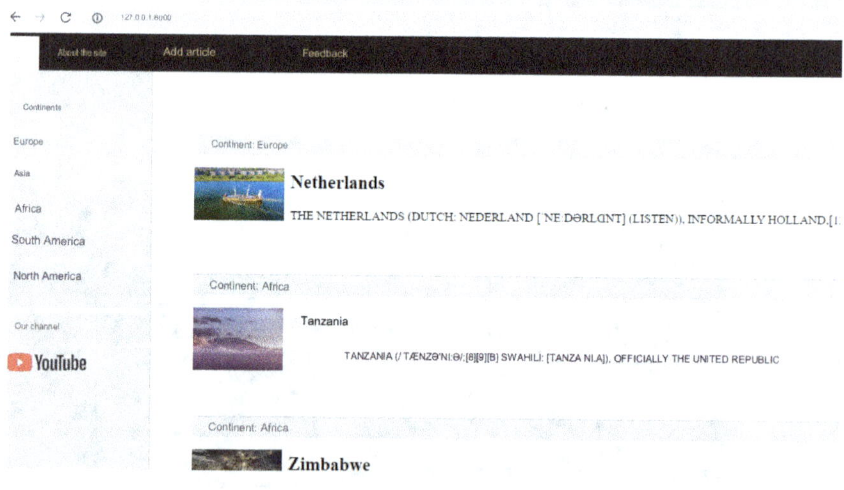

But that's not all.

The '**Continents**' tab should be selected.

Let's add one more line to our class.

```python
def get_context_data(self, *, object_list=None, **kwargs):
    context = super().get_context_data(**kwargs)
```

context['menu'] = menu

context['title'] = 'Home Page'

context['cat_selected'] = 0

return context

Since we're passing the context in this function, let's remove the line above:

extra_context = {'title': 'Home Page'}

and instead, within the function itself, let's use

context['title'] = 'Home Page'.

```
16    class Dir_travelHome(ListView):
17        model = Dir_travel
18        template_name = 'traveler/index.html'
19        context_object_name = 'posts'
20
21
22        def get_context_data(self, *, object_list=None, **kwargs):
23            context = super().get_context_data(**kwargs)
24            context['menu'] = menu
25            context['title'] = 'Main page '
26            context['cat_selected'] = 0
27            return context
```

Let's refresh/update the page.

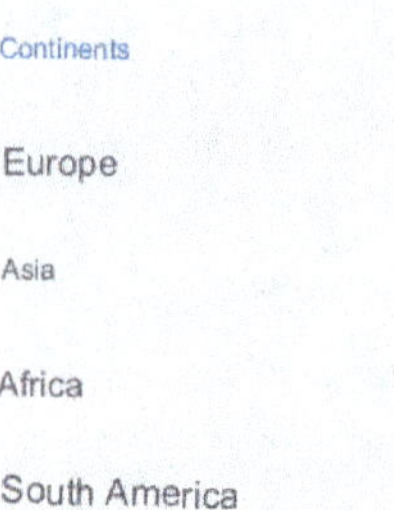

Let's make it so that on the home page, we have all the articles marked for publication. Right now, we have all the articles.

We'll use a specific method

def get_queryset(self):

return Dir_travel.objects.filter(is_published=True)

We return from our model only those records where... **is_published=True.**

```
29    def get_queryset(self):
30        return Dir_travel.objects.filter(is_published=True)
```

To test the functionality of this method, let's go to the admin panel in the browser and uncheck the checkboxes in the **'Publication'** field for some articles.

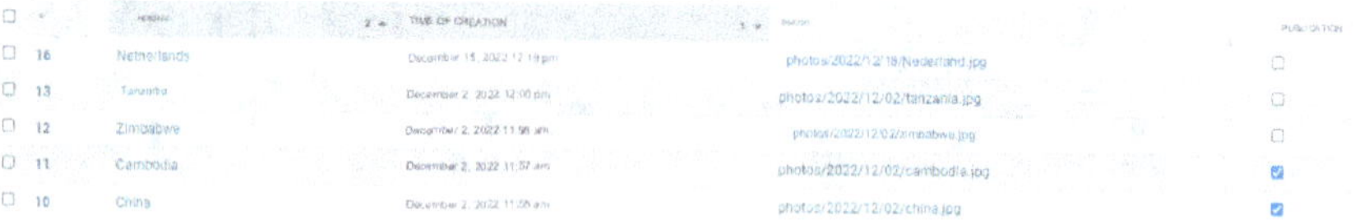

However, upon exiting the admin panel and returning to the home page, those articles for which we unchecked the boxes will disappear. Just remember to save this action in the admin panel.

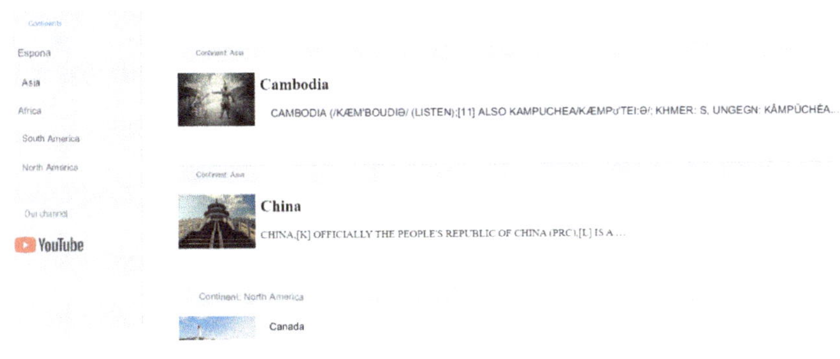

To display the list by separate categories, let's create a similar class instead of a function.

```python
class Dir_travelCategory(ListView):

    model = Dir_travel

    template_name = 'traveler/index.html'

    context_object_name = 'posts'


    def get_queryset(self):

        return Dir_travel.objects.filter(cat__slug=self.kwargs['cat_slug'], is_published=True)
```

```python
class Dir_travelCategory(ListView):
    model = Dir_travel
    template_name = 'traveler/index.html'
    context_object_name = 'posts'

    def get_queryset(self):
        return Dir_travel.objects.filter(cat__slug=self.kwargs['cat_slug'], is_published=True)
```

In the method def **get_queryset(self):**, we select records from the **Dir_travel** table only those that correspond to the category specified by the slug **'cat_slug'**.

Remember, in our urls.py, we've indicated an identifier. However, we want to specify a slug.

```python
urlpatterns = [
```

```
path('', Dir_travelHome.as_view(), name='home'),
path('about/', about, name='about'),
path('addpage/', addpage, name='add_page'),
path('contact/', addpage, name='contact'),
path('login/', login, name='login'),
path('post/<slug:post_slug>/', show_post, name='post'),
path('category/<int:cat_id>/', show_category, name='category'),
]
```

We'll change the last entry to:

Furthermore, through the parameter **kwargs['cat_slug'],** we can retrieve all the parameters of our route. That is, when an instance of the **Dir_travelCategory** class is formed for a specific request, through the link self

return Dir_travel.objects.filter(cat__slug=self.kwargs['cat_slug'], is_published=True)

we access the kwargs dictionary and refer to the constant **'cat_slug'**.

And now, we should select from the Dir_travelCategory table all records for which the **'cat_slug'** coincides with the slug of categories **cat__slug**

return Dir_travel.objects.filter(cat__slug=self.kwargs['cat_slug'], is_published=True)

cat__slug means that for the cat object in the Dir_travel model, there is a reference to the Category model.

cat = models.ForeignKey('Category', on_delete=models.PROTECT, null=True, verbose_name="Category")

and we refer to the slug field of the categories table cat.

Then, in **urls.py**, let's change

path('category/slug:cat_slug/', Dir_travelCategory.as_view(), name='category'),

and finally, in **models.py**, let's change

```
def get_absolute_url(self):
    return reverse('category', kwargs={'cat_slug': self.slug})
```

We'll refresh/update the page

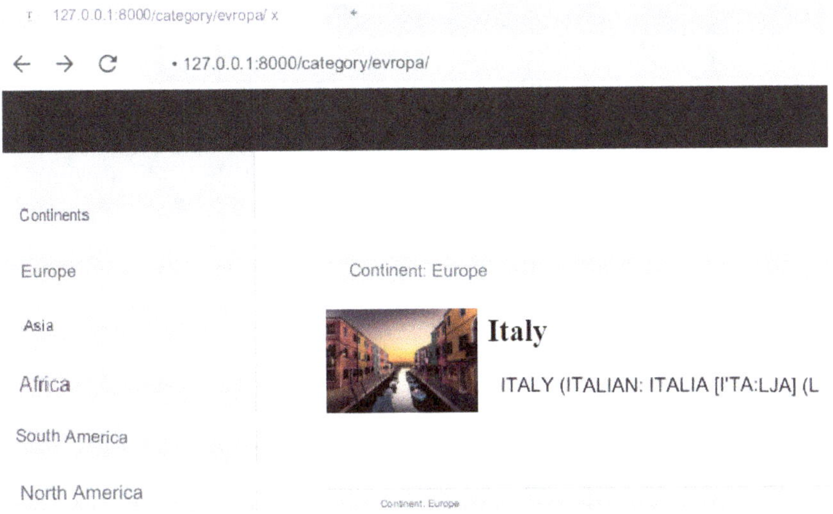

The title, main horizontal menu, and the left sidebar highlighting the category we are currently in aren't displaying. Let's fix that.

def get_context_data(self, *, oblect_list=None, **kwargs):

context = super().get_context_data(**kwargs)

context['title'] = ' Category - ' + str(context['posts'][0].cat)

context['menu'] = menu

context['cat_selected'] = context['posts'][0].cat_id

return context

```
def get_context_data(self, *, oblect_list=None, **kwargs):
    context = super().get_context_data(**kwargs)
    context['title'] = 'Category - ' + str(context['posts'][0].cat)
    context['menu'] = menu
    context['cat_selected'] = context['posts'][0].cat_id
    return context
```

context = super().get_context_data(kwargs)** – We form the data context that is already created by the base **ListView** class.

context['title'] = 'Category - ' + str(context['posts'][0].cat)

In this line, posts represent the collection of read records, where we take the first record **[0]** and access the **'cat'** attribute, which returns the category's name. We convert all of this into a string using str and add it to the string **'Category - '**.

context['cat_selected'] = context['posts'][0].cat_id – We do the same, but this time we fetch the identifier of the selected category, **cat_id**.

And we return return context.

Let's check how this will work.

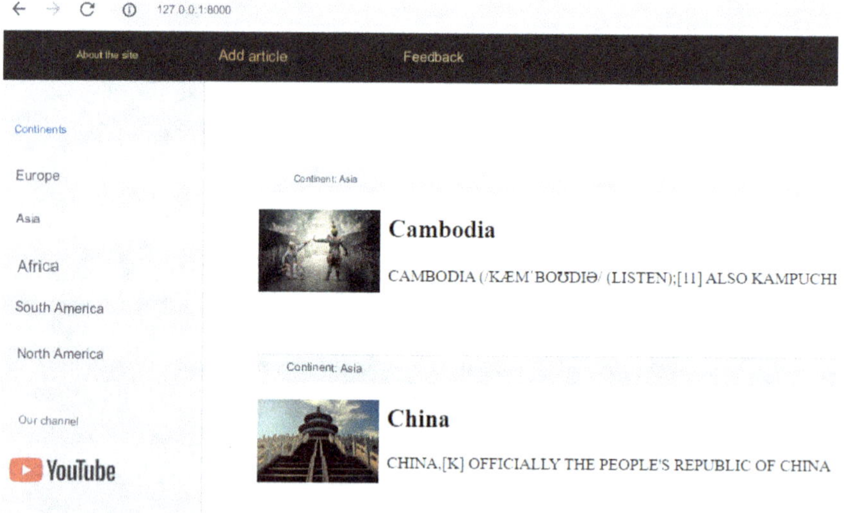

It seems everything is working as intended. If you navigate to the **'Europe'** category, you'll notice that everything works just as planned.

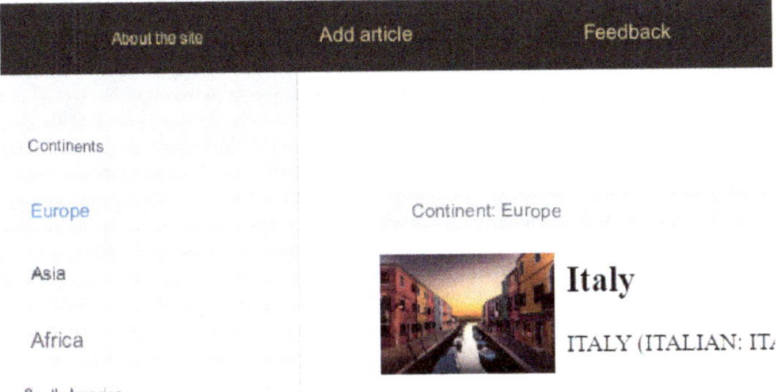

However, there is one nuance. Let's type in the browser's address bar a non-existing slug, for example

http://127.0.0.1:8000/category/aziya5/

 У нас возникнет ошибка

← → C   ⓘ   127.0.0.1:8000/category/aziya5/

IndexError at /category/aziya5/

list index out of range

```
Request Method:     GET
    Request URL:    http://127.0.0.1:8000/category/aziya5/
  Django Version:   4.1.1
  Exception Type:   IndexError
 Exception Value:   list index out of range
Exception Location: C:\Python\Django\travels\venv\lib\site-packages\django\db\models\query.py, line 446, in __getitem__
   Raised during:   traveler.views.Dir_travelCategory
Python Executable:  C:\Python\Django\travels\venv\Scripts\python.exe
  Python Version:   3.10.7
     Python Path:   ['C:\\Python\\Django\\travels\\travels',
                     'C:\\Python\\python310.zip',
                     'C:\\Python\\DLLs',
                     'C:\\Python\\lib',
                     'C:\\Python',
                     'C:\\Python\\Django\\travels\\venv',
                     'C:\\Python\\Django\\travels\\venv\\lib\\site-packages']
     Server time:   Sun, 25 Dec 2022 10:48:15 +0000
```

Traceback Switch to copy-and-paste view

```
C:\Python\Django\travels\venv\lib\site-packages\django\core\handlers\exception.py, line 55, in inner

    55.                 response = get_response(request)
```

Written

Exception Value: list index out of range

This occurs because if we don't have any existing articles **(Posts),** we can't access the first entry using **context['posts'][0].cat_id** since it doesn't exist.

If there are no entries in our list, let's generate a **404** error.

To do this, we'll add the following attribute

```
class Dir_travelCategory(ListView):

    model = Dir_travel

    template_name = 'traveler/index.html'

    context_object_name = 'posts'

    allow_empty = False
```

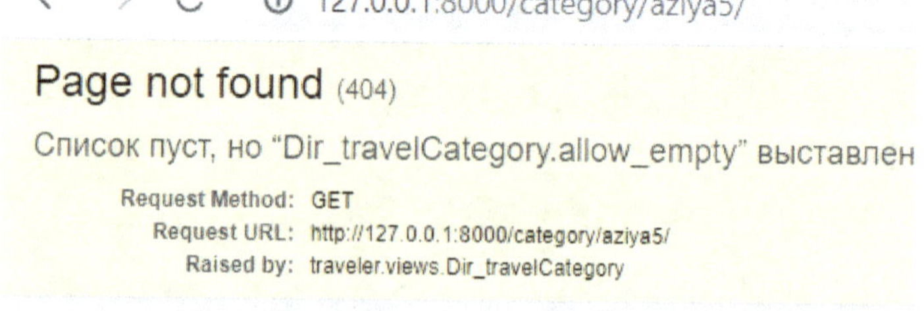

We'll refresh the page and see that when the page doesn't exist, a **404** error occurs.

Continuing our exploration of class capabilities, let's look at another class called **DetailView**, responsible for displaying a specific post.

First, let's import it.

*from django.views.generic import ListView, **DetailView***

```
1    from django.http import HttpResponse
2    from django.shortcuts import render, redirect, get_object_or_404
3    from django.http import Http404
4    from django.views.generic import ListView, DetailView
```

Then, let's find the function responsible for displaying a specific post, delete all its content, and write a class.

class ShowPost(DetailView):

  model = Dir_travel

  template_name =' traveler/post.html'

```
64      class ShowPost(DetailView):
65          model = Dir_travel
66          template_name = 'traveler/post.html'
```

All lines are repeated from the previous example, so everything should be clear.

Next, let's move to the list of routes in urls.py and change the name from the function to the class

*path('post/<slug:post_slug>/', **ShowPost.as_view()**, name='post'),*

```
11    path('post/<slug:post_slug>/', ShowPost.as_view(), name='post'),
12    path('category/<slug:cat_slug>/', Dir_travelCategory.as_view(), name='category'),
```

 Let's see how it works by going to the home page and refreshing it.

AttributeError at /post/italy/

Generic detail view ShowPost must be called with either an object pk or a slug in the URLconf.

```
        Request Method: GET
           Request URL: http://127.0.0.1:8000/post/italy/
        Django Version: 4.1.1
        Exception Type: AttributeError
       Exception Value: Generic detail view ShowPost must be called with either an object pk or a slug in the URLconf.
    Exception Location: C:\Python\Django\travels\venv\lib\site-packages\django\views\generic\detail.py, line 46, in get_object
         Raised during: traveler.views.ShowPost
     Python Executable: C:\Python\Django\travels\venv\Scripts\python.exe
        Python Version: 3.10.7
           Python Path: ['C:\\Python\\Django\\travels\\travels',
                         'C:\\Python\\python310.zip',
                         'C:\\Python\\DLLs',
                         'C:\\Python\\lib',
                         'C:\\Python',
                         'C:\\Python\\Django\\travels\\venv',
                         'C:\\Python\\Django\\travels\\venv\\lib\\site-packages']
           Server time: Mon, 26 Dec 2022 15:30:42 +0000
```

Let's change in the line

path('post/slug:post_slug/', ShowPost.as_view(), name='post'),

post_slug

 to just slug

and refresh the page.

Everything should work, but without displaying posts and the horizontal menu.

This means that this variable is used by default to obtain the slug.

But what if we want to keep everything as it is, without changing the variable?!

To do this, we'll apply a special attribute in our class.

class ShowPost(DetailView):

  model = Dir_travel

  template_name = 'traveler/post.html'

  slug_url_kwarg = 'post_slug'

```
64      class ShowPost(DetailView):
65          model = Dir_travel
66          template_name = 'traveler/post.html'
67          slug_url_kwarg = 'post_slug'
```

Let's refresh the page, and no errors appear. Let's move on. Since the **post.html** template uses **{{post.title}}** in the tag, we need to specify this explicitly in our class.

class ShowPost(DetailView):

   model = Dir_travel

   template_name = 'traveler/post.html'

   slug_url_kwarg = 'post_slug'

   context_object_name = 'post'

```python
class ShowPost(DetailView):
    model = Dir_travel
    template_name = 'traveler/post.html'
    slug_url_kwarg = 'post_slug'
    context_object_name = 'post'
```

Upon refreshing the page, the entire article with the photograph is already displayed. Now, we just need to pass the menu list and the tab title.

def get_context_data(self, *, oblect_list=None, **kwargs):

   context = super().get_context_data(kwargs)**

   context['title'] = context['post']

   context['menu'] = menu

   return context

```python
def get_context_data(self, *, oblect_list=None, **kwargs):
    context = super().get_context_data(**kwargs)
    context['title'] = context['post']
    context['menu'] = menu
    return context
```

Let's refresh the page, and we'll have a fully functional page ready with all the components.

Let's consider another class for working with forms. To start, let's import the **CreateView** class.

from django.http import HttpResponse

from django.shortcuts import render, redirect, get_object_or_404

from django.http import Http404

*from django.views.generic import ListView, DetailView, **CreateView***

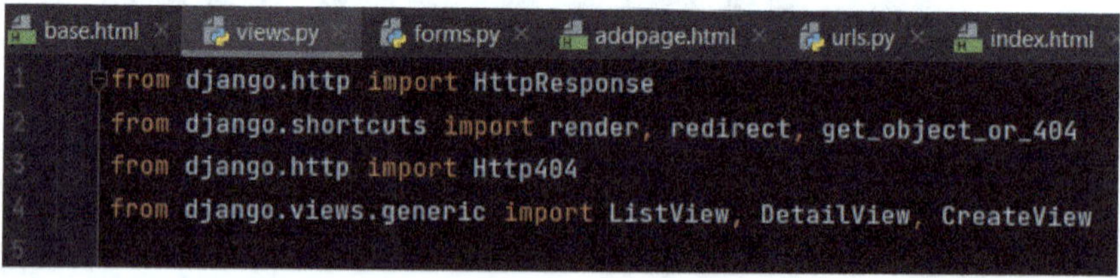

```
base.html   views.py   forms.py   addpage.html   urls.py   index.html
1  from django.http import HttpResponse
2  from django.shortcuts import render, redirect, get_object_or_404
3  from django.http import Http404
4  from django.views.generic import ListView, DetailView, CreateView
5
```

Next, to add a new post, let's create our own class based on **CreateView**. Let's comment out the addpage function and instead create a class called **AddPage.**

```
class AddPage(CreateView):
    form_class = AddPostForm
    template_name = 'traveler/addpage.html'
```

Then, in the **urls.py** file, we associate it with a route

```
path('addpage/', AddPage.as_view(), name='add_page'),
```

```
5  urlpatterns = [
6      path('', Dir_travelHome.as_view(), name='home'),
7      path('about/', about, name='about'),
8      path('addpage/', AddPage.as_view(), name='add_page'),
```

To display the title and horizontal menu, let's add a method **get_context_data** similar to the previous classes

```
class AddPage(CreateView):
    form_class = AddPostForm
    template_name = 'traveler/addpage.html'

    def get_context_data(self, *, oblect_list=None, **kwargs):
        context = super().get_context_data(**kwargs)
        context['title'] = 'Add Article'
        context['menu'] = menu
        return context
```

```python
36    class AddPage(CreateView):
37        form_class = AddPostForm
38        template_name = 'traveler/addpage.html'
39
40        def get_context_data(self, *, oblect_list=None, **kwargs):
41            context = super().get_context_data(**kwargs)
42            context['title'] = 'Adding an article'
43            context['menu'] = menu
44            return context
```

Let's go to the browser, refresh the page, and try adding a new article.

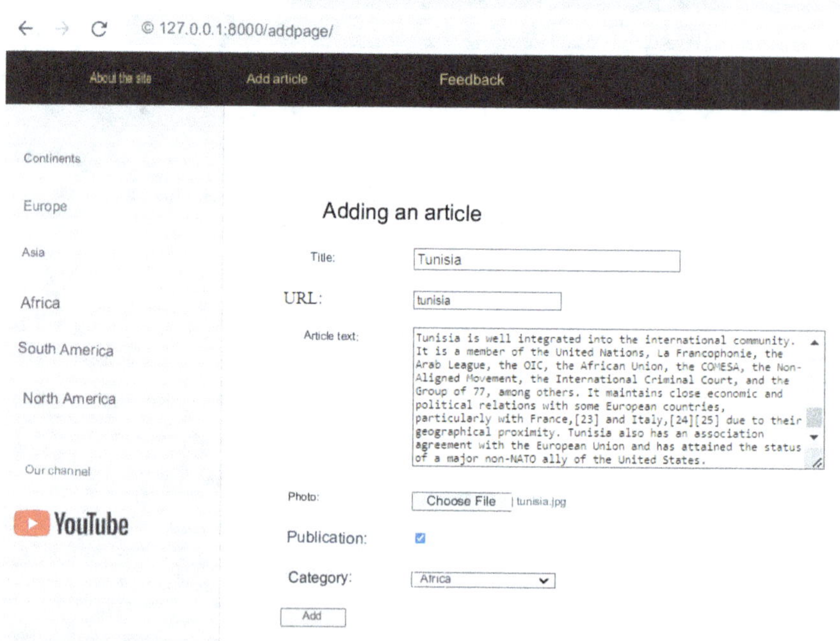

Looks like the article has been added!

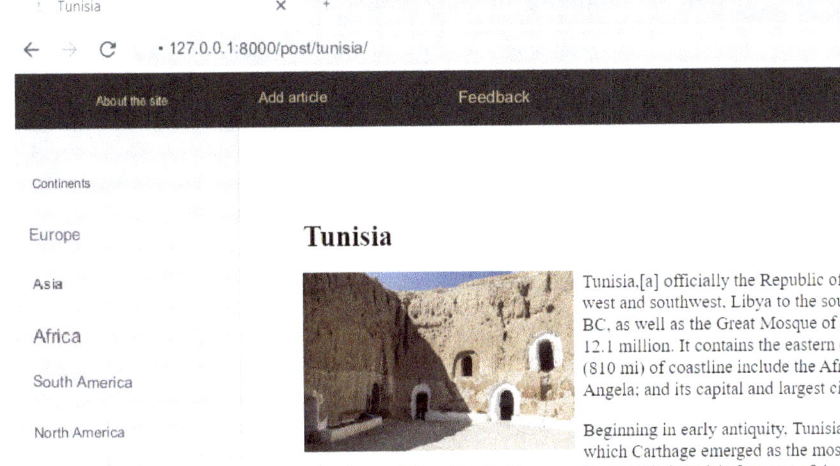

Compare the code in the view function with the view class, and it's easy to notice that the code has become noticeably smaller and simpler. Some code is duplicated in all our classes, and later we'll compose them using mixins.

After adding a post, Django redirects using the **get_absolute_url** method in the **models.py** file. If for any reason this method is not defined, in the **AddPage** class, you just need to add one line:

success_url = reverse_lazy('home')

Using the **reverse_lazy** method, we redirect to the home page.

And don't forget to import it.

from django.urls import reverse_lazy

Main commands of Django ORM

Let's consider the main **ORM** commands with related tables. As an example, let's consider the previously created models **Dir_travel** and **Category**, which are linked by a foreign key **field cat_id**.

With such rich functionality in **Django's ORM**, the need to resort to **SQL** queries will be rare. This system also allows querying any database type - **SQLite, MySQL, PostgreSQL, Oracle** - without being dependent on the database type.

For more detailed information, you can refer to the link **https://django.fun/ru/docs/django-orm-cookbook/2.0/.**

Next, let's consider **QuerySet** methods - a list of objects of a specific model. **QuerySet** enables reading data from the database, filtering, and changing their order.

To demonstrate **Django's ORM** functionality, let's move to the terminal and start the **Django** shell using the command...

Python manage.py shell

```
(venv) PS C:\Python\Django\travels> cd travels
(venv) PS C:\Python\Django\travels\travels> Python manage.py shell
Python 3.10.7 (tags/v3.10.7:6cc6b13, Sep  5 2022, 14:08:36) [MSC v.1933 64 bit (AMD64)] on win32
Type "help", "copyright", "credits" or "license" for more information.
(InteractiveConsole)
>>>
```

Next, let's import all our models that we'll be working with.

*from traveler.models import ***

Let's check if everything is working correctly by selecting all entries from the **Dir_travel** table, using the command...

Dir_travel.objects.all()

```
>>> from traveler.models import *
>>> Dir_travel.objects.all()
<QuerySet [<Dir_travel: Tunisia>, <Dir_travel: Tanzania>, <Dir_travel: Netherlands>, <Dir_travel: Tanzania>, <Dir_travel: Zimbabwe>, <Dir_travel: Cambodia>, <Dir_travel: China>, <Dir_travel: Canada>, <Dir_travel: United States>, <Dir_travel: Mexico>, <Dir_travel: Peru>, <Dir_travel: Brazil>, <Dir_travel: Italy>, <Dir_travel: Germany>, <Dir_travel: Poland>, <Dir_travel: Ukraine>]>
>>>
```

All entries are sorted as defined in the **Meta** class

```python
24        class Meta:
25            verbose_name = "All countries "
26            verbose_name_plural = "All countries "
27            ordering = ['-time_create', 'title']
```

Line '27'

ordering = ['-time_create', 'title']

If not all entries are needed but only some, this can be done using slice syntax. Let's select the first 3 entries.

Dir_travel.objects.all()[:3]

```
>>> Dir_travel.objects.all()[:3]
<QuerySet [<Dir_travel: Tunisia>, <Dir_travel: Tanzania>, <Dir_travel: Netherlands>]>
>>>
```

All these queries are executed not in **Python** but on the **SQL** query level. This can be confirmed further. First, let's import the following module

from django.db import connection

and refer to the next collection

connection.queries

```
>>> from django.db import connection
>>> connection.queries
[{'sql': 'SELECT "traveler_dir_travel"."id", "traveler_dir_travel"."title", "traveler_dir_travel"."slug", "traveler_dir_travel"."content", "traveler_dir_travel"."photo", "traveler_dir_travel"."time_create", "traveler_dir_travel"."time_update", "traveler_dir_travel"."is_published", "traveler_dir_travel"."cat_id" FROM "traveler_dir_travel" ORDER BY "traveler_dir_travel"."time_create" DESC, "traveler_dir_travel"."title" ASC LIMIT 21', 'time': '0.000'}, {'sql': 'SELECT "traveler_dir_travel"."id", "traveler_dir_travel"."title", "traveler_dir_travel"."slug", "traveler_dir_travel"."content", "traveler_dir_travel"."photo", "traveler_dir_travel"."time_create", "traveler_dir_travel"."time_update", "traveler_dir_travel"."is_published", "traveler_dir_travel"."cat_id" FROM "traveler_dir_travel" ORDER BY "traveler_dir_travel"."time_create" DESC, "traveler_dir_travel"."title" ASC LIMIT 3', 'time': '0.000'}]
>>>
```

At the end of the entry, we see...

Yes, the first three entries were selected from the database

Dir_travel.objects.all()[2:5]

```
>>> Dir_travel.objects.all()[2:5]
<QuerySet [<Dir_travel: Netherlands>, <Dir_travel: Tanzania>, <Dir_travel: Zimbabwe>]>
```

```
LIMIT 3 OFFSET 2',
```

Let's change the order of sorting the entries based on a specific field, for instance, the primary key **(pk).**

Dir_travel.objects.order_by('pk')

```
>>> Dir_travel.objects.order_by('pk')
<QuerySet [<Dir_travel: Ukraine>, <Dir_travel: Poland>, <Dir_travel: Germany>, <Dir_travel: Italy>, <Dir_travel: Brazil>, <Dir_travel: Peru>, <Dir_travel: Mexico>, <Dir_travel: United
States>, <Dir_travel: Canada>, <Dir_travel: China>, <Dir_travel: Cambodia>, <Dir_travel: Zimbabwe>, <Dir_travel: Tanzania>, <Dir_travel: Netherlands>, <Dir_travel: Tanzania>, <Dir_trav
el: Tunisia>]>
```

As we can see, all entries are arranged according to this field. Let's reverse the order completely

Dir_travel.objects.order_by('-pk')

Or using the **reverse** method

Dir_travel.objects.reverse()

```
>>> Dir_travel.objects.reverse()
<QuerySet [<Dir_travel: Ukraine>, <Dir_travel: Pola
States>, <Dir_travel: Canada>, <Dir_travel: China>,
el: Tunisia>]>
>>> Dir_travel.objects.order_by('pk')
<QuerySet [<Dir_travel: Ukraine>, <Dir_travel: Pola
States>, <Dir_travel: Canada>, <Dir_travel: China>,
el: Tunisia>]>
>>> Dir_travel.objects.order_by('-pk')
<QuerySet [<Dir_travel: Tunisia>, <Dir_travel: Tanza
ravel: Canada>, <Dir_travel: United States>, <Dir_t
el: Ukraine>]>
>>>
```

Next, let's observe the practical application of the **filter** method, for example, selecting multiple entries based on specific conditions.

Dir_travel.objects.filter(pk__lte=2)

If for any reason you've closed the terminal, it's necessary to repeat the commands we previously entered, namely entering the Django terminal and importing all models.

```
(venv) PS C:\Python\Django\travels\travels> python manage.py shale
Unknown command: 'shale'. Did you mean shell?
Type 'manage.py help' for usage.
(venv) PS C:\Python\Django\travels\travels> python manage.py shell
Python 3.10.7 (tags/v3.10.7:6cc6b13, Sep  5 2022, 14:08:36) [MSC v.1933 64 bit (AMD64)] on win32
Type "help", "copyright", "credits" or "license" for more information.
(InteractiveConsole)
>>> from traveler.models import *


KeyboardInterrupt
>>> from traveler.models import*
>>>
```

And after that, let's repeat entering the command

Dir_travel.objects.filter(pk__lte=2)

```
>>> Dir_travel.objects.filter(pk__lte=2)
<QuerySet [<Dir_travel: Poland>, <Dir_travel: Ukraine>]>
>>>
```

Using this filter, we select all records where the primary key is less than or equal to '2'.

pk__lte=2

If you need to select a single record, then use the **'get'** method

Dir_travel.objects.get(pk =2)

And it uses the unique field by which this record is selected. It's important to note that when using the **'filter'** method, we get back a **QuerySet** collection, whereas with the **'get'** method, we receive an instance of our model.

Let's see how processing of related data from different tables occurs. First, let's select one record.

w = Dir_travel.objects.get(pk =1)

Then, the variable 'w' will reference this record. In this variable, we have access to the following properties:

All fields that exist in our model, specifically from **w.title** to **w.is_published.**
We can refer to the record's identifier using **w.pk** or **w.id**.
Access the category identifier through the property **w.cat_id**.
Access the **Category** model class property using w.cat with the corresponding value **id = cat_id**.
For example, let's execute the command **w.cat**

Indeed, we see a reference to the category.

Next, we can access any property of the **Category** table, for instance, **w.cat.name**

Note that if we refer to a field we hadn't previously selected, Django will execute an extra **SQL** query to retrieve its value.

Next, we'll craft a query using the primary **Category** model to obtain all associated posts. For instance, let's choose the '**Europe**' category and all records linked to it in the **Dir_travel** model. For this, Django automatically creates a special property for any primary model:

<secondary_model>_set

This property enables us to select all associated records. Let's illustrate this with an example. First, let's select the first category from the **Category** model

c = Category.objects.get(pk=1)

And then we'll output **'c'**

```
(venv) PS C:\Python\Django\travels\travels> Python manage.py shell
Python 3.10.7 (tags/v3.10.7:6cc6b13, Sep  5 2022, 14:08:36) [MSC v.1933 64 bit (AMD64)] on win32
Type "help", "copyright", "credits" or "license" for more information.
(InteractiveConsole)
>>> from traveler.models import *
>>> c = Category.objects.get(pk=1)
>>> c
<Category: Europe    >
>>>
```

Using the mechanism of reverse linking, let's read all posts associated with this category from the **Dir_travel** model.

And then the command...

c.dir_travel_set

Please note that the name of our model is written in lowercase. If written with uppercase, we'll get the following. And with the subsequent command, we'll correct this.

```
>>> c.Dir_travel_set
Traceback (most recent call last):
  File "<console>", line 1, in <module>
AttributeError: 'Category' object has no attribute 'Dir_travel_set'
>>> c.dir_travel_set
<django.db.models.fields.related_descriptors.create_reverse_many_to_one_manager.<locals>.RelatedManager object at 0x00000169F39C5270>
>>>
```

We obtained an object through which we can select all **Dir_travel** posts. Let's select all posts

c.dir_travel_set.all()

```
>>> c.dir_travel_set.all()
<QuerySet [<Dir_travel: Netherlands>, <Dir_travel: Italy>, <Dir_travel: Germany>, <Dir_travel: Poland>, <Dir_travel: Ukraine>]>
>>>
```

Field filters.

< Attribute name >__gte – Greater than or equal to comparison (>=);

< Attribute name >__lte – Less than or equal to comparison (<=);

Those are called lookups: **__gte and __lte**, which allow us to select records based on conditions of **>= or <=** respectively**.**

For instance, let's move to the terminal and execute the following command where the primary key is greater than or equal to 2.

Dir_travel.objects.filter(pk__gte=2)

```
>>> Dir_travel.objects.filter(pk__gte=2)
<QuerySet [<Dir_travel: Tunisia>, <Dir_travel: Tanzania>, <Dir_travel: Netherlands>, <Dir_travel: Tanzania>, <Dir_travel: Zimbabwe>, <Dir_travel: Cambodia>, <Dir_travel: China>, <Dir_travel: Canada>, <Dir_travel: United States>, <Dir_travel: Mexico>, <Dir_travel: Peru>, <Dir_travel: Brazil>, <Dir_travel: Italy>, <Dir_travel: Germany>, <Dir_travel: Poland>]>
>>>
```

Let's introduce a few more filters for familiarity. For example, one that allows searching records by a text fragment. In this case, let's say it's **'Ge'**

Dir_travel.objects.filter(title__contains='Ge')

```
>>> Dir_travel.objects.filter(title__contains='Ge')
<QuerySet [<Dir_travel: Germany>]>
>>>
```

The second filter does the same thing but disregards case sensitivity.

Dir_travel.objects.filter(title__icontains='GE')

```
>>> Dir_travel.objects.filter(title__icontains='GE')
<QuerySet [<Dir_travel: Germany>]>
>>>
```

Keep in mind that in the **SQLite** database engine, this filter doesn't work with Russian characters. However, in other database systems, there are no such issues.

Another filter allows selecting records by the primary key and its **ID.**

Dir_travel.objects.filter(pk__in=[1,3,4])

```
>>> Dir_travel.objects.filter(pk__in=[1,3,4])
<QuerySet [<Dir_travel: Italy>, <Dir_travel: Germany>, <Dir_travel: Ukraine>]>
>>>
```

You can also use two conditions simultaneously

Dir_travel.objects.filter(pk__in=[1,3,4], is_published=True)

```
>>> Dir_travel.objects.filter(pk__in=[1,3,4], is_published=True)
<QuerySet [<Dir_travel: Italy>, <Dir_travel: Germany>, <Dir_travel: Ukraine>]>
>>>
```

These conditions should be true simultaneously. This filter can also be used for a foreign key. For instance, let's refer to the foreign key and retrieve all records from the first and second categories.

Dir_travel.objects.filter(cat__in=[1, 2])

```
>>> Dir_travel.objects.filter(cat__in=[1, 2])
<QuerySet [<Dir_travel: Netherlands>, <Dir_travel: Cambodia>, <Dir_travel: China>, <Dir_tra
vel: Italy>, <Dir_travel: Germany>, <Dir_travel: Poland>, <Dir_travel: Ukraine>]>
>>>
```

Let's approach this a bit differently. First, let's read the categories for which we'd like to select records.

cats = Category.objects.all()

And then...

Dir_travel.objects.filter(cat__in=cats)

```
>>> cats = Category.objects.all()
>>> Dir_travel.objects.filter(cat__in=cats)
<QuerySet [<Dir_travel: Tunisia>, <Dir_travel: Tanzania>, <Dir_travel: Netherlands>, <Dir_t
ravel: Tanzania>, <Dir_travel: Zimbabwe>, <Dir_travel: Cambodia>, <Dir_travel: China>, <Dir
_travel: Canada>, <Dir_travel: United States>, <Dir_travel: Mexico>, <Dir_travel: Peru>, <D
ir_travel: Brazil>, <Dir_travel: Italy>, <Dir_travel: Germany>, <Dir_travel: Poland>, <Dir_
travel: Ukraine>]>
>>>
```

Let's see how to use the **Q** class to create conditions not based on **AND**, but on **OR** and **NOT.**

Using this class allows for the application of the following approaches:

1. **&** - Logical **AND** (priority 2)
2. **|** - Logical **OR** (priority 3)
3. **~** - Logical **NOT** (priority 1)

Let's go to the terminal and import the **Q** class. We'll select all records where the primary key is less than **5** and the category equals **2.**

Dir_travel.objects.filter(pk__lt=5, cat_id=2)

The output will be...

<QuerySet []>

```
>>> from django.db.models import Q
>>> Dir_travel.objects.filter(pk__lt=5, cat_id=2)
<QuerySet []>
>>>
```

We received an empty list because all records where **pk<5** belong to the first category. However, if we combine these two conditions using **OR**, i.e., to select records where **pk<5 OR cat_id=2**, then we'll obtain the list of records.

Dir_travel.objects.filter(Q(pk__lt=5) | Q(cat_id=2))

```
>>> Dir_travel.objects.filter(Q(pk__lt=5) | Q(cat_id=2))
<QuerySet [<Dir_travel: Cambodia>, <Dir_travel: China>, <Dir_travel: Italy>, <Dir_travel: Germany>
, <Dir_travel: Poland>, <Dir_travel: Ukraine>]>
>>>
```

The very first example can be presented differently, using the **Q** class

Dir_travel.objects.filter(Q(pk__lt=5) & Q(cat_id=2))

```
>>> Dir_travel.objects.filter(Q(pk__lt=5) & Q(cat_id=2))
<QuerySet []>
```

And let's apply the final operator that reverses the condition.

Dir_travel.objects.filter(~Q(pk__lt=5) | Q(cat_id=2))

```
>>> Dir_travel.objects.filter(~Q(pk__lt=5) | Q(cat_id=2))
<QuerySet [<Dir_travel: Tunisia>, <Dir_travel: Tanzania>, <Dir_travel: Netherlands>, <Dir_travel:
Tanzania>, <Dir_travel: Zimbabwe>, <Dir_travel: Cambodia>, <Dir_travel: China>, <Dir_travel: Canad
a>, <Dir_travel: United States>, <Dir_travel: Mexico>, <Dir_travel: Peru>, <Dir_travel: Brazil>]>
>>>
```

In the **Django ORM,** there are several methods for quickly retrieving records from a table.

To get the first record from a selection, you can use the following method

Dir_travel.objects.first()

```
>>> Dir_travel.objects.first()
<Dir_travel: Tunisia>
>>>
```

If you select all records, you'll see that this particular record comes first.

Dir_travel.objects.all()

```
>>> Dir_travel.objects.all()
<QuerySet [<Dir_travel: Tunisia>, <Dir_travel: Tanzania>, <Dir_travel: Netherlands>, <Dir_travel:
Tanzania>, <Dir_travel: Zimbabwe>, <Dir_travel: Cambodia>, <Dir_travel: China>, <Dir_travel: Canad
a>, <Dir_travel: United States>, <Dir_travel: Mexico>, <Dir_travel: Peru>, <Dir_travel: Brazil>, <
Dir_travel: Italy>, <Dir_travel: Germany>, <Dir_travel: Poland>, <Dir_travel: Ukraine>]>
>>>
```

We can change the sorting order by **pk** and then select the first record.

Dir_travel.objects.order_by('pk').all()

```
>>> Dir_travel.objects.order_by('pk').all()
<QuerySet [<Dir_travel: Ukraine>, <Dir_travel: Poland>, <Dir_travel: Germany>, <Dir_travel: Italy>
, <Dir_travel: Brazil>, <Dir_travel: Peru>, <Dir_travel: Mexico>, <Dir_travel: United States>, <Di
r_travel: Canada>, <Dir_travel: China>, <Dir_travel: Cambodia>, <Dir_travel: Zimbabwe>, <Dir_trave
l: Tanzania>, <Dir_travel: Netherlands>, <Dir_travel: Tanzania>, <Dir_travel: Tunisia>]>
>>>
```

Dir_travel.objects.order_by('pk').first()

```
>>> Dir_travel.objects.order_by('pk').first()
<Dir_travel: Ukraine>
>>>
```

or

Dir_travel.objects.order_by('-pk').first()

```
>>> Dir_travel.objects.order_by('-pk').first()
<Dir_travel: Tunisia>
>>>
```

We can also take the last entry

Dir_travel.objects.order_by('pk').last()

```
>>> Dir_travel.objects.order_by('pk').last()
<Dir_travel: Tunisia>
>>>
```

or

Dir_travel.objects.order_by('-pk').last()

```
>>> Dir_travel.objects.order_by('-pk').last()
<Dir_travel: Ukraine>
>>>
```

Furthermore, if our table contains fields named **time_create** and **time_update**, we can apply the following queries for selection:

For instance, if we need to retrieve the entry with the latest date....

Dir_travel.objects.latest('time_update')

```
>>> Dir_travel.objects.latest('time_update')
<Dir_travel: Tunisia>
>>>
```

Or we'll select the entry that was most recently added to the database

Dir_travel.objects.earliest('time_update')

```
>>> Dir_travel.objects.earliest('time_update')
<Dir_travel: Ukraine>
>>>
```

Moreover, if we need to select the next or previous entry relative to the current record, there are specific methods available.

Let's say we're selecting a certain entry from the table...

w = Dir_travel.objects.get(pk=6)

We want to retrieve the previous and next records relative to this entry. To achieve this, we need to utilize a specific method

get_previous_by_

w.get_previous_by_time_update()

So, first, we specify this method with an underscore at the end, and then the name of the field based on which we are seeking the previous entry.

```
>>> w.get_previous_by_time_update()
<Dir_travel: Brazil>
>>>
```

And for selecting the next entry

w.get_next_by_time_update()

```
>>> w.get_next_by_time_update()
<Dir_travel: Mexico>
>>>
```

Additionally, in these methods, conditions regarding the next and previous entries can also be specified. For instance, let's select the next entry where the primary **key (pk)** is greater than or equal to 7

w.get_next_by_time_update(pk__gt=4)

```
>>> w.get_next_by_time_update(pk__gt=4)
<Dir_travel: Mexico>
>>>
```

Let's consider the following two methods:

1. **exists()** – Checking the existence of a record.
2. **count()** – Getting the count of entries.

Don't forget! If you've exited the Django terminal, write the command

Python manage.py shell

After that, we import all our models

*from traveler.models import **

And after these two simple commands, we can continue practicing. Let's add another category to the table.

Category.objects.create(name='Asia', slug='asia')

```
>>> Category.objects.create(name='Asia', slug='asia')
<Category: Asia>
>>>
```

For this newly created category, there are no posts yet. Let's test the **exists()** method for this category. This method should return False if there are no records.

new = Category.objects.get(pk=6)

```
>>> new = Category.objects.get(pk=6)
>>> new
<Category: Asia>
>>>
```

To retrieve associated records from the **Dir_travel** table, we use the method **dir_travel_set**. Remember to start this method with a lowercase letter.

```
>>> new.dir_travel_set.exists()
False
>>>
```

In this case, this method will return **False**. If you check another category, you'll get the value **True.**

c1 = Category.objects.get(pk=1)

And onward we go

c1.dir_travel_set.exists()

```
>>> c1 = Category.objects.get(pk=1)
>>> c1
<Category :Europe    >
>>> c1.dir_travel_set.exists()
True
>>>
```

To find out the number of entries for a specific category, we use the second method by analogy.

c1.dir_travel_set.count()

```
>>> c1.dir_travel_set.count()
5
>>>
```

And for the new category

new.dir_travel_set.count()

```
>>> new.dir_travel_set.count()
0
>>>
```

These methods can be applied to any selections. For instance, let's choose some entries where the primary **key (pk)** is greater than 3 and count the number of these entries.

Dir_travel.objects.filter(pk__gt=3).count()

```
>>> Dir_travel.objects.filter(pk__gt=3).count()
13
>>>
```

Next, let's consider several aggregate functions.

In the simplest case, an aggregate function looks like this:

Dir_travel.objects.count()

This one simply returns the count of posts. Other aggregate commands are written within a special method

aggregate()

For example, if we want to see what the minimum value of a field is... **cat_id**

Dir_travel.objects. aggregate(Min('cat_id'))

In this case, we want to compute the minimum **'cat_id'** field.

To use any aggregate function, you need to import it first.

from django.db.models import *

```
>>> Dir_travel.objects.aggregate(Min('cat_id'))
{'cat_id__min': 1}
>>>
```

From the screenshot, we can see that the minimum **cat_id** is 1. Alternatively, we can specify multiple functions separated by commas

Dir_travel.objects.aggregate(Min('cat_id'), Max('cat_id'))

```
>>> Dir_travel.objects.aggregate(Min('cat_id'), Max('cat_id'))
{'cat_id__min': 1, 'cat_id__max': 5}
>>>
```

If we want to get different key names in the dictionary instead of...

{'cat_id__min': 1, 'cat_id__max': 5}

Then you should write it as follows

Dir_travel.objects.aggregate(cat_min=Min('cat_id'),cat_max= Max('cat_id'))

```
>>> Dir_travel.objects.aggregate(cat_min=Min('cat_id'),cat_max= Max('cat_id'))
{'cat_min': 1, 'cat_max': 5}
>>>
```

You can also perform standard mathematical operations.

Dir_travel.objects.aggregate(res=Sum('cat_id') - Count('cat_id'))

```
>>> Dir_travel.objects.aggregate(res=Sum('cat_id') - Count('cat_id'))
{'res': 27}
>>>
```

So, we sum the **'cat_id'** values and then subtract the count of **'cat_id'** from that sum. Or we can calculate the arithmetic mean of the **'cat_id'** field

Dir_travel.objects.aggregate(res=Avg('cat_id'))

We can also apply an aggregate function not to all records but by using a specific subset or selection.

Dir_travel.objects.filter(pk__gt=4).aggregate(res=Avg('cat_id'))

```
>>> Dir_travel.objects.filter(pk__gt=4).aggregate(res=Avg('cat_id'))
{'res': 3.25}
>>>
```

So, we select all records where the primary key is greater than 4, and then we apply an aggregate function to this subset.

In all our selections above, all fields were automatically chosen, and only those fields we explicitly mentioned were displayed in the console. For instance, if we display fields with **pk=1,** we'll get...

w = Dir_travel.objects.get(pk=1)

w.title, w.slug

```
>>> w = Dir_travel.objects.get(pk=1)
>>> w
<Dir_travel: Ukraine>
>>> w.title
'Ukraine'
>>> w.slug
'ukraine'
>>>
```

But what if we don't want that, and we only need the fields that we explicitly specify? There's a special method for this, like....

Dir_travel.objects.values('title', 'cat_id').get(pk=1)

```
>>> Dir_travel.objects.values('title', 'cat_id').get(pk=1)
{'title': 'Ukraine', 'cat_id': 1}
>>>
```

This kind of query will execute faster than the previous one. We can also utilize associated data.

Dir_travel.objects.values('title', 'cat__name').get(pk=1)

We select the 'title' field and choose the 'name' field associated with the primary model 'Category' for the first record with **pk=1.**

```
>>> Dir_travel.objects.values('title', 'cat__name').get(pk=1)
{'title': 'Ukraine', 'cat__name': 'Europe '}
>>>
```

So we retrieved associated data from both tables. Alternatively, we can select associated data: **'title'** from the **Dir_travel** table and 'name' from the **Category** table.

w = Dir_travel.objects.values('title', 'cat__name')

```
>>> w = Dir_travel.objects.values('title', 'cat__name')
>>> w
<QuerySet [{'title': 'Tunisia', 'cat__name': 'Africa'}  , {'title': 'Tanzania', 'cat__name': 'Africa'}, {'tit
le': 'Netherlands', 'cat__name': 'Europe'}, {'title': 'Tanzania', 'cat__name': 'Africa'}, {'title': 'Zimbab
we', 'cat__name': 'Africa'}, {'title': 'Cambodia', 'cat__name': 'Asia'}, {'title': 'China', 'cat__name':
'Asia'}, {'title': 'Canada', 'cat__name': 'North America'}  , {'title': 'United States', 'cat__name': '
North America'}, {'title': 'Mexico', 'cat__name': 'South America'},  {'title': 'Peru', 'cat__name': '
'}, {'title': 'Brazil', 'cat__name':  'South America'}, {'title': 'Italy', 'cat__name': 'Europe'}, {'tit
le': 'Germany', 'cat__name': 'Europe'}, {'title': 'Poland', 'cat__name': 'Europe'}, {'title': 'Ukraine', 'c
at__name': 'Europe'}]>
>>>
```

For clarity, we can output the list using a for loop.

for p in w:

...   print(p['title'], p['cat__name'])

```
>>> for p in w:
...          print(p['title'], p['cat__name'])
...
Tunisia Africa
Tanzania Africa
Netherlands Europe
Tanzania Africa
Zimbabwe Africa
Cambodia Asia
China Asia
Canada North America
United States North America
Mexico South America
Peru South America
Brazil South America
Italy Europe
Germany Europe
Poland Europe
Ukraine Europe
>>>
```

Here's how **Django's ORM** generally looks. Above, only the principles of various methods within this **ORM** were shown, and this material can only serve as a stepping stone for a more ambitious study of this topic using the official documentation.

Mixins - eliminating code duplication.

Let's extract all the code we have in the view classes into a separate class called a **Mixin**. **Mixins** are designed for consistent operation with objects.

For a better understanding of what mixins are, let's imagine a situation with an online store that has several different products, each sharing a set of identical characteristics. These might include weight, price, dimensions, identifier, and so on. For each product, you could create a separate class listing all these similar characteristics. However, for more concise code and better comprehension, you can extract the repetitive characteristics into a separate class, place it separately, and thereby avoid cluttering the code.

In Python, thanks to the mechanism of multiple inheritance, mixins can be added as a separate base class with certain considerations. In our case, the already created classes inherit some methods from the base classes.

For instance, the class

Dir_travelHome inherits from ListView.

To utilize the functionality of mixins, this class needs to be specified first. That is, if for some reason we have repeating attributes in the first inherited class (mixin) and in the second base class, the attributes from the class positioned first will be applied.

class Dir_travelHome(DataMixin, ListView)

Let's eliminate code duplication in practice.

We'll open **views.py** and, upon reviewing the code, we'll find that there is duplicated code

*def get_context_data(self, *, object_list=None, **kwargs):*

*context = super().get_context_data(**kwargs)*

context['menu'] = menu

context['title'] = 'Homepage'

context['cat_selected'] = 0

return context

```python
class Dir_travelHome(ListView):
    model = Dir_travel
    template_name = 'traveler/index.html'
    context_object_name = 'posts'


    def get_context_data(self, *, object_list=None, **kwargs):
        context = super().get_context_data(**kwargs)
        context['menu'] = menu
        context['title'] = 'Homepage'
        context['cat_selected'] = 0
        return context


    def get_queryset(self):
        return Dir_travel.objects.filter(is_published=True)


def about(request):
    return render(request, 'traveler/about.html', {'menu': menu, 'title': 'About the site'})
```

All of this can be optimized. First, let's define the class DataMixin.

In **Django**, all additional utility classes are typically specified in a separate file, which we'll name utils.

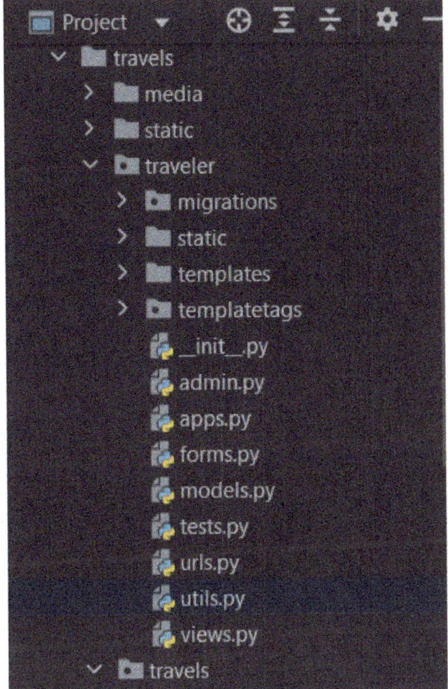

Next, in the **views.py** file, we'll cut out the fragment

```
menu = [{'title': " About the website ", 'url_name': 'about'},
    {'title': " Add article ", 'url_name': 'add_page'},
    {'title': " Feedback ", 'url_name': 'contact'},
    {'title': " Sign in ", 'url_name': 'login'}
]
```

And move it to the created **utils.py** file.

Below, we'll define the class **DataMixin**

```
class DadtaMixin:

    def get_user_context(self, **kwargs):

        context = kwargs

        cats = Category.objects.all()

        context['menu'] = menu

        context['cats'] = cats

        if 'cat_selected' not in context:

            context['cat_selected'] = 0

        return context
```

```
 3    menu = [{'title': "About the site", 'url_name': 'about'},
 4            {'title': "Add article ",  'url_name': 'add_page'},
 5            {'title': "Feedback ",  'url_name': 'contact'},
 6            {'title': "To come ", 'url_name': 'login'}
 7    ]
 8
 9    class DadtaMixin:
10        def get_user_context(self, **kwargs):
11            context = kwargs
12            cats = Category.objects.all()
13            context['menu'] = menu
14            context['cats'] = cats
15            if 'cat_selected' not in context:
16                context['cat_selected'] = 0
17            return context
```

The method **get_user_context** will create a default template context.

We'll start with **context = kwargs** to form an initial dictionary from the named parameters passed to the **get_user_context** function. Next, we'll create a list of categories: **cats = Category.objects.all().**

Previously, we were creating custom templates in the file **traveler_tags.py**

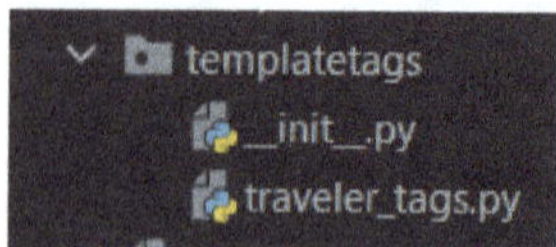

And using the tag **show_categories**

```python
14    @register.inclusion_tag('traveler/list_categories.html')
15    def show_categories(sort=None, cat_selected=0):
16        if not sort:
17            cats = Category.objects.all()
18        else:
19            cats = Category.objects.order_by(sort)
20        return {"cats": cats, "cat_selected": cat_selected}
```

In the **base.html** template, we were already displaying our categories

{% show_categories cat_selected=cat_selected %}

```html
41            <li><a href="{% url 'home' %}">Континенты</a></li>
42    {% endif %}
43
44    {% show_categories cat_selected=cat_selected %}
45
46        <li class="share">
47        <p>Наш канал</p>
48        <a class="share-yt" href="#"></a>
49        </li>
```

Let's do the following: Remove the line

{% show_categories cat_selected=cat_selected %}

And instead, we'll specify the output of categories using the category **cats**

{% for c in cats %}

{% if c.pk == cat_selected %}

<li class="selected">{{c.name}}</li>

{% else %}

<li> <a href="{{ c.get_absolute_url }}">{{c.name}}</a></li>

```
{% endif %}
{% endfor %}
```

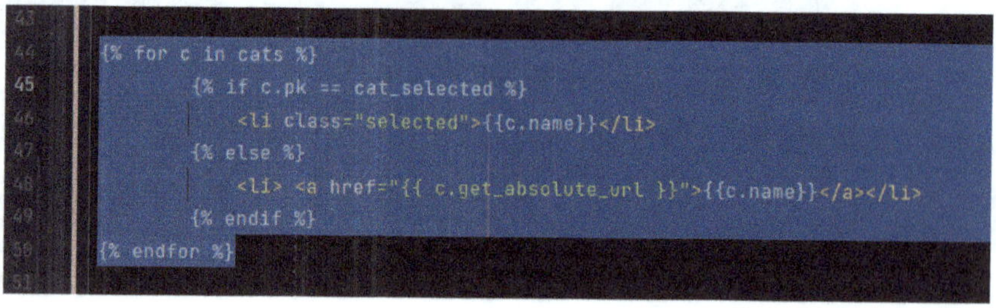

```
44    {% for c in cats %}
45        {% if c.pk == cat_selected %}
46            <li class="selected">{{c.name}}</li>
47        {% else %}
48            <li> <a href="{{ c.get_absolute_url }}">{{c.name}}</a></li>
49        {% endif %}
50    {% endfor %}
```

So, as it was initially for us. And this collection will be passed to the template because we're forming such a context.

context['cats'] = cats

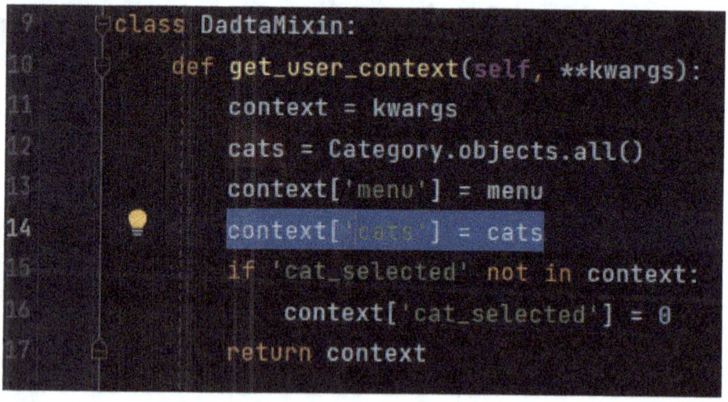

```
9     class DadtaMixin:
10        def get_user_context(self, **kwargs):
11            context = kwargs
12            cats = Category.objects.all()
13            context['menu'] = menu
14            context['cats'] = cats
15            if 'cat_selected' not in context:
16                context['cat_selected'] = 0
17            return context
```

So that we can use the **Category** model, let's import it

```
class DataMixin:
    def get_user_context(self, **kwargs):
        context = kwargs
        cats = Category.objects.all()
```

```
context['menu'] = menu
context['cats'] = cats
if 'cat_selected' not in context:
    context['cat_selected'] = 0
return context
```

from .model import *

```python
from .models import *

menu = [{'title': "About the site", 'url_name': 'about'},
        {'title': "Add article ", 'url_name': 'add_page'},
        {'title': "Feedback ", 'url_name': 'contact'},
        {'title': "To come ", 'url_name': 'login'}
]


class DataMixin:
    def get_user_context(self, **kwargs):
        context = kwargs
        cats = Category.objects.all()
        context['menu'] = menu
        context['cats'] = cats
        if 'cat_selected' not in context:
            context['cat_selected'] = 0
        return context
```

Next, we set

context['cat_selected'] = 0

and check if 'cat_selected' not in

context. If we somehow define the ****kwargs** key within the parameters of the function def **get_user_context(self, **kwargs),**

then in the context if **'cat_selected'** not in context, this key will be present, and in this case, we won't override it. If this key is absent, then by default, we create

context['cat_selected'] = 0.

Finally, we return the context using return context.

Now, moving to **views.py**, let's begin by importing everything we've defined in utils:

from .utils import *

```
 8          from .forms import *
 9          from .models import *
10          from .utils import *
```

Next, in the class **Dir_travelHome**,

we'll start by specifying our mixin first. After that, we'll eliminate duplication.

```
class Dir_travelHome(DataMixin, ListView):

    model = Dir_travel

    template_name = 'traveler/index.html'

    context_object_name = 'posts'


def get_context_data(self, *, object_list=None, **kwargs):

    context = super().get_context_data(**kwargs)

    c_def = self.get_user_context(title='Homepage')

    return  dict(list(context.items()) + list(c_def.items()))
```

```
13          class Dir_travelHome(DataMixin, ListView):
14              model = Dir_travel
15              template_name = 'traveler/index.html'
16              context_object_name = 'posts'
17
18
19              def get_context_data(self, *, object_list=None, **kwargs):
20                  context = super().get_context_data(**kwargs)
21                  c_def = self.get_user_context(title='Main page')
22                  return  dict(list(context.items()) + list(c_def.items()))
```

We call the **get_user_context** method using self because we can access all the methods of the base class.

We pass it one named parameter,

title='Homepage'.

Everything else will be automatically added to the context. The required common context will be determined by both dictionaries – context and **c_def**.

Now we need to merge these two dictionaries by creating a list from the first and second dictionaries:

dict(list(context.items()) + list(c_def.items())).

Let's see how all this will work. We'll run it as we remember, using the terminal command

Python manage.py runserver

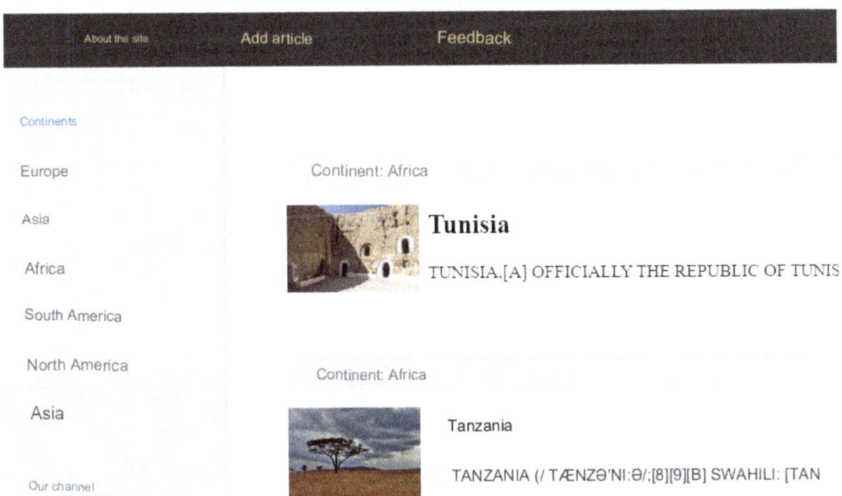

We see what the **Dir_travelHome** view class generates, and everything works the same as before.

Let's repeat this operation for all the other view classes, inheriting similarly from the previous **DataMixin** class.

```python
32  class AddPage(DataMixin, CreateView):
33      form_class = AddPostForm
34      template_name = 'traveler/addpage.html'
35
36      def get_context_data(self, *, oblect_list=None, **kwargs):
37          context = super().get_context_data(**kwargs)
38          c_def = self.get_user_context(title='Main page')
39          return dict(list(context.items()) + list(c_def.items()))
```

And don't forget to change the title, where we'll write **'Add an article**.' Then, we do the same thing.

```python
class ShowPost(DataMixin, DetailView):

    model = Dir_travel

    template_name = 'traveler/post.html'

    slug_url_kwarg = 'post_slug'

    context_object_name = 'post'


    def get_context_data(self, *, oblect_list=None, **kwargs):

        context = super().get_context_data(**kwargs)

        c_def = self.get_user_context(title= context['post'])

        return dict(list(context.items()) + list(c_def.items()))
```

```python
72  class ShowPost(DataMixin, DetailView):
73      model = Dir_travel
74      template_name = 'traveler/post.html'
75      slug_url_kwarg = 'post_slug'
76      context_object_name = 'post'
77
78      def get_context_data(self, *, oblect_list=None, **kwargs):
79          context = super().get_context_data(**kwargs)
80          c_def = self.get_user_context(title= context['post'])
81          return dict(list(context.items()) + list(c_def.items()))
```

The post title **(title = context['post'])** is formed based on the context

context = super().get_context_data(kwargs),**

which in turn was formed based on the **method ().get_context_data** of the base class **DetailView**.

Let's move on to the next class

```python
class Dir_travelCategory(DataMixin, ListView):
    model = Dir_travel
    template_name = 'traveler/index.html'
    context_object_name = 'posts'
    allow_empty = False

    def get_queryset(self):
        return Dir_travel.objects.filter(cat__slug=self.kwargs['cat_slug'], is_published=True)

    def get_context_data(self, *, oblect_list=None, **kwargs):
        context = super().get_context_data(**kwargs)
        c_def = self.get_user_context(title='Категория - ' + str(context['posts'][0].cat),
                    cat_selected = context['posts'][0].cat_id)
        return dict(list(context.items()) + list(c_def.items()))
```

```python
class Dir_travelCategory(DataMixin, ListView):
    model = Dir_travel
    template_name = 'traveler/index.html'
    context_object_name = 'posts'
    allow_empty = False

    def get_queryset(self):
        return Dir_travel.objects.filter(cat__slug=self.kwargs['cat_slug'], is_published=True)

    def get_context_data(self, *, oblect_list=None, **kwargs):
        context = super().get_context_data(**kwargs)
        c_def = self.get_user_context(title='Category - ' + str(context['posts'][0].cat),
                    cat_selected = context['posts'][0].cat_id)
        return dict(list(context.items()) + list(c_def.items()))
```

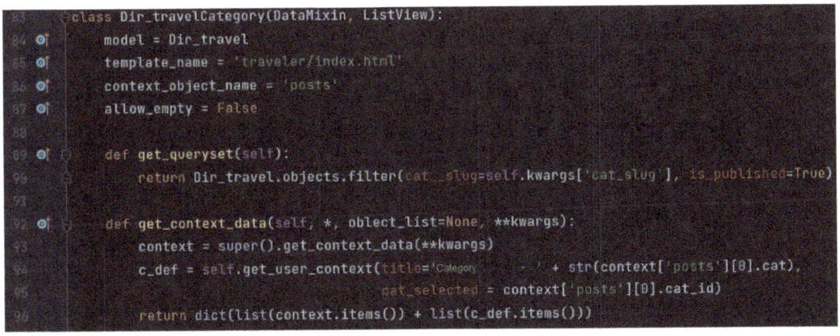

Let's check if everything works as intended. Open and refresh the page.

Ensure that everything works exactly as it did before the current changes. When working with mixins, you can use not only methods but also extract common attributes.

In **Django**, alongside view classes, you can use multiple mixins. Let's consider a mixin example related to user authentication, called **LoginRequiredMixin**. It allows restricting access to pages for unauthorized users.

For more details, you can read the documentation here:
https://docs.djangoproject.com/en/4.1/topics/auth/default/

This mixin can be used in conjunction with the view class. On our page, there is a tab **'Add an article'**

Adding an article

Title:

URL:

Article text:

Photo: Choose File | File not selected

Publication: ☑

Category: | Category not selected ▾

Add

We would like to allow only authorized users to add articles and restrict access to this page for everyone else.

To work with this mixin, it needs to be imported.

from django.contrib.auth.mixins import LoginRequiredMixin

```
from django.contrib.auth.mixins import LoginRequiredMixin
```

Then we'll add **LoginRequiredMixin** to the **AddPage** class, which handles the authentication page.

```
class AddPage(LoginRequiredMixin, DataMixin, CreateView):

    form_class = AddPostForm

    template_name = 'traveler/addpage.html'
```

⚠ This mixin is already in effect. Let's verify by refreshing the page.

Page not found (404)

Request Method: GET
Request URL: http://127.0.0.1:8000/accounts/login/?next=/addpage/

Using the URLconf defined in `travels.urls`, Django tried these URL patterns, in this order:

The page is not found.

This could indicate that we are not authenticated. If we go to the admin panel, authenticate, and then click on the **'Add an article'** tab, everything should work.

If we log out from the admin panel and then refresh the page with the form, it will again show a **404** page. That's what this mixin is responsible for.

But let's make our page more user-friendly. In other words, if the user is not authenticated, they should be redirected to the admin panel, where they can enter their login and password or authenticate.

To do this, in the **AddPage** class, we'll include the following attribute

```
class AddPage(LoginRequiredMixin, DataMixin, CreateView):

    form_class = AddPostForm

    template_name = 'traveler/addpage.html'

    login_url = '/admin'
```

```
33    class AddPage(LoginRequiredMixin, DataMixin, CreateView):
34        form_class = AddPostForm
35        template_name = 'traveler/addpage.html'
36        login_url = '/admin'
```

Which specifies the redirection address for an unregistered user.

However, this isn't the best practice to write it this way.

Therefore, let's use the following function

login_url = reverse_lazy('home')

So that we can use names to construct routes and, in this case, redirect to the main page.

But first, let's import this function

from django.urls import reverse_lazy

```
3    from django.http import Http404
4    from django.urls import reverse_lazy
5    from django.views.generic import ListView, DetailView, CreateView
```

Or, if we don't want to redirect to the main page but explicitly indicate that an unauthorized user cannot add an article, we can redirect them to page **303**.

raise_exception = True

```
33   class AddPage(LoginRequiredMixin, DataMixin, CreateView):
34       form_class = AddPostForm
35       template_name = 'traveler/addpage.html'
36       login_url = reverse_lazy('home')
37       raise_exception = True
```

And then, if the user is not authorized, they will see the page

403 Forbidden

If the user logs in

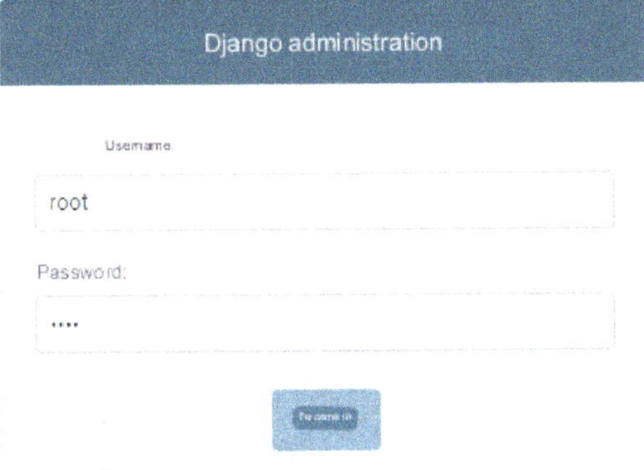

And clicks on the **'Add Article'** tab, they will see

Adding an article

This mixin only works in conjunction with view classes.

If we're using view functions, to restrict access, we should use a decorator.

In this case

@login_required

We'll restrict unauthorized users from accessing the '**About**' page

@login_required

def about(request):

 return render(request, 'traveler/about.html', {'menu': menu, 'title': ' About page'})

```
36      @login_required
31    ⊟def about(request):
32          return render(request, 'traveler/about.html', {'menu': menu, 'title': 'About the site'})
```

And, of course, this decorator needs to be imported.

from django.contrib.auth.decorators import login_required

```
4      from django.urls import reverse_lazy
5      from django.contrib.auth.decorators import login_required
6      from django.views.generic import ListView, DetailView, CreateView
```

Now, if the user tries to access the '**About**' page without being logged in, they will encounter an issue

Without dwelling on this, let's ensure that unauthorized users don't see the '**Add Article**' tab.

However, as soon as a user logs in, this tab automatically appears, providing the ability to create a post.

The easiest way to implement this functionality is through **DataMixin**, as it helps us pass the main menu

```
3   menu = [{'title': "About the ", 'url_name': 'about'},
4          {'title': "Add article ", 'url_name': 'add_page'}
5          {'title': "Feedback ", 'url_name': 'contact'},
6          {'title': "To come in ", 'url_name': 'login'}
```

Instead of the line

context['menu'] = menu

in the class **DataMixin**

we'll add the following few lines

```
class DataMixin:
  def get_user_context(self, **kwargs):
    context = kwargs
    cats = Category.objects.all()

    user_menu = menu.copy()
    if not self.request.user.is_authenticated:
      user_menu.pop(1)
    context['menu'] = user_menu

    context['cats'] = cats
    if 'cat_selected' not in context:
      context['cat_selected'] = 0
```

```python
class DataMixin:

    def get_user_context(self, **kwargs):
        context = kwargs
        cats = Category.objects.all()


        user_menu = menu.copy()
        if not self.request.user.is_authenticated:
            user_menu.pop(1)
        context['menu'] = user_menu


        context['cats'] = cats
        if 'cat_selected' not in context:
            context['cat_selected'] = 0
```

When the **get_user_context** method is called, we make a copy of the dictionary with **user_menu = menu.copy(),** that is, the entire collection

menu = [{'title': " About page ", 'url_name': 'about'},

{'title': " Add Article ", 'url_name': 'add_page'},

{'title': " Feedback ", 'url_name': 'contact'},

{'title': " Log In ", 'url_name': 'login'}

We save the link to this menu in the variable **user_menu.**

Then, if

if not self.request.user.is_authenticated:

i.e., if **is_authenticated** is **False**, the user is not authenticated. If **True**, then they are authenticated accordingly.

If the user is not authenticated, it means we remove the second element from the **user_menu** collection using **user_menu.pop(1),** which is at index **1**.

{'title': " Add Article ", 'url_name': 'add_page'},

For unauthorized users, we won't have this line, but for authorized ones, it will be present.

And in the context, we're already passing a link to this menu *context['menu'] = user_menu*

Let's go to our website and check.

If the user is not logged in, this menu item shouldn't be present. If we access the admin panel and log in, this menu item should appear.

And let's make one more improvement.

Let's go to the website and click on the '**Antarctica**' tab.

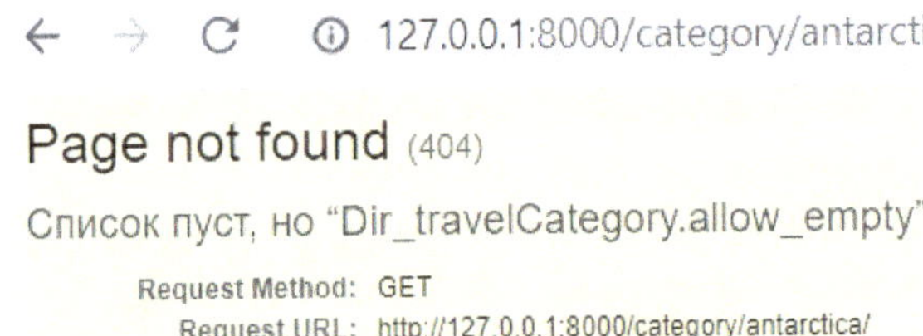

As we can see, the page isn't found because there are no posts in this category. Let's make it so that if any category doesn't have any posts, it doesn't need to be displayed.

Let's go to the **DataMixin** class and change the line

cats = Category.objects.all()

to

cats = Category.objects.annotate(Count('dir_travel'))

For the Count function to work, it needs to be imported

from django.db.models import Count

```
10  o↓  class DataMixin:
11          def get_user_context(self, **kwargs):
12              context = kwargs
13              cats = Category.objects.all()
14              cats = Category.objects.annotate(Count('dir_travel'))
```

```
1      from .models import *
2      from django.db.models import Count
```

Now, in the **'cats'** collection, we have another property related to the number of posts associated with this category. We can use this attribute at the template level.

Let's go to **base.html** and where the categories are displayed, let's add a condition

{% for c in cats %}

{% if c.dir_travel__count > 0 %}

    {% if c.pk == cat_selected %}

      <li class="selected">{{c.name}}</li>

    {% else %}

      <li> <a href="{{ c.get_absolute_url }}">{{c.name}}</a></li>

    {% endif %}

{% endif %}

{% endfor %}

```
44    {% for c in cats %}
45    {% if c.dir_travel__count > 0 %}
46            {% if c.pk == cat_selected %}
47                <li class="selected">{{c.name}}</li>
48            {% else %}
49                <li> <a href="{{ c.get_absolute_url }}">{{c.name}}</a></li>
50            {% endif %}
51    {% endif %}
52    {% endfor %}
```

If the object **'c'**, which is an element of the **'cats'** collection, has a value for the property **c.dir_travel__count > 0**, indicating that this category has at least one post,

then we display this post.

Now, we're only displaying categories that have at least one post.

Let's update our website.

Continents

Asia

Africa

Europe

North America

South America

Our channel

And, as you can see, the category without any posts is absent.

Pagination

Pagination, or as often called, paging, is needed when there's a long list of posts on a page that impairs text readability. This option allows breaking long lists into multiple pages and displaying navigational links at the bottom for each page, presented as easily accessible links.

For more details on pagination, you can read at the following link...

https://django.fun/ru/docs/django/4.1/topics/pagination/

It's worth noting that this option can be applied using various approaches.

1. Can be used separately.
2. In ListView, where pagination is already embedded.
3. Pagination handling in the template.
4. For view functions.
5. Using attributes and methods of the Paginator class

Let's go over the first approach.

We'll open the **Python** console and, first of all, import

from django.core.paginator import Paginator

We'll use it with some list.

We'll take an arbitrary list, for example...

Dir_travel = ['ukraine', 'poland', 'austria', 'germany', 'italy', 'spain', 'hungary']

```
Python 3.10.7 (tags/v3.10.7:6cc6b13, Sep  5 2022, 14:08:36) [MSC v.1933 64 bit (AMD64)] on win32
>>> from django.core.paginator import Paginator
>>> Dir_travel = ['ukraine', 'poland', 'austria', 'germany', 'italy', 'spain', 'hungary']
```

And we'll work with this list.

First, we'll create an instance of the **Paginator** class

p = Paginator(Dir_travel, 3)

To do this, we pass the Dir_travel list to its constructor, with which it will work.

3 - the number of items per page.

Now we can work with the properties of this class.

For example, let's determine the number of items in this list.

p.count

```
>>> p = Paginator(Dir_travel, 3)
>>> p.count
7
```

We'll obtain the number of pages

p.num_pages

We'll get **3, since 7/3 = 3** pages where elements will be displayed.

If we want to work with the first page, the object 'p' has such a method

p1 = p.page(1)

page(1) – The page number we want to work with.

And now the link p1 will refer to the first page.

We'll get a list of this first page

p1.object_list

```
>>> p1 = p.page(1)
>>> p1.object_list
['ukraine', 'poland', 'austria']
```

We can determine if there's a next page using the method...

p1.has_next()

```
>>> p1.has_next()
True
```

We can determine if there's a previous page using the command...

p1.has_previous()

```
>>> p1.has_previous()
False
```

We can determine if there's any pagination at all using the command...

p1.has_other_pages()

```
>>> p1.has_other_pages()
True
```

We'll determine the number of the next page

p1.next_page_number()

```
>>> p1.next_page_number()
2
```

Now let's see how all of this can be used on our website.

As we remember, the **Dir_travelHome** class is responsible for displaying the main page, which is inherited from the base class **ListView**.

So, pagination is already built into this base class.

We just need to add one line

paginate_by = 3

Where the number 3 represents the quantity of items per page.

```
16   class Dir_travelHome(DataMixin, ListView):
17       paginate_by = 3
18       model = Dir_travel
19       template_name = 'traveler/index.html'
20       context_object_name = 'posts'
```

If we load the web server and navigate to the main page, refreshing it, we'll see only three posts.

However, if we use view functions instead of classes, we'll need to write a bit more code.

def about(request):

  contact_list = Dir_travel.objects.all()

  paginator = Paginator(contact_list, 3)

  page_number = request.GET.get('page')

  page_obj = paginator.get_page(page_number)

  return render(request, 'traveler/about.html', {'page_obj': page_obj, 'menu': menu, 'title': 'About the site'})

```python
def about(request):
    contact_list = Dir_travel.objects.all()
    paginator = Paginator(contact_list, 3)
    page_number = request.GET.get('page')
    page_obj = paginator.get_page(page_number)
    return render(request, 'traveler/about.html', {'page_obj': page_obj, 'menu': menu, 'title': 'О сайте'})
```

contact_list = Dir_travel.object.all() – We display a list of countries

paginator = Paginator(contact_list, 3) – We create a **Paginator** class

In order for us to use it, we need to import it

from django.core.paginator import Paginator

```python
from django.contrib.auth.mixins import LoginRequiredMixin
from django.core.paginator import Paginator
```

page_number = request.Get.get('page') – We retrieve the page number from the current **GET request**, where we take the **'page'** parameter formed within this request.

page_obj = paginator.get_page(page_number) – The list of elements on the current page, where we access the instance of the **paginator** class and utilize a function... **get_page** We access the page obtained from the **GET** request, **'page_number,'** and then the **'page_obj'** list should be passed to the template

return render(request, 'traveler/about.html', {**'page_obj': page_obj**, menu': menu, 'title': 'About the site'})

Next, let's open the **about.html** template and set up the display of the list.

{% extends 'traveler/base.html' %}

{% block content %}

<h1>{{title}}</h1>

{% for contact in page_obj %}

* {{ contact }} *

{% endfor %}

{% endblock %}

```
1    {% extends 'traveler/base.html' %}
2
3    {% block content %}
4    <h1>{{title}}</h1>
5
6    {% for contact in page_obj %}
7    <p>{{ contact }}</p>
8    {% endfor %}
9
10   {% endblock %}
```

We iterate through the **page_obj** collection and display it as paragraphs ** {{ contact }} **

Let's open the **'About the site'** page and check how everything is functioning.

About the site

Tunisia

Tanzania

Netherlands

So, we've obtained a list of the first three countries. If we want to move to the next page, we need to specify the next page in the **GET** request using the **'page'** parameter

127.0.0.1:8000/about/?page=2

About the site

Tanzania

Zimbabwe

Cambodia

And so on.

Next, let's display a list of links to different pages. To do this, let's go to the **about.html** template and add the following lines of code.

```
<nav>
  <ul>
    {% for p in page_obj.paginator.page_range %}
    <li>
      <a href="?page={{ p }}">{{ p }}</a>
    </li>
    {% endfor %}
  </ul>
</nav>
```

```
10    <nav>
11      <ul>
12          {% for p in page_obj.paginator.page_range %}
13          <li>
14              <a href="?page={{ p }}">{{ p }}</a>
15          </li>
16          {% endfor %}
17      </ul>
18    </nav>
19
20    {% endblock %}
```

We access the **page_obj** object, which is a reference to a specific page in the paginator, and then we access the paginator property and its **page_range** method, which returns an iterator allowing us to generate page numbers. We return this iterator without parentheses because in templates, all methods are called exactly in this manner. The templating engine will call this method itself. Next, using the 'for' tag, we'll generate, at each iteration, the page number as a regular list

<li>

<a href="?page={{ p }}">{{ p }}</a>

</li>

Let's navigate to the page and see how everything works.

About the site

Italy

Germany

Poland

- 1
- 2
- 3
- 4
- 5
- 6

Next, we won't improve anything further, as it was just an example of pagination working with a view function. Let's move on to view classes and do the same thing, but this time on the home page. We've already done something on the home page, namely, splitting it into three posts. Let's add links to pages, just as we did in the previous example. Let's open the **base.html** template, which is responsible for displaying pages on our site, and add the following lines

```
<nav class="list-pages">
  <ul>
    {% for p in paginator.page_range %}
    <li class="page-num">
      <a href="?page={{ p }}">{{ p }}</a>
    </li>
    {% endfor %}
  </ul>
</nav>
```

```html
71   <nav class="list-pages">
72       <ul>
73           {% for p in paginator.page_range %}
74           <li class="page-num">
75               <a href="?page={{ p }}">{{ p }}</a>
76           </li>
77           {% endfor %}
78       </ul>
79   </nav>
```

Followed the same pattern as the previous example. Added a few styles

class="list-pages"

class="page-num"

To make them work, you need to add them to **styles.css**

```css
.list-pages {
    text-align: center;
    margin: 0 0 20px 0;
}
.list-pages ul {
    margin: 20px 0 0 0;
    padding: 0;
    list-style: none;
}
.list-pages ul li {
    display: inline-block;
    margin: 0 20px 0 0;
}
.list-pages a {
    color: #000;
    font-size: 24px;
```

```css
        text-decoration: none;
}
.list-pages .page-num, .page-num-selected {
        display: inline-block;
        width: 60px;
        height: 44px;
        padding: 16px 0 0 0;
        border: 1px solid #d0d0d0;
        border-radius: 30px;
}
.list-pages .page-num:hover {
        box-shadow: 3px 3px 1px #d0d0d0;
}
.list-pages .page-num-selected {
        border: none;
        color: #000;
        font-size: 20px;
}
.list-pages .page-num-selected:hover {
        box-shadow: none;
```

Next, using a 'for' loop, we iterate through the **page_range** iterator. We access it directly through the paginator object because in classes, in the base class **ListView**, the paginator object is automatically passed to the index.html template. Now let's see how all of this will be displayed. Let's open our site.

1   2   3   4   5

Alright, sure, it's indeed better.

The **index.html** template is responsible for the main page. It's quite logical to ask why we placed the code in the base.html template.

It's all about practicality and following the 'Don't Repeat Yourself' paradigm. The thing is, over time, there might be a need for pagination in continent-specific categories, if not already present. To avoid duplicating code, it's more practical to write it once. If we navigate through categories, for example, 'Europe,' we won't find pagination there. We'll fix that later.

There's another aspect to consider. While using pagination to select a page, we don't see which page we're currently on. We need to somehow highlight this number by disabling the link. This way, it stands out among other buttons that are highlighted as links.

So, let's open **base.html** and make some modifications to our code

```
<nav class="list-pages">
  <ul>
    {% for p in paginator.page_range %}
    {% if page_obj.number == p %}
    <li class="page-num page-num-selected">{{ p }}</li>
    {% else %}
    <li class="page-num">
      <a href="?page={{ p }}">{{ p }}</a>
    </li>
    {% endif %}
    {% endfor %}
  </ul>
</nav>
```

```
71  <nav class="list-pages">
72      <ul>
73          {% for p in paginator.page_range %}
74          {% if page_obj.number == p %}
75          <li class="page-num page-num-selected">{{ p }}</li>
76          {% else %}
77          <li class="page-num">
78              <a href="?page={{ p }}">{{ p }}</a>
79          </li>
80          {% endif %}
81          {% endfor %}
82      </ul>
83  </nav>
```

If the current page number matches the number '**p**'...

{% if page_obj.number == p %}

Then we display this list item as plain text

<li class="page-num page-num-selected">{{ p }}</li>

Additionally, let's add styles for formatting

class="page-num page-num-selected"

It's all provided in the **style.css** file.

Otherwise **{% else %}**

The same list as before

<li class="page-num">

<a href="?page={{ p }}">{{ p }}</a>

</li>

Let's go to the main page and refresh.

1   2   3   4   5

That's exactly how it was intended.

Let's add our pagination to all pages of the site to avoid duplicating code. For displaying categories, we rely on...

Dir_travelCategory

If you take a closer look, in...

class Dir_travelCategory(DataMixin, ListView):

and

class Dir_travelHome(DataMixin, ListView):

there's a common class called **DataMixin**. That's where we'll define the attribute...

paginate_by = 3

and consequently remove it from **Dir_travelHome**. As a result, we'll have...

class DataMixin:

  paginate_by = 3

```python
class DataMixin:
    paginate_by = 3
    def get_user_context(self, **kwargs):
        context = kwargs
        cats = Category.objects.all()
        cats = Category.objects.annotate(Count('dir_travel'))
```

Let's navigate to the page and ensure everything is functioning as intended. If we visit a page with fewer than three posts, we'll see the number 1 without a link because there are no more posts, indicating that in this case, there's only one page

1

Let's ensure that when there are 3 or fewer posts—meaning the entire list fits on one page—we don't need to display any list. Let's navigate to the **base.html** template and use a specific method.

has_other_pages

{% if page_obj.has_other_pages %}

```
66    <!-- Блок контента -->
67        <div class="content-text">
68    {% block content %}
69    {% endblock %}
70    {% if page_obj.has_other_pages %}
71    <nav class="list-pages">
72        <ul>
73            {% for p in paginator.page_range %}
74            {% if page_obj.number == p %}
75            <li class="page-num page-num-selected">{{ p }}</li>
76            {% else %}
77            <li class="page-num">
78                <a href="?page={{ p }}">{{ p }}</a>
79            </li>
80            {% endif %}
81            {% endfor %}
82        </ul>
83    </nav>
84    {% endif %}
85        </div>
```

This method returns True if there are multiple pages and False if there's only one page.

There's another aspect to consider. If we have a lot of posts, there will be many corresponding links. It would be optimal to display, for example, two numbers on the left and two numbers on the right.

How can we do this? In our template, we have the **'page_obj'** object with its **'number'** property, indicating the current page being displayed. Additionally, in the template, we iterate over the 'p' element using a 'for' loop

{% for p in paginator.page_range %}

We can set boundaries for this **'p'** page using the **'add'** filter to display the list. For instance, we can subtract **2**

page_obj.number|add:-2

and increase by **2**

page_obj.number|add:2

Let's see how we can do this at the **base.html** template level

```html
<nav class="list-pages">

  <ul>

    {% for p in paginator.page_range %}

    {% if page_obj.number == p %}

    <li class="page-num page-num-selected">{{ p }}</li>

    {% elif p >= page_obj.number|add:-2 and page_obj.number|add:2 %}

    <li class="page-num">

      <a href="?page={{ p }}">{{ p }}</a>

    </li>

    {% endif %}

    {% endfor %}


</nav>
```

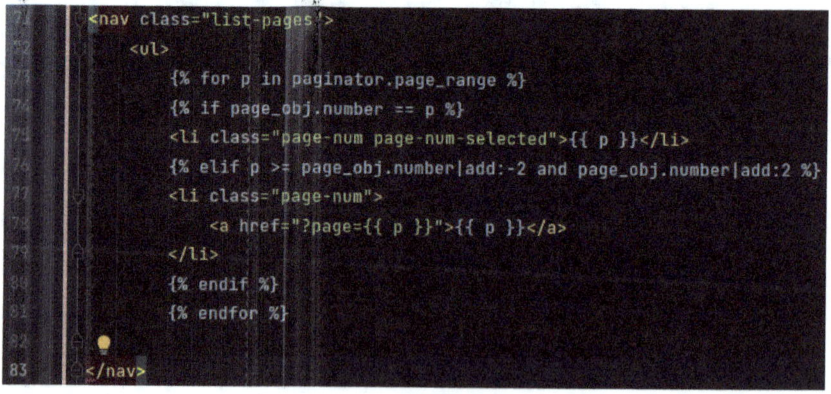

```html
<nav class="list-pages">
    <ul>
        {% for p in paginator.page_range %}
        {% if page_obj.number == p %}
        <li class="page-num page-num-selected">{{ p }}</li>
        {% elif p >= page_obj.number|add:-2 and page_obj.number|add:2 %}
        <li class="page-num">
            <a href="?page={{ p }}">{{ p }}</a>
        </li>
        {% endif %}
        {% endfor %}

</nav>
```

If the object **p** is not the currently selected page and falls within the selected range, i.e., greater than or equal to **-2** and less than or equal to **+2**

```
>= page_obj.number|add:-2 and page_obj.number|add:2
```

Then we display the link

```html
<li class="page-num">
  <a href="?page={{ p }}">{{ p }}</a>
</li>
```

Let's add two more buttons that allow navigating to the previous page and the next one.

```
{% if page_obj.has_previous %}
    <li class="page-num">
      <a href="?page={{ page_obj.previous_page_number }}">&lt;</a>
    </li>
{% endif %}
```

```
74        {% if page_obj.has_previous %}
75        <li class="page-num">
76            <a href="?page={{ page_obj.previous_page_number }}">&lt;</a>
77        </li>
78        {% endif %}
```

We're checking here if the previous page exists

page_obj.previous_page_number

using the method **previous_page**_number. If it returns True, we can display this button as an angled bracket '<' and form the link using the **previous_page_number**.

In a similar manner, let's add a button for the next page.

```
{% if page_obj.has_next %}
    <li class="page-num">
      <a href="?page={{ page_obj.next_page_number }}">&gt;</a>
    </li>
{% endif %}
```

```
90        {% if page_obj.has_next %}
91        <li class="page-num">
92            <a href="?page={{ page_obj.next_page_number }}">&gt;</a>
93        </li>
94        {% endif %}
```

We're checking if there's a next page **has_next**

And create a link to the next page if it exists

next_page_number

as well as the right angled bracket

>

Let's go to the website and refresh

User registration on the website

To access additional features, users can undergo a registration process through a specialized form. For instance, to have a personal account or leave comments. We have the following fields available, detailed information about which can be found on the website in the admin panel.

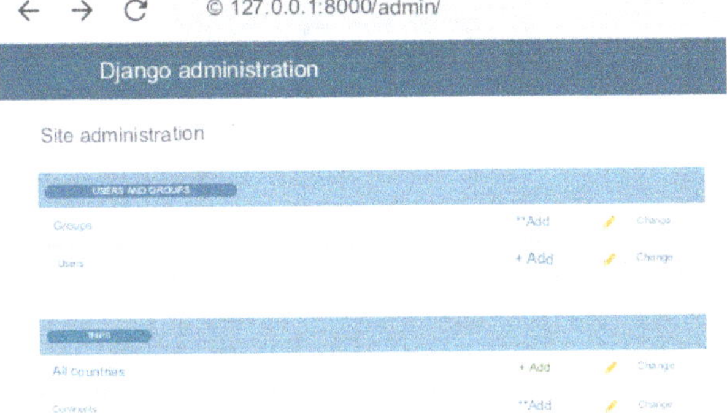

Click on the 'Users' tab, then select the registered user 'root'. Currently, we only have one registered user.

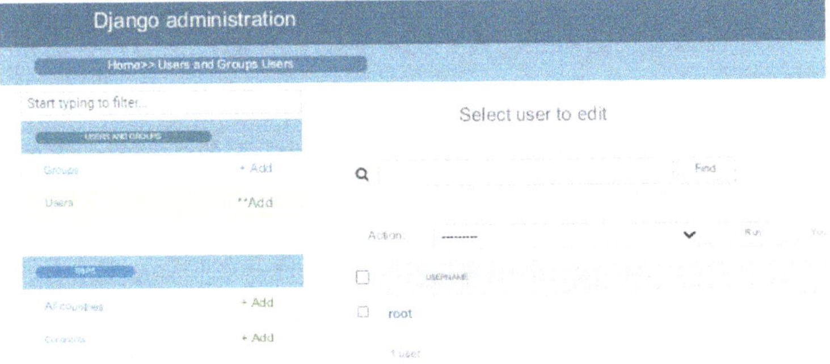

On the next screenshot, we can see all the available fields.

Change user

root

Username: root

Obligatory field. No more than 150 characters. Only letters

Password: algorithm: pkdf2_sha256 iterations: 390000 salt:

Passwords are stored encrypted, so there is no

Personal information

Name:

Surname:

E-mail address: root@gmail.com

As seen in the screenshot, the following fields are available to us: Username, Password, First Name, Last Name, and Email Address. Additionally, there is a status displayed below

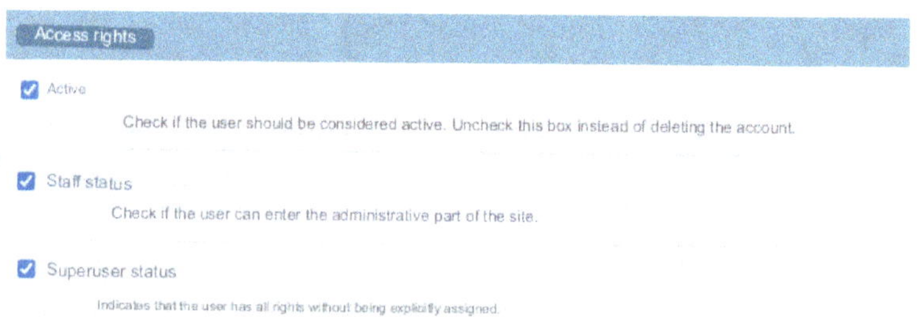

So, we can request all these fields from the user during registration. Let's start by adding a link for new user registration.

First, let's navigate to the base.html template and locate where the main menu is displayed. Then, we'll slightly modify this block.

```
{% for m in menu %}
    <li><a href="{% url m.url_name %}">{{m.title}}</a></li>
```

```
{% endfor %}
    <li class='last'><a href="{% url 'register' %}">Регистрация</a> | <a href="{% url 'login' %}">Войти</a></li>
```

```
{% for m in menu %}
        <li><a href="{% url m.url_name %}">{{m.title}}</a></li>
{% endfor %}
        <li class="last"><a href="{% url 'register' %}"> Registration    </a> | <a href="{% url 'login' %}">To come</a></li>
```

Let's go to **utils.py** and remove the last item from the main menu

```
menu = [{'title': " About the website ", 'url_name': 'about'},
    {'title': " Add an article ", 'url_name': 'add_page'},
    {'title': " Feedback ", 'url_name': 'contact'}
    ]
```

```
menu = [{'title': "About the site", 'url_name': 'about'},
        {'title': "Add article ", 'url_name': 'add_page'},
        {'title': "Feedback ", 'url_name': 'contact'}
        ]
```

Additionally, for the Registration button to work, we need to define the **'register'** URL route. Let's navigate to urls.py and add the line

```
path('login/', login, name='login'),
path('register/', login, name='register'),
```

```
path('login/', login, name='login'),
path('register/', login, name='register'),
```

Let's go to the website and refresh the page.

Everything is functioning. However, the registration isn't operational yet as it currently uses a simple placeholder function. Let's fix that.

Navigate to urls.py and replace the line with:

path('register/', login, name='register'),

=>

path('register/', RegisterUser.as_view(), name='register'),

```
10          path('login/', login, name='login'),
11        💡 path('register/', RegisterUser.as_view(), name='register'),
12          path('post/<slug:post_slug>/', ShowPost.as_view(), name='post'),
```

Next, let's go to the **views.py** file and define the RegisterUser view class. Since this class will work with a form that will be inputting data into the database, we'll inherit from the standard **CreateView** class. Additionally, we'll include the standard **DataMixin** mixin.

class RegisterUser(DataMixin, CreateView):

  form_class = UserCreationForm

  template_name = 'traveler/register.html'

  success_url = reverse_lazy('login')

```
115     class RegisterUser(DataMixin, CreateView):
116         form_class = UserCreationForm
117         template_name = 'traveler/register.html'
118         success_url = reverse_lazy('login')
```

form_class - This attribute will reference the standard **Django UserCreationForm**, which is used for user registration.

template_name = 'traveler/register.html' - Link to the template we'll be using.

success_url = reverse_lazy('login') - Redirect to the URL upon successful user registration.

Next, let's prepare the context for the template. This should be familiar to us already.

*def get_context_data(self, *, oblect_list=None, **kwargs):*

*context = super().get_context_data(**kwargs)*

c_def = self.get_user_context(title=' Registration ')

return dict(list(context.items()) + list(c_def.items()))

```
115      class RegisterUser(DataMixin, CreateView):
116          form_class = UserCreationForm
117          template_name = 'traveler/register.html'
118          success_url = reverse_lazy('login')
119
120          def get_context_data(self, *, oblect_list=None, **kwargs):
121              context = super().get_context_data(**kwargs)
122              c_def = self.get_user_context(title='Registration ')
123              return dict(list(context.items()) + list(c_def.items()))
```

Next, we need to import the **UserCreationForm** class so that we can use it.

from django.contrib.auth.forms import UserCreationForm

```
7      from django.contrib.auth.mixins import LoginRequiredMixin
8      from django.contrib.auth.forms import UserCreationForm
9      from django.core.paginator import Paginator
```

And let's create the **register.html** template. Add our template to the app.

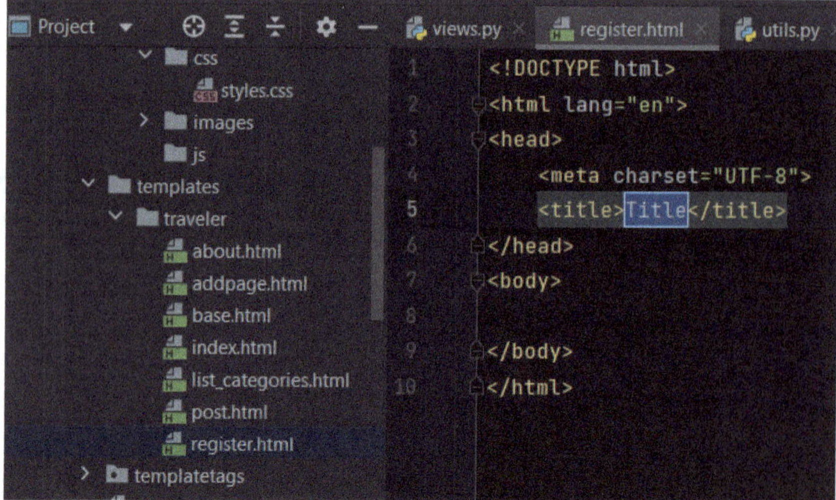


```html
<!DOCTYPE html>
<html lang="en">
<head>
    <meta charset="UTF-8">
    <title>Title</title>
</head>
<body>

</body>
</html>
```

Instead of the standard code, let's add the following lines.

```
{% extends 'traveler/base.html' %}

{% block content %}
<h1>{{title}}</h1>
<form method="post">
    {% csrf_token %}
    {{ form.as_p }}
    <button type="submit"> Registration </button>
</form>
{% endblock %}
```

```
1    {% extends 'traveler/base.html' %}
2
3    {% block content %}
4    <h1>{{title}}</h1>
5
6    <form method="post">
7        {% csrf_token %}
8        {{ form.as_p }}
9        <button type="submit">Registration </button>
10   </form>
11
12   {% endblock %}
```

Expanding the base template

{% extends 'traveler/base.html' %}

Displaying a first-level heading

<h1>{{title}}</h1>

Below is all standard.

Let's see how this will work.

Let's go to our website and click on the '**Registration**' link.

Registration

Username: Required [   ] field. No more than 150 characters. Letters, numbers, and @/./+/-/_ symbols only.

Password: [   ]

- The password should not be too similar to your other personal information.
- Your password must contain at least 8 characters.
- The password should not be too simple or common.
- The password cannot contain only numbers.

Password confirmation: [   ] To confirm, please enter your password again.

[Registration]

The standard form with three fields is displayed.

Let's improve the appearance of the form.

To do this, we will create our own form class in the **forms.py** file

```python
class RegisterUserForm(UserCreationForm):
    class Meta:
        model = User
        fields = ['username', 'password1', 'password2']
        widgets = {
            'username': forms.TextInput(attrs={'class': 'form-input'}),
            'password1': forms.PasswordInput(attrs={'class': 'form-input'}),
            'password2': forms.PasswordInput(attrs={'class': 'form-input'}),
        }
```

```python
class RegisterUserForm(UserCreationForm):
    class Meta:
        model = User
        fields = ['username', 'password1', 'password2']
        widgets = {
            'username': forms.TextInput(attrs={'class': 'form-input'}),
            'password1': forms.PasswordInput(attrs={'class': 'form-input'}),
            'password2': forms.PasswordInput(attrs={'class': 'form-input'}),
        }
```

Let's import the base class **UserCreationForm**, which we'll be extending

```python
from django.contrib.auth.forms import UserCreationForm
```

```python
from django.contrib.auth.forms import UserCreationForm
from django.contrib.auth.models import User
```

Also, let's import the **User** model

```python
from django.contrib.auth.models import User
```

We specify the fields that will be displayed in our form.

```python
fields = ['username', 'password1', 'password2']
```

and the formatting for each of these fields' widgets. The names of these fields, namely **'username', 'password1', 'password2'**, can be found as follows:

Access the admin panel and then navigate to users

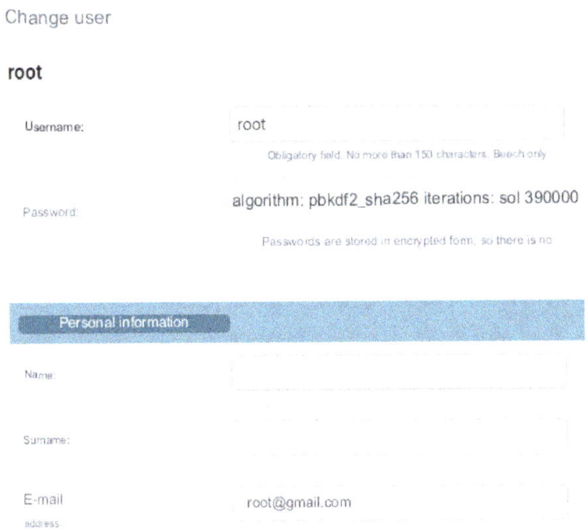

Change user

root

Username: root

Obligatory field. No more than 150 characters. Beech only

Password: algorithm: pbkdf2_sha256 iterations: sol 390000

Passwords are stored in encrypted form, so there is no

Personal information

Name:

Surname:

E-mail address: root@gmail.com

Next, hover over the '**Username**' field, right-click, and select '**Inspect**' to open the code inspector. Look for the line

```
▼<label class="required" for="id_username">
    "Имя пользователя:"
    ::after
  </label>
  <input type="text" name="username" value="root" class="vTextField" maxlength=
  "150" autocapitalize="none" autocomplete="username" required id="id_username">
    == $0
 ▶<div class="help" id="id_username_helptext"> ⋯ </div>
  </div>
</div>
```

Similarly, locate the other fields. For instance, to identify the password names, click on the **form**

hash: OK758m** ***********************************

This user's password, but you can change it using this form.

And navigate

Change password: root

Enter a new password for the root user.

Password:

The password should not be too similar to your other personal information.
Your password must contain at least 8 characters.
The password should not be too simple and common.
The password cannot consist only of numbers.

The password again):

To confirm, please enter your password again.

And launch the code inspector for the **'Password'** field

```
<input type="password" name="password1" autocomplete="new-password" autofocus
required id="id_password1"> == $0
```

And 'Password' (once again)

```
<input type="password" name="password2" autocomplete="new-password" required id=
"id_password2"> == $0
```

This way, using the browser, you can view the names of all fields. In the **view.py** file, we should use this form. Accordingly, in the **RegisterUser** class, we'll modify the line...

```
class RegisterUser(DataMixin, CreateView):

    form_class = RegisterUserForm

    template_name = 'traveler/register.html'

    success_url = reverse_lazy('login')


    def get_context_data(self, *, oblect_list=None, **kwargs):

        context = super().get_context_data(**kwargs)

        c_def = self.get_user_context(title=' Registration ')

        return dict(list(context.items()) + list(c_def.items()))
```

```python
115    class RegisterUser(DataMixin, CreateView):
116        form_class = RegisterUserForm
117        template_name = 'traveler/register.html'
118        success_url = reverse_lazy('login')
119
120        def get_context_data(self, *, oblect_list=None, **kwargs):
121            context = super().get_context_data(**kwargs)
122            c_def = self.get_user_context(title='Registration')
123            return dict(list(context.items()) + list(c_def.items()))
```

Let's also add styles for all fields since the standard **Django** method didn't apply styles to all fields.

Registration

Username: [________________________]   Obligatory field. No more

Password: [______________]

- The password should not be too similar to your other personal information.
- Your password must contain at least 8 characters.
- The password should not be too simple and common.
- The password cannot consist only of numbers.

Password confirmation: [______________] | Please enter to confirm

[Registration]

As we can see, styles were only applied to the **Username field**. Therefore, we'll assign styles somewhat differently.

```python
class RegisterUserForm(UserCreationForm):
    username = forms.CharField(label='Login', widget=forms.TextInput(attrs={'class': 'form-input'}))

    email = forms.EmailField(label='Email', widget=forms.EmailInput(attrs={'class': 'form-input'}))

    password1 = forms.CharField(label='Password', widget=forms.PasswordInput(attrs={'class': 'form-input'}))

    password2 = forms.CharField(label='Confirm password', widget=forms.PasswordInput(attrs={'class': 'form-input'}))
```

class Meta:

model = User

fields = ('username', 'email', 'password1', 'password2')

```python
class RegisterUserForm(UserCreationForm):
    username = forms.CharField(label='Login', widget=forms.TextInput(attrs={'class': 'form-input'}))
    email = forms.EmailField(label='Email', widget=forms.EmailInput(attrs={'class': 'form-input'}))
    password1 = forms.CharField(label='Password', widget=forms.PasswordInput(attrs={'class': 'form-input'}))
    password2 = forms.CharField(label='Password repeat', widget=forms.PasswordInput(attrs={'class': 'form-input'}))

    class Meta:
        model = User
        fields = ('username', 'email', 'password1', 'password2')
```

Next, let's open the **register.html** file and make some adjustments.

Instead of the line

{{ form.as_p }}

Let's write it manually

{% extends 'traveler/base.html' %}

{% block content %}
<h1>{{title}}</h1>

<form method="post">
{% csrf_token %}

{% for f in form %}
<p><label class="form-label" for="{{ f.id_for_label }}">{{f.label}}: </label>{{ f }}</p>
<div class="form-error">{{ f.errors }}</div>
{% endfor %}

<button type="submit"> Registration </button>

```
</form>

{% endblock %}
```

```
1    {% extends 'traveler/base.html' %}
2
3    {% block content %}
4    <h1>{{title}}</h1>
5
6    <form method="post">
7        {% csrf_token %}
8
9        {% for f in form %}
10       <p><label class="form-label" for="{{ f.id_for_label }}">{{f.label}}: </label>{{ f }}</p>
11       <div class="form-error">{{ f.errors }}</div>
12       {% endfor %}
13
14           <button type="submit">Registration </button>
15   </form>
16
17   {% endblock %}
```

We're going through all the form fields

{% for f in form %}

And manually constructing all these fields

<p><label class="form-label" for="{{ f.id_for_label }}">{{f.label}}: </label>{{ f }}</p>

If there are any errors, they will be displayed using

<div class="form-error">{{ f.errors }}</div>

Let's go to the website, refresh the page, and immediately enter the details for the new user

Registration

Login: user_1

Email: y@i.com

Password:

Password repeat:

The entered password is too short. It must contain at least 8 characters. The entered password is too wide.
The entered password consists of numbers only.

Registration

Registration

Login: user_1

A user with the same name already exists.

Email: y@i.com

Password:

Password repeat:

The entered passwords do not match.

Registration

As we can see, the system shows us errors if we've done something incorrectly. If everything is done correctly, it will redirect us to the next page

← → C ⓘ 127.0.0.1:8000/login/

Authorization

That's because we specified it that way

```
115     class RegisterUser(DataMixin, CreateView):
116         form_class = RegisterUserForm
117         template_name = 'traveler/register.html'
118         success_url = reverse_lazy('login')
```

If you go to the admin panel and click on the **Users** tab, you'll see the following window

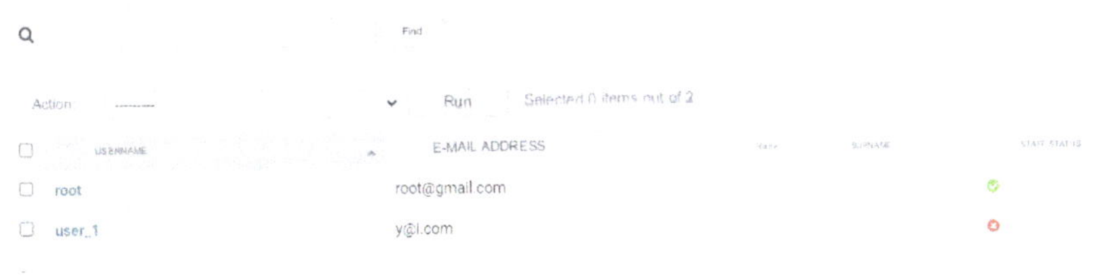

If you click on the username, you'll see the following window with settings

Change user

user_1

Username:

user_1

Obligatory field. No more than 150 characters. Only b

Password:

algorithm: pkdf2_sha256 iterations: 390000 sa

Passwords are stored encrypted, so no

Personal information

Name:

Surname:

E-mail
address

y@i.com

Access rights

☑ Active Check if the user should be considered active. Remove this checkbox

☐ Staff status
Check if the user can enter the administrative part of the site.

User authorization

First, in the **views.py** file, let's add a view responsible for the authorization form.

```python
class LoginUser(DataMixin, LoginView):
    form_class = AuthenticationForm
    template_name = 'traveler/login.html'

    def get_context_data(self, *, oblect_list=None, **kwargs):
        context = super().get_context_data(**kwargs)
        c_def = self.get_user_context(title=' Authorization ')
        return dict(list(context.items()) + list(c_def.items()))
```

```python
class LoginUser(DataMixin, LoginView):
    form_class = AuthenticationForm
    template_name = 'traveler/login.html'

    def get_context_data(self, *, oblect_list=None, **kwargs):
        context = super().get_context_data(**kwargs)
        c_def = self.get_user_context(title='Authorization ')
        return dict(list(context.items()) + list(c_def.items()))
```

This class will inherit from two base classes: **DataMixin** and **LoginView**. **LoginView** contains all the logic for the authorization of a new user. As we already know, to make this class work, it is necessary to import.

```python
from django.contrib.auth.views import LoginView
```

```python
from django.contrib.auth.views import LoginView
```

AuthenticationForm is the standard authentication form also provided by **Django.**

We also need to import it.

from django.contrib.auth.forms import AuthenticationForm

```
 9        from django.contrib.auth.forms import AuthenticationForm
10        from django.contrib.auth.views import LoginView
```

Our class, which we have just created, will use the logic of the **LoginView** class and the form of the **AuthenticationForm** class. The form will be displayed in the template **template_name = 'traveler/login.html'**.

And for creating the context for this template

*def get_context_data(self, *, oblect_list=None, **kwargs):*

*context = super().get_context_data(**kwargs)*

c_def = self.get_user_context(title=' Authorization ')

return dict(list(context.items()) + list(c_def.items()))

Let's create the **login.html** template

```
 1    {% extends 'traveler/base.html' %}
 2
 3    {% block content %}
 4    <h1>{{title}}</h1>
 5
 6    <form method="post">
 7        {% csrf_token %}
 8        {{ form.as_p }}
 9
10    <button type="submit">to come in</button>
11    </form>
12
13    {% endblock %}
```

It's a standard one. Let's create it similarly to the template for registration. Next, let's connect the view class to the route. Go to **urls.py** and add the line.

path('login/', loginUser.as_view(), name='login'),

```
10            path('login/', LoginUser.as_view(), name='login'),
11            path('register/', RegisterUser.as_view(), name='register'),
```

And finally, comment out or delete the function that was responsible for the placeholder page.

```
71    def login(request):
72        return HttpResponse("Authorization ")
```

We go to the website, click **'Login'**, and the standard authorization form is displayed.

Authorization

Username:

Password:

And this form is already functional.

If you enter the data of a previously registered user into the fields, the corresponding page will be displayed

Page not found (404)

Request Method: GET
Request URL: http://127.0.0.1:8000/accounts/profile/

Since we don't have a handler for that address, we see the **404** page.

Let's redirect to the main page of the site. Open **views.py**, find **LoginUser**, and add the method

def get_success_url(self):

return reverse_lazy('home')

```python
class LoginUser(DataMixin, LoginView):
    form_class = AuthenticationForm
    template_name = 'traveler/login.html'

    def get_context_data(self, *, oblect_list=None, **kwargs):
        context = super().get_context_data(**kwargs)
        c_def = self.get_user_context(title='Authorization ')
        return dict(list(context.items()) + list(c_def.items()))

    def get_success_url(self):
        return reverse_lazy('home')
```

It will be called if the user entered the login and password correctly, i.e., the form passed validation, and we redirect to the main page. Let's see how it will work. Open the authorization form and enter the user's data.

Authorization

Username: user_2

Password: ••••••••••

And we are on the main page. If you go to

http://127.0.0.1:8000/admin/,

you will see

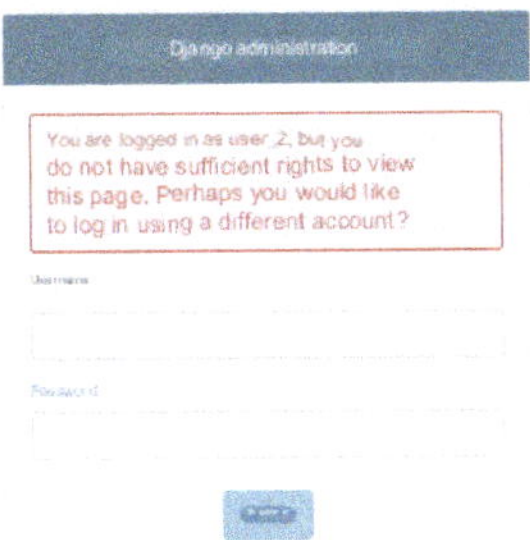

You can also do the same thing a bit differently, in the configuration package. Let's check how it works and then revert it back. Comment out the last lines

def get_success_url(self):

   return reverse_lazy('home')

Open the **settings.py** file and add the line

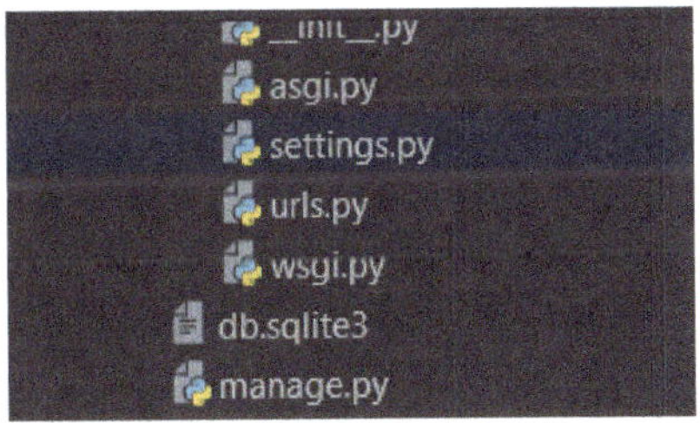

LOGIN_REDIRECT_URL = '/'

```
127    DEFAULT_AUTO_FIELD = 'django.db.models.BigAutoField'
128
129
130    MEDIA_ROOT = os.path.join(BASE_DIR, 'media')
131    MEDIA_URL = '/media/'
132
133    LOGIN_REDIRECT_URL = '/'
```

If you log in with the credentials of a registered user again, everything will work exactly as in the previous example. That is, you can do it one way or another. Let's improve the appearance of the authorization form. Let's create another authentication form class and name it

LoginUserForm

In the **forms.py** file, let's write the class

class LoginUserForm(AuthenticationForm):

   username = forms.CharField(label=' Login ', widget=forms.TextInput(attrs={'class': 'form-input'}))

   password = forms.CharField(label=' Password ', widget=forms.PasswordInput(attrs={'class': 'form-input'}))

```python
class LoginUserForm(AuthenticationForm):
    username = forms.CharField(label='Логин', widget=forms.TextInput(attrs={'class': 'form-input'}))
41  password = forms.CharField(label='Пароль', widget=forms.PasswordInput(attrs={'class': 'form-input'}))
```

We will extend the base class **AuthenticationForm**. It needs to be imported

from django.contrib.auth.forms import AuthenticationForm

The class **'class Meta:'** as in the form above does not need to be created.

You can add more fields, for example, the email field. But we won't add it now. Next, go to **views.py** and in the **LoginUser** class, insert our **LoginUserForm** class instead of **AuthenticationForm**. We imported this class at the very beginning. At this stage, we can remove that line.

class LoginUser(DataMixin, LoginView):

   form_class = LoginUserForm

   template_name = 'traveler/login.html'

```python
125     class LoginUser(DataMixin, LoginView):
126         form_class = LoginUserForm
127         template_name = 'traveler/login.html'
```

Let's not stop here and continue improving the form. Open **login.html** and instead of

{{ form.as_p }},

write the following lines

{% for f in form %}

<p><label class="form-label" for="{{ f.id_for_label }}">{{f.label}}: </label>{{ f }}</p>

<div class="form-error">{{ f.errors }}</div>

{% endfor %}

```
{% for f in form %}
<p><label class="form-label" for="{{ f.id_for_label }}">{{f.label}}: </label>{{ f }}</p>
<div class="form-error">{{ f.errors }}</div>
{% endfor %}
```

Additionally, at the top, we will display general errors during user authentication (incorrect login and password)

<div class="form-error">{{ form.non_field_errors }}</div>

```
{% csrf_token %}
<div class="form-error">{{ form.non_field_errors }}</div>
```

Let's go to the website and check the functionality of this form. Enter incorrect login and password

Authorization

Please enter the correct username and password. Both fields can be case sensitive.

Login:

Password:

This line, highlighted in red, appeared thanks to the code

<div class="form-error">{{ form.non_field_errors }}</div>

Next, if the user is authenticated, there is no need to display the **Registration** and **Login** links; instead, display the **Logout** link and a welcome message.

Registration | To come in

Let's implement this. Go to the base template, **base.html**, and find the section where the main menu is displayed.

```
15      {% block mainmenu %}
16
17          <div class="header">
18              <ul id="mainmenu" class="m
19              <li class="logo"><a href="
20      {% for m in menu %}
21                  <li><a href="{% url m.url
22      {% endfor %}
23                  <li class="last"><a href=
24              </ul>
25              <div class="clear"></div>
26          </div>
27      {% endblock mainmenu %}
```

And before the line

<li class="last"><a href="{% url 'register' %}"> Registration </a> | <a href="{% url 'login' %}"> Log In </a></li>

Let's write an additional condition. If the current user is authenticated...

{% if request.user.is_authenticated %}

...then

<li class="last"> {{user.name}} | <a href="{% url 'logout' %}"> Logout </a></li>

...we will display their name **{{user.username}}** ...and a link **<a href="{% url 'logout' %}"> Logout </a>**

Otherwise **{% else %}**

<li class="last"><a href="{% url 'register' %}"> Registration </a> | <a href="{% url 'login' %}"> Log In </a></li>

```
24    {% if request.user.is_authenticated %}
25        <li class="last"> {{user.username}} | <a href="{% url 'logout' %}">To come</a></li>
26    {% else %}
27    <li class="last"><a href="{% url 'register' %}">Registration </a> | <a href="{% url 'login' %}">To come</a></li>
28    {% endif %}
```

Let's add the 'logout' route. Go to **urls.py** and add the corresponding line of code

path('logout/', logout_user, name='logout'),

```
10        path('login/', LoginUser.as_view(), name='login'),
11        path('logout/', logout_user, name='logout'),
12        path('register/', RegisterUser.as_view(), name='register'),
```

Define the **logout_user** function in **views.py**

def logout_user(request):

  logout(request)

  return redirect('login')

```
138    def logout_user(request):
139        logout(request)
140        return redirect('login')
```

There is no need to write a whole class, as the function itself is very simple. This function calls the standard logout function, which needs to be imported.

from django.contrib.auth import logout

Go to the website, log in with your username **user_4**

If you click Logout, you will be redirected to the

http://127.0.0.1:8000/login/

page and see on the right

and

127.0.0.1:8000/login/

Let's make another improvement. It would be logical for the user to be automatically authenticated upon registration.

Go to **views.py**, find the **RegisterUser** class, and add the following at the end

```python
class RegisterUser(DataMixin, CreateView):
    form_class = RegisterUserForm
    template_name = 'traveler/register.html'
    success_url = reverse_lazy('login')


    def get_context_data(self, *, oblect_list=None, **kwargs):
        context = super().get_context_data(**kwargs)
        c_def = self.get_user_context(title=' Registration ')
        return dict(list(context.items()) + list(c_def.items()))


    def form_valid(self, form):
        user = form.save()
        login(self.request, user)
        return redirect('home')
```

```
124         def form_valid(self, form):
125             user = form.save()
126             login(self.request, user)
127             return redirect('home')
```

The **form_valid** method is called upon successful validation of the new user registration form.

We save the form to the database

```python
user = form.save()
```

By calling **login(self.request, user),** we authenticate the user and redirect them to the homepage

```python
return redirect('home')
```

And, of course, don't forget to import the function **login**

```python
from django.contrib.auth import login
```

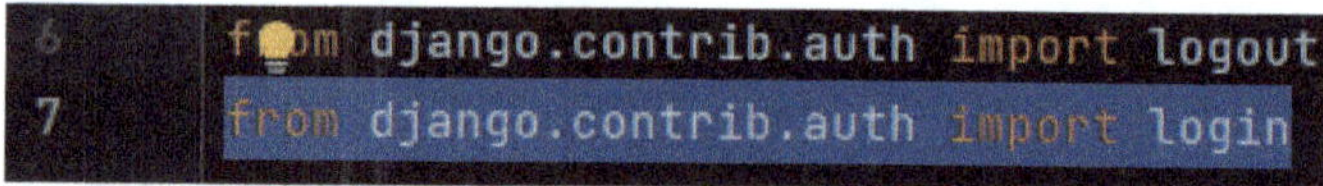
```
6        from django.contrib.auth import logout
7        from django.contrib.auth import login
```

To test, register a new user, and if everything goes smoothly, they will be already authenticated.

Registration

Login:	user_6
Email:	g@i.com
Password:	••••••••••••••
Password repeat:	•••••••••••••

Registration

Everything is as intended

user_6 | Go out

You can read more details about authentication at the following link

https://docs.djangoproject.com/en/4.1/topics/auth/default/

Caching pages

SQL queries are executed to generate pages for our website. It's important to understand that each client request involves the creation of pages and corresponding **SQL** queries.

Let's say your website is visited by 100-200, or even 1000-2000 people per day, and there's potential for even more. For a typical website, the norm might be several hundred thousand, or even a million queries per day. How can you reduce the load on your website and database?

To address this, caching mechanisms for pages were introduced. You can find more detailed information at the following link:
https://docs.djangoproject.com/en/4.1/topics/cache/

The idea behind caching is that if page updates are infrequent and there are numerous requests for the same page, it makes sense to generate the page the first time and serve the previously generated **HTML** document on subsequent requests.

This significantly reduces the load on databases and servers.

Memory caching

Caching in **Django** can be implemented either at the memory level using Memcached, at the database level, or at the file system caching level – the most common caching method. Let's consider this method for organizing file system caching.

Navigate to settings.py and define a dictionary. Find the standard lines of code in the documentation, copy them, and paste them in

```
CACHES = {
  'default': {
    'BACKEND': 'django.core.cache.backends.filebased.FileBasedCache',
    'LOCATION': 'c:/foo/bar',
  }
}
```

Next, we need to specify the path to the root folder of the cache itself.

Replace

'LOCATION': 'c:/foo/bar' with **'LOCATION': os.path.join(BASE_DIR, 'travels_cache').**

'travels_cache' is an arbitrary name for the folder that needs to be created.

BASE_DIR is a constant that holds the root directory of the project.

```
134  CACHES = {
135      'default': {
136          'BACKEND': 'django.core.cache.backends.filebased.FileBasedCache',
137          'LOCATION': os.path.join(BASE_DIR, 'travels_cache')
138      }
139  }
```

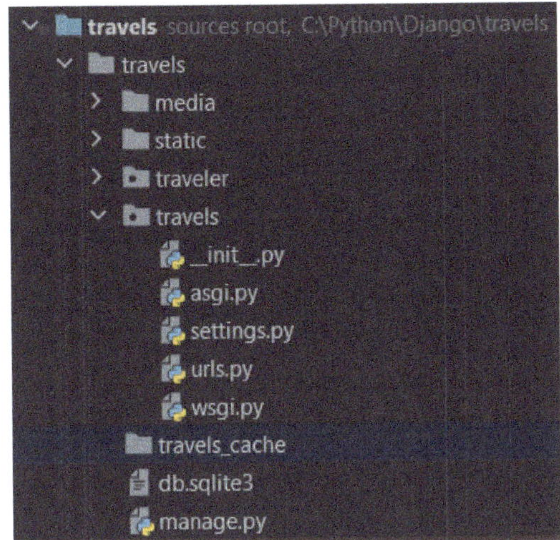

If you read the caching documentation, various parameters are presented – you can cache the entire site.

However, we will cache individual types of pages at the class (or view) level.

This means we can cache individual classes (views). We'll be working with classes.

Open the **urls.py** file. Let's start with caching the **main page**.

Import the decorator

from django.views.decorators.cache import cache_page

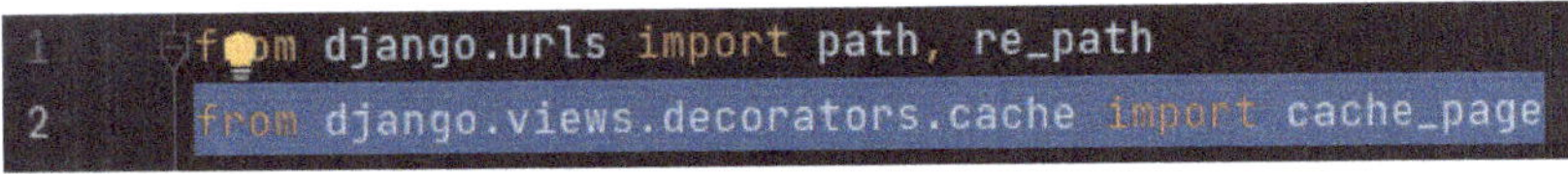

```python
1  from django.urls import path, re_path
2  from django.views.decorators.cache import cache_page
```

Based on this decorator, both functions and classes can be cached.

Let's cache the main page

path('', cache_page(60)(Dir_travelHome.as_view()), name='home'),

```python
6  urlpatterns = [
7      path('', cache_page(60)(Dir_travelHome.as_view()), name='home'),
8      path('about/', about, name='about'),
```

cache_page(60) – The cache will be stored for 60 seconds.

(Dir_travelHome.as_view()), - The view class that we are caching.

Let's check how this will work.

After loading the page, go to the cache folder created earlier in our project, and you'll see two files that store the cached page

If we refresh the page, as we expect, there should be no **SQL** query,

and the page generation time will be significantly reduced. This query will work again exactly after 1 minute.

If the content of the page changes during this time, the user won't notice any difference upon refresh because their page will be generated from the cache.

If the page is dynamically changing, for example, a page with comments, caching such a page is not advisable.

Caching at the request level

Let's go to urls.py and bring back the line...

path('', cache_page(60)(Dir_travelHome.as_view()), name='home'),

to its initial state

path('', Dir_travelHome.as_view(), name='home'),

Next, let's consider another method – template-level caching, where we can cache individual fragments.

For example, let's cache the sidebar, as it requires a single **SQL** query for its formation. Right before the sidebar, load the tag...

{% load cache %}

Next...

{% cache 60 sidebar %} – We write the tag, pass the time 60 seconds, and the name of the cache itself **(key) - 'sidebar'**, under which the cache will be stored.

```
37   {% load cache %}
38       <td valign="top" class="left-chapters">
39
40       <ul id="leftchapters">
41   {% cache 60 sidebar %}
42   {% if cat_selected == 0 %}
43           <li class="selected">Continents </li>
44   {% else %}
45           <li><a href="{% url 'home' %}">Continents </a></li>
46   {% endif %}
47
48   {% for c in cats %}
49   {% if c.dir_travel__count > 0 %}
50           {% if c.pk == cat_selected %}
51               <li class="selected">{{c.name}}</li>
52           {% else %}
53               <li> <a href="{{ c.get_absolute_url }}">{{c.name}}</a></li>
54           {% endif %}
55   {% endif %}
56   {% endfor %}
57   {% endcache %}
```

At the point where the sidebar formation ends, write the tag...

{% endcache %}

That's it.

Everything should work as intended. Let's consider one more caching method.

Low-level API caching

Let's remove the recent changes, as in the previous example. There are the following functions

cache.set() – saving arbitrary data to the cache by key.

cache.get() – retrieving arbitrary data from the cache by key.

cache.add() – sets a new value in the cache if it doesn't exist there yet.

cache.get_or_set() – fetches data from the cache, and if it doesn't exist, automatically adds the default value.

cache.delete() – deleting data from the cache by key.

cache.clear() – complete cache clearance.

Let's go to **utils.py**, find the **DataMixin** class, and cache the **SQL query**

cats = Category.objects.annotate(Count('dir_travel'))

Import the module

from django.core.cache import cache

```python
2        from django.db.models import Count
3        from django.core.cache import cache
```

Next

cats = cache.get('cats')

   if not cats:

      cats = Category.objects.annotate(Count('dir_travel'))

      cache.set('cats', cats, 60)

```python
14            cats = cache.get('cats')
15            if not cats:
16                cats = Category.objects.annotate(Count('dir_travel'))
17                cache.set('cats', cats, 60)
```

Read the **'cats'** collection using the **get**('cats') function with the key **'cats'**. Perform a check.

If the value of 'cats' is **'None**,' indicating that the data has not been read, then we will read this data from the table

cats = Category.objects.annotate(Count('dir_travel'))

We'll cache the data

cache.set('cats', cats, 60)

It's important to remember that this caching tool should be enabled at the final stages of website development.

Caching can hide many **SQL** queries and thereby mislead the developer.

Feedback form

Our website looks quite finished. However, if you click on the link...

we will end up on a placeholder page

Let's fix that.

Go to the **views.py** file, and instead of the function...

```python
def contact(request):
  return HttpResponse("Feedback ")
```

let's define a view class to generate this page.

```python
class ContactFormView(DataMixin, FormView):
  form_class = ContactForm
  template_name = 'traveler/contact.html'
  success_url = reverse_lazy('login')

  def get_context_data(self, *, oblect_list=None, **kwargs):
    context = super().get_context_data(**kwargs)
    c_def = self.get_user_context(title='Feedback')
    return dict(list(context.items()) + list(c_def.items()))

  def form_valid(self, form):
    print(form.cleaned_data)
    return redirect('home')
```

```python
class ContactFormView(DataMixin, FormView):
    form_class = ContactForm
    template_name = 'traveler/contact.html'
    success_url = reverse_lazy('login')

    def get_context_data(self, *, oblect_list=None, **kwargs):
        context = super().get_context_data(**kwargs)
        c_def = self.get_user_context(title='Feedback')
        return dict(list(context.items()) + list(c_def.items()))

    def form_valid(self, form):
        print(form.cleaned_data)
        return redirect('home')
```

This class will inherit from the standard classes **DataMixin** and **FormView**.

FormView is a standard base class for forms that are not tied to a model, hence it won't interact with the database.

If the form is successful, it will redirect to the home page. **'def get_context_data'** forms the context for the template, and we're already familiar with it.

'def form_valid' is called when the user correctly fills in all the fields of the contact form.

Let's add **ContactForm** in the **forms.py** file.

```python
class ContactForm(forms.Form):
    name = forms.CharField(label='Имя', max_length=255)
    email = forms.EmailField(label='Email')
    content = forms.CharField(widget=forms.Textarea(attrs={'cols': 60, 'rows': 10}))
```

```python
class ContactForm(forms.Form):
    name = forms.CharField(label='Name', max_length=255)
    email = forms.EmailField(label='Email')
    content = forms.CharField(widget=forms.Textarea(attrs={'cols': 60, 'rows': 10}))
```

This class will inherit from the general **Form** class and will contain three fields.

Next, let's associate the **ContactFormView** with the route

```python
path('contact/', ContactFormView.as_view(), name='contact'),
```

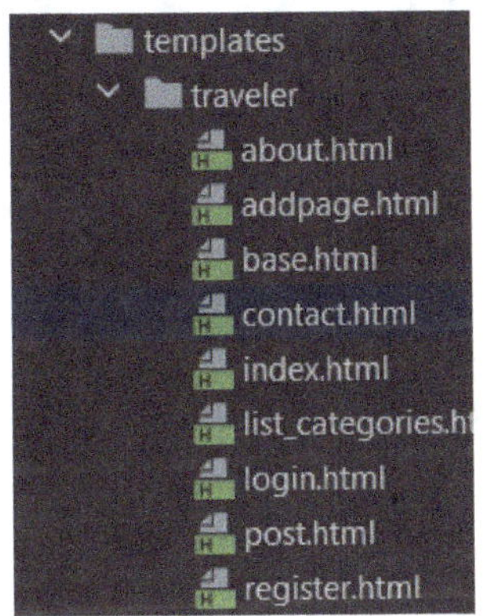

Next, let's add the template.


```django
{% extends 'traveler/base.html' %}

{% block content %}
<h1>{{title}}</h1>

<form method="post">
    {% csrf_token %}
<div class="form-error">{{ form.non_field_errors }}</div>
{% for f in form %}
<p><label class="form-label" for="{{ f.id_for_label }}">{{f.label}}: </label>{{ f }}</p>
<div class="form-error">{{ f.errors }}</div>
{% endfor %}
```

```
<button type="submit"> Send </button>

</form>


{% endblock %}
```

```django
1   {% extends 'traveler/base.html' %}
2
3   {% block content %}
4   <h1>{{title}}</h1>
5
6   <form method="post">
7           {% csrf_token %}
8   <div class="form-error">{{ form.non_field_errors }}</div>
9   {% for f in form %}
10  <p><label class="form-label" for="{{ f.id_for_label }}">{{f.label}}: </label>{{ f }}</p>
11  <div class="form-error">{{ f.errors }}</div>
12  {% endfor %}
13
14          <button type="submit">Send </button>
15  </form>
16
17  {% endblock %}
```

We won't repeat the process as we've added it multiple times.

Let's go to our website, click on '**Feedback**,' and see...

Feedback

Name:

Email:

Content:

Send

If you fill out the form with any data and submit it, you will be redirected to the home page, as intended

return redirect('home')

Let's go to the terminal and find the message that displays all the data we submitted in the form

```
[10/Mar/2023 12:39:15] "GET /contact/ HTTP/1.1" 200 3024
{'name': 'MAX     ', 'email': 'mr@ukr.net', 'content': 'Hello!'}
[10/Mar/2023 12:42:43] "POST /contact/ HTTP/1.1" 302 0
```

Fine-tuning the admin panel for the developed website

More details can be found on the website
https://docs.djangoproject.com/en/4.1/ref/contrib/admin/.

 Let's see how to customize the styling of the admin panel.

admin/base_site.html is the base template for creating admin panel pages. Let's take a look at its content.

Navigate to the venv directory, then lib, followed by the site-packages directory. In this directory, find **django,** then contrib, then admin. Inside the admin directory, locate the templates folder, go into the admin folder, and there you'll find the file **base_site.html**.

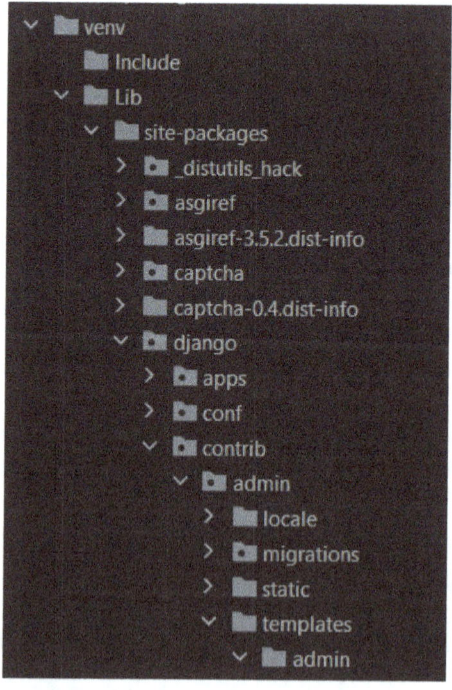

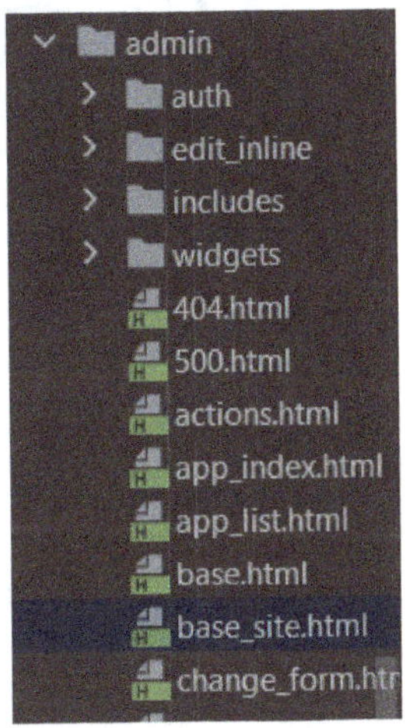

And its contents

```
{% extends "admin/base.html" %}

{% block title %}{% if subtitle %}{{ subtitle }} | {% endif %}{{ title }} | {{ site_title|default:_('Django site admin'

{% block branding %}
<h1 id="site-name"><a href="{% url 'admin:index' %}">{{ site_header|default:_('Django administration') }}</a></h1>
{% endblock %}

{% block nav-global %}{% endblock %}
```

We can make changes directly in this file, but it is not the best practice. It's better to override it directly in our project.

To override this file, let's create a folder at the root of our project called 'templates.' Inside this directory, create a folder named 'admin'.

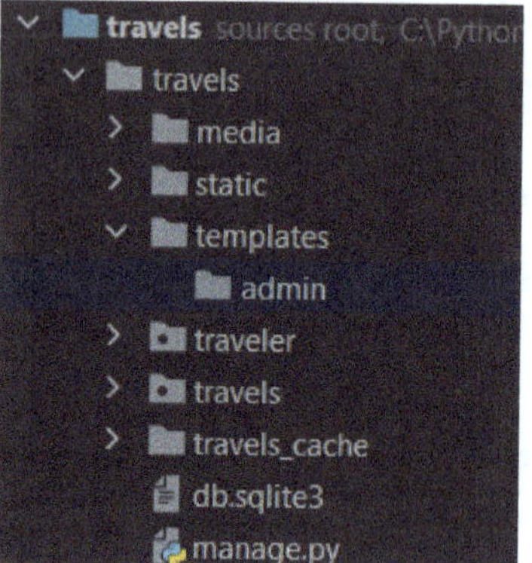

If you place a file named base_site.html in this directory, it will override the file with the exact same name that we looked at earlier.

And copy all the contents from the previous file into this one.

{% extends "admin/base.html" %}

{% block title %}{% if subtitle %}{{ subtitle }} | {% endif %}{{ title }} | {{ site_title|default:_('Django site admin') }}{% endblock %}

{% block branding %}

<h1 id="site-name"><a href="{% url 'admin:index' %}">{{ site_header|default:_('Django administration') }}</a></h1>

{% endblock %}

{% block nav-global %}{% endblock %}

Since the new path to this file is non-standard, we need to explicitly specify it in the settings.py file under the **TEMPLATES** section.

'DIRS': [os.path.join(BASE_DIR, 'templates')],

```
56    TEMPLATES = [
57        {
58            'BACKEND': 'django.template.backends.django.DjangoTemplates',
59            'DIRS': [os.path.join(BASE_DIR, 'templates')],
60            'APP_DIRS': True,
61            'OPTIONS': {
```

Reload the server.

And, as we can see, nothing has changed.

We see the same admin panel, but now it's our own, not the built-in one. And now we can override it without affecting the existing built-in panel.

What do we see in this template?!

{% block title %} – block for the title.

{% block branding %} - Django administration

Django administration

{% block nav-global %} – Navigation block.

Let's add our own styling. If you open the higher-level template **base.html**, you'll see the block:

{% block extrastyle %}{% endblock %}

If we write styles in this block, they will be applied in the **<head>** section accordingly. Let's place it somewhere near the beginning.

The content of this block will link to our style sheet, which will add new styles to the admin panel.

```
{% extends "admin/base.html" %}

{% load static %}

{% block extrastyle %}

<link rel="stylesheet" href="{% static 'css/admin.css' %}">

{% endblock %}
```

```
{% block title %}{% if subtitle %}{{ subtitle }} | {% endif %}{{ title }} | {{ site_title|default:_('Django site admin') }}{% endblock %}
```

```
{% block branding %}

<h1 id="site-name"><a href="{% url 'admin:index' %}">{{ site_header|default:_('Django administration') }}</a></h1>

{% endblock %}
```

```
{% block nav-global %}{% endblock %}
```

Include it

{% load static %}

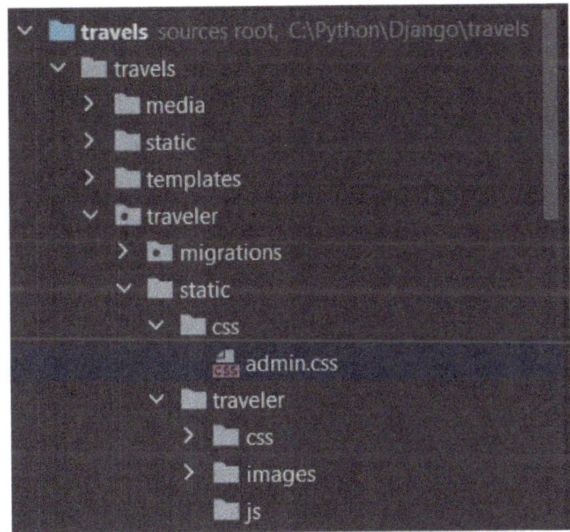

```
{% extends "admin/base.html" %}
{% load static %}
{% block extrastyle %}
<link rel="stylesheet" href="{% static 'css/admin.css' %}">
{% endblock %}

{% block title %}{% if subtitle %}{{ subtitle }} | {% endif %}{{ title }} | {{ site_title|default:_('Django site admin') }}{% endblock %}

{% block branding %}
<h1 id="site-name"><a href="{% url 'admin:index' %}">{{ site_header|default:_('Django administration') }}</a></h1>
{% endblock %}

{% block nav-global %}{% endblock %}
```

Next, we should specify **'css/admin.css'**

If you go to the admin page, refresh, and use the file inspector, you will see that our file is successfully linked

```
<link rel="stylesheet" href="/static/admin/css/nav_sidebar.css">
<script src="/static/admin/js/nav_sidebar.js" defer></script>
<link rel="stylesheet" href="/static/css/admin.css">
```

How to find out which selectors are used, for example, to change the color of the header?

Django administration

Using the browser, let's inspect the element code

```
▼<div id="header"> flex == $0
```

Copy the **id='header'**.

With this identifier, we can now work with the header. Go to our **admin.css** file and add the selector. In it, change the background color to any arbitrary color.

#header {

  background: #088A08;

}

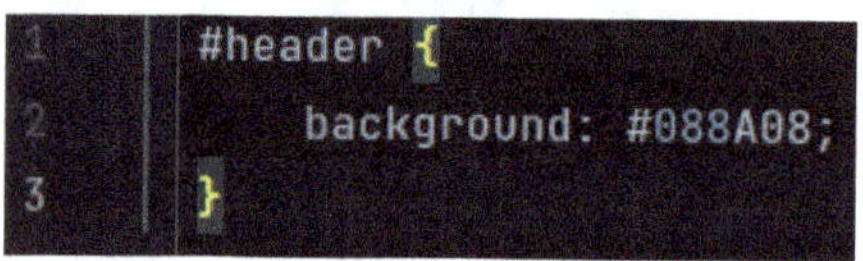

Go to the admin panel page and refresh

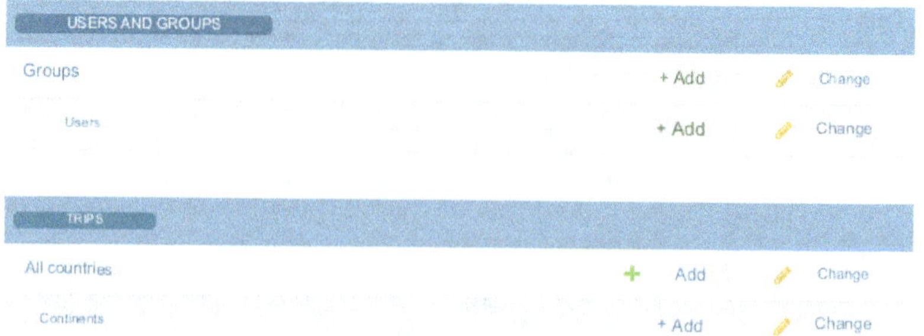

Let's proceed. For example, if we want to assign the same color to the categories below

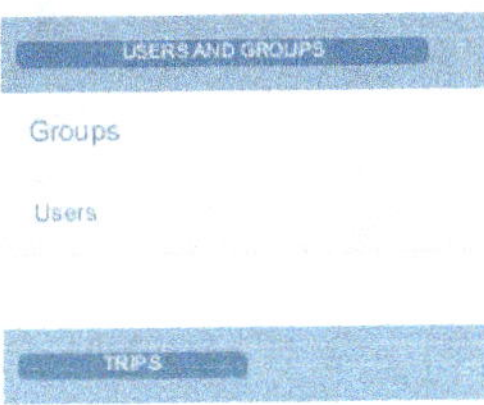

To do this, first highlight **'Users and Groups'** and invoke the inspector

```
▶<div id="header"> ⋯ </div>  flex          text-transform: uppercase;
  <!-- END Header -->                     }
▼<div class="main" id="main">  flex       .module h2, .module caption, .inline-group h2 {
  ▼<div class="content">                      margin: ▶ 0;
    <!-- Content -->                          padding: ▶ 8px;
    ▼<div id="content" class="colMS">         font-weight: 400;
      <h1>Администрирование сайта</h1>        font-size: 0.8125rem;
      ▼<div id="content-main">               text-align: left;
        ▼<div class="app-auth module">       background: ▶ ▉var(--primary);
          ▼<table>                           color: ▢var(--header-link-color);
            ▶<caption> ⋯ </caption> == $0   }
            ▶<tbody> ⋯ </tbody>              caption {                          user
            </table>                            display: table-caption;
                                                text-align: -webkit-center;
                                              }
```

On the right, in the styles, we see the line:

```
.module h2, .module caption, .inline-group h2 {
```

Copy **.module** caption and paste it into our styles

```
#header, .module caption {
  background: #088A08;
}
```

```
1    #header, .module caption {
2        background: #088A08;
3    }
```

Refresh the page in the browser

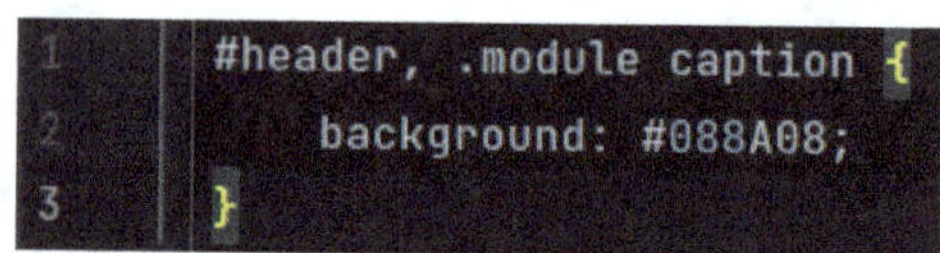

Keep in mind that pages are cached, so it's best to refresh using the **Ctrl+F5** key combination. In this case, the cache will be cleared.

This way, you can change the design and color scheme of our admin panel. If we need to change the actual title...

it's better to do it through **admin.py**. Let's add two additional attributes

admin.site.site_title = 'Admin Panel for Travels'

admin.site.site_header = 'Travel Site Management'

```python
    list_filter = ('is_published', 'time_create')
    prepopulated_fields = {"slug": ("title",)}


class CategoryAdmin(admin.ModelAdmin):
    list_display = ('id', 'name')
    list_display_links = ('id', 'name')
    search_fields = ('name',)
    prepopulated_fields = {"slug": ("name",)}


admin.site.register(Dir_travel, Dir_travelAdmin)
admin.site.register(Category, CategoryAdmin)

admin.site.site_title =
admin.site.site_header =
```

Refresh the page

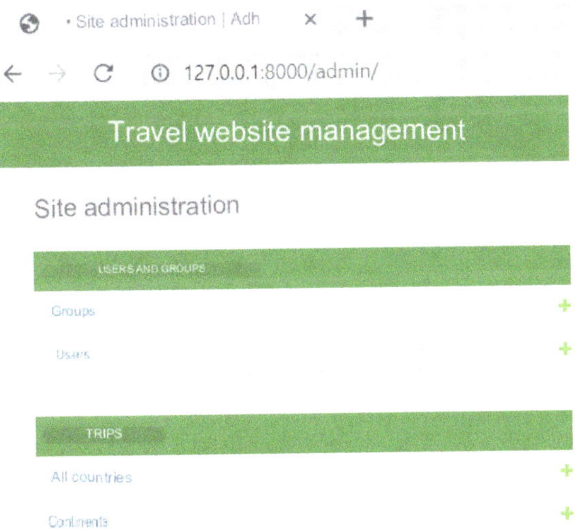

The full list of these attributes can be found in the documentation. Let's make the display of our thumbnails directly in the list

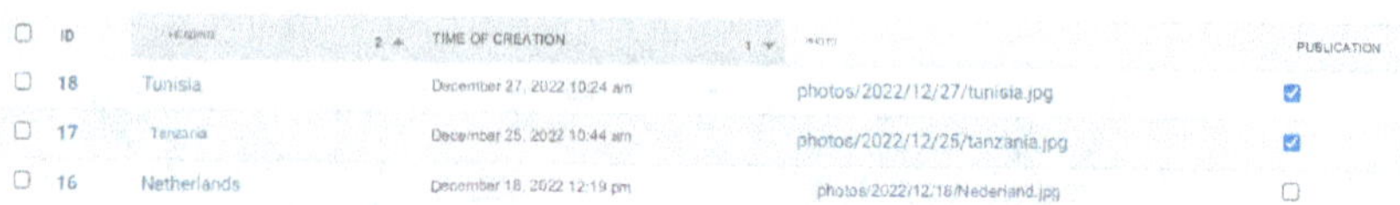

ID	HEADING	TIME OF CREATION		PUBLICATION
18	Tunisia	December 27, 2022 10:24 am	photos/2022/12/27/tunisia.jpg	☑
17	Tanzania	December 25, 2022 10:44 am	photos/2022/12/25/tanzania.jpg	☑
16	Netherlands	December 18, 2022 12:19 pm	photos/2022/12/18/Nederland.jpg	☐

To do this, in the **admin.py** file, find the **Dir_travelAdmin** class and add a special method that returns **HTML** code. We will then use this code instead of paths

photos/2022/12/27/tunisia.jpg

photos/2022/12/25/tanzania.jpg

def get_html_photo(self, object):

return mark_safe(f"<img src='{object.photo.url}' width=50>")

```python
class Dir_travelAdmin(admin.ModelAdmin):
    list_display = ('id', 'title', 'time_create', 'photo', 'is_published')
    list_display_links = ('id', 'title')
    search_fields = ('title', 'content')
    list_editable = ('is_published',)
    list_filter = ('is_published', 'time_create')
    prepopulated_fields = {"slug": ("title",)}

    def get_html_photo(self, object):
        return mark_safe(f"<img src='{object.photo.url}' width=50>")
```

object – a parameter that will refer to the current entry in the list.

mark_safe – a function that indicates not to escape

the tags **"<img src='{object.photo.url}' width=50>").** This function needs to be imported.

from django.utils.safestring import mark_safe

```python
from django.contrib import admin
from django.utils.safestring import mark_safe
```

Next, in the line

list_display = ('id', 'title', 'time_create', 'photo', 'is_published')

replace '**photo**' with '**get_html_photo**

*list_display = ('id', 'title', 'time_create', '**get_html_photo**', 'is_published')*

Not all of our posts have a photo. Accordingly, we can encounter an exception.

To prevent this, let's add one more line

if object.photo:

return mark_safe(f"<img src='{object.photo.url}' width=50>")

```python
class Dir_travelAdmin(admin.ModelAdmin):
    list_display = ('id', 'title', 'time_create', 'get_html_photo', 'is_published')
    list_display_links = ('id', 'title')
    search_fields = ('title', 'content')
    list_editable = ('is_published',)
    list_filter = ('is_published', 'time_create')
    prepopulated_fields = {"slug": ("title",)}

    def get_html_photo(self, object):
        if object.photo:
            return mark_safe(f"<img src='{object.photo.url}' width=50>")
```

Go to the site and refresh the page. If everything is done correctly, we should see thumbnails

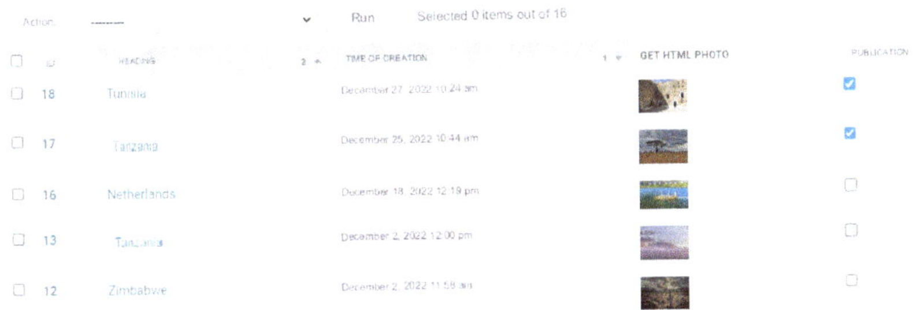

If there are no images in any post, we will see dashes. Let's make it so that instead of showing '**GET HTML PHOTO**', the thumbnail is displayed.

To do this, let's add another attribute in our class.

get_html_photo.short_description = " Thumbnail "

```python
def get_html_photo(self, object):
    if object.photo:
        return mark_safe(f"<img src='{object.photo.url}' width=50>")

get_html_photo.short_description = "Miniature"
```

After refreshing the page, we'll see...

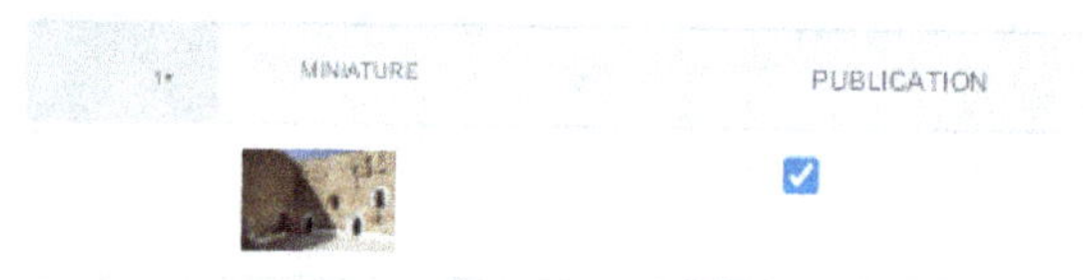

Such transformations can be done not only with photos but with any other information as well. Let's display photos even during editing.

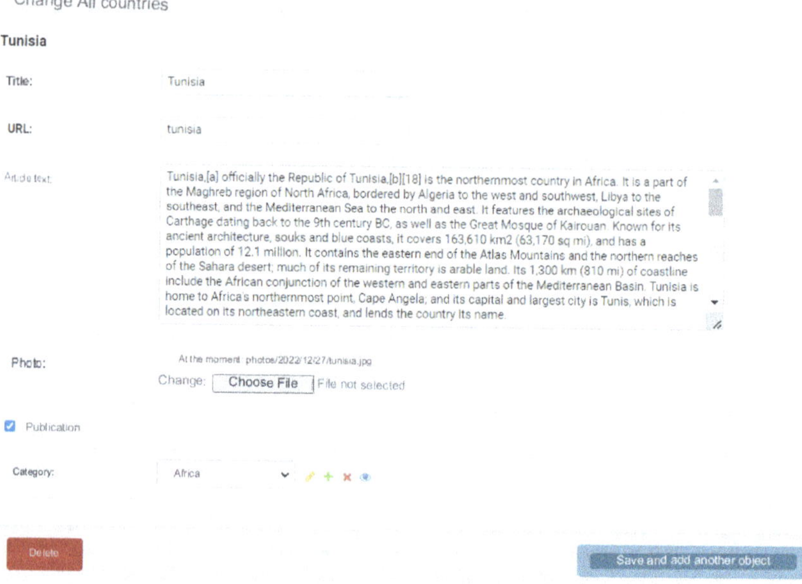

To do this, in the same **Dir_travelAdmin** class, add the following attribute:

fields = ('title', 'slug', 'cat', 'content', 'photo', 'is_published')

```
12    list_filter = ('is_published', 'time_create')
13    prepopulated_fields = {"slug": ("title",)}
14    fields = ('title', 'slug', 'cat', 'content', 'photo', 'is_published')
```

This attribute contains the order and list of editable fields.

Let's also add non-editable, read-only fields.

readonly_fields = ('time_create', 'time_update')

And only after that, we can specify them in the collection **fields**

*fields = ('title', 'slug', 'cat', 'content', 'photo', 'is_published', **'time_create', 'time_update'**)*

```
14    fields = ('title', 'slug', 'cat', 'content', 'photo', 'is_published', 'time_create', 'time_update')
15    readonly_fields = ('time_create', 'time_update')
```

Let's refresh our page.

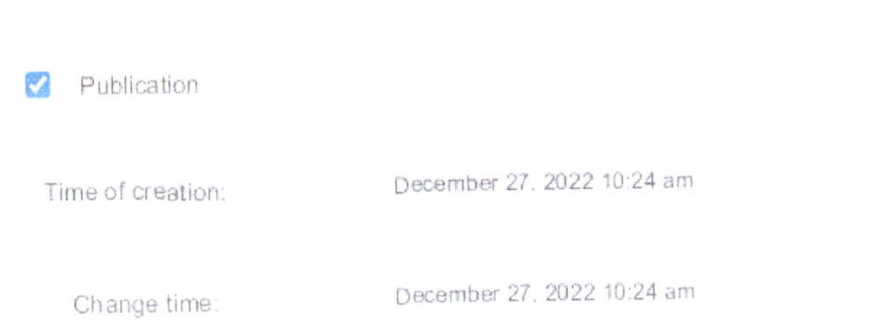

Let's add a thumbnail that will be a read-only field.

As we already know, in the **readonly_fields** attribute, add the name of our method with the photo: **readonly_fields = ('time_create', 'time_update', 'get_html_photo'),**

and then add this thumbnail after the 'photo' field

*fields = ('title', 'slug', 'cat', 'content', 'photo', **'get_html_photo'**, 'is_published', 'time_create', 'time_update')*

```
    fields = ('title', 'slug', 'cat', 'content', 'photo', 'get_html_photo', 'is_published', 'time_create', 'time_update')
    readonly_fields = ('time_create', 'time_update', 'get_html_photo')
```

Next, refresh the page

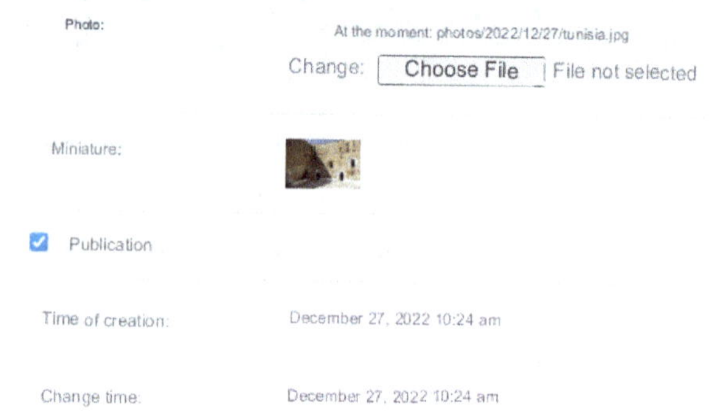

As we can see, everything is working.

You can find more details about all the attributes in the documentation provided above.

Alright, that's probably it!

You will need to deploy (publish) your site on a so-called production server. Practice this on your own. I can recommend an excellent server, **PythonAnywhere**, where you can deploy your site quite easily and for free (with some limitations).

The information provided should be more than enough for a good and reliable start.

For confident growth in this industry, you will need additional resources and daily hard work, overcoming laziness and, at times, despair. But if you see a goal in front of you, go towards it without turning aside. Your hard work will be rewarded. May the force be with you!

___Volodymyr Zadorozhnyi © 2023